THE MEANING OF HISTORY

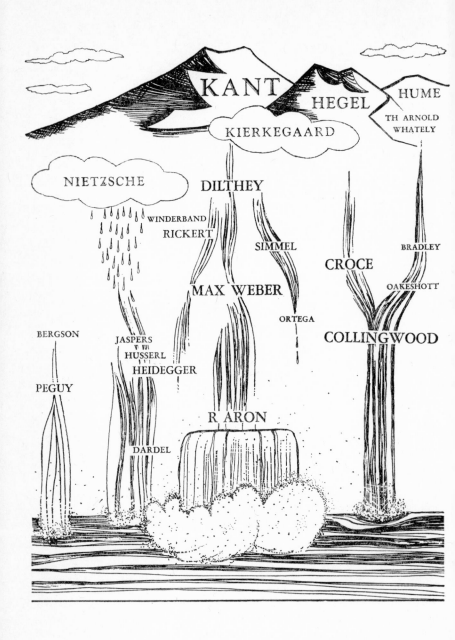

HENRI-IRÉNÉE MARROU

The Meaning of History

HELICON

Baltimore — Dublin

Helicon Limited,
20 Upr. Fitzwilliam Street,
Dublin 2, Ireland

Helicon Press, Inc.
1120 N. Calvert Street
Baltimore, Maryland 21202

Originally published in French under the
title *De la connaissance historique* by
Editions du Seuil, Paris, 1959,
4th edition, revised

translation by ROBERT J. OLSEN

PRINTED IN THE REPUBLIC OF IRELAND BY
HELY THOM, LIMITED, DUBLIN, IRELAND

CONTENTS

THE MEANING OF HISTORY

The Critical Philosophy of History

This little book is offered as a philosophical introduction to the study of history. An attempt will be made to find the answers to certain fundamental questions. What is historical truth? What are the degrees and limits of this truth? All human knowledge has its limits, and the same effort that establishes its validity also determines the useful extent and area of its exercise. What conditions are necessary for its elaboration? In short, what is the proper role of the human intellect in the study of history?

This introduction is addressed to the student who is now ready for research, and who wants to know what it will mean for him to become a historian. It is meant for the honest and reasonable man making practical use of our scientific production, who is legitimately concerned to know the real value of history before integrating it with other knowledge. It is quite permissible for a philosopher to glance over the technicians' shoulders if he is curious to know what they think of their technique. But we shall confine ourselves to a very elementary level.

There can be no attempt to investigate for their own sake the special problems which the structure of a historical study may present to the logician. While acknowledging this structure summarily, we shall simply indicate the practical principles that must govern the historian's task. The effort of critical analysis should lead to a theory of duty, a kind of deontology for the use of the "apprentice" and the "journeyman," a treatise on the virtues of the historian.

An introduction to historical studies, however, can hardly go beyond the most general principles. In fact, at a very early stage the method must be diversified in specializations in order to adapt itself to the variety of the historical object and its conditions of apprehension. Consequently, comments will be found here that are prefatory to any attempt to provide a rational elaboration of history. I hope that no one will be surprised if I speak as a philosopher even though I am a historian by profession, for this is my right and my duty. It is time to react against the inferiority complex (and the superiority complex also, since psychology has revealed this ambivalence which morality calls a ruse of pride) that historians have too long maintained with regard to philosophy.

In his opening lecture at the Collège de France (1933), Lucien Febvre said, with a note of irony, "I have often allowed the remark to pass, that historians do not have great philosophical needs."[1] Matters have not improved very much since then. Re-publishing in 1953 his book of 1911, *La synthèse en histoire,* Henri Berr tossed a rather strange compliment at me in the Appendix. He said, "In an issue of the *Revue de Métaphysique et de Morale* devoted to 'Problems of History' (July–October, 1949), the only article tainted with philosophy is the one by H. I. Marrou. . . ."[2]

We must put an end to these outmoded reflexes and break free from the torpor in which positivism has too long held historians (and their colleagues of the "exact" sciences also). Our profession is burdensome, overwhelming us with technical servitudes. It tends eventually to produce the mentality of the specialized insect in those who are its practitioners. Instead of helping the scholar to react against professional deformation, positivism gave him

1. Reprinted in *Combats pour l'histoire* (1953), p. 4.
2. *La synthèse en histoire* (new edition, 1953), p. 288.

a quiet conscience, and he could say, "I am only a historian, and not a philosopher at all. I cultivate my own little
garden and practice my profession honestly. I do not med-
dle in matters that are beyond me: *ne sutor ultra crepidam
. . . Altiora ne quaesieris!*"* But this was simply lowering
himself to the status of an unskilled laborer. The scholar
who makes use of a method when he knows nothing of its
logical structure, or who applies rules without knowing
how to gauge their efficacy, becomes like a worker who
has charge of a factory machine, controlling its operation
but quite incapable of making repairs—and even less able
to construct it. We must sternly repudiate any such attitude
of mind because it constitutes one of the gravest dangers
threatening the future of our Western civilization, already
on the verge of foundering in an atrocious technological
barbarism.

In parody of the Platonic maxim, we shall inscribe over
the portals of our Propylaea: "Let no one enter here who
is not a philosopher," that is to say, unless he has first reflected on the nature of history and the vocation of the
historian. The soundness of a scientific discipline requires
that the scholar possess a certain methodological solicitude,
a real concern to become cognizant of the procedural technique, and some desire to reflect on problems relevant to
the "theory of knowledge" which the technique implies.

We must try to dispel any misunderstanding, for ambiguity of vocabulary has contributed considerably to
prolonging the uneasiness which we hope will be overcome.
We are not attempting to present a "philosophy of history"
in the Hegelian sense, as a speculation on the evolution of
humanity in general, in order to discover its laws—or its
meaning, as we would be more likely to say nowadays.

---

* "Let the cobbler stick to his last . . . Don't reach for things that are
above you!"

Instead, our concern is to develop a "critical philosophy of history"[3] which will be a reflection *on* history, devoted to the examination of logical and gnosiological problems that arise from the historian's line of thought. It will enter into that "philosophy of the sciences" whose legitimacy or fecundity no one today would question. It will be in the same relation to the "philosophy of history" as the critical philosophy of mathematics, physics, etc., is to *Naturphilosophie*[4] which, in romantic idealism, was developed in a way that was parallel to the *Philosophy of History*: as a speculative effort to penetrate the mystery of the universe.

The problem of historical truth is a matter that concerns not only the internal betterment of our discipline, for beyond the narrow circle of historians themselves it also concerns every reasonable and educated man. There is in question nothing less than history's right to have a place in his education, a place that is increasingly disputed today. While our science continues to develop along the lines of a growing technical competence, applying its methods which are constantly more demanding to enquiries that are increasingly more far-reaching, some have begun "to be discouraged by the very meager and perhaps illusory results obtained."[5]

It is unnecessary to take inventory of the evidence attesting this "crisis of history," but we should keep in mind that everything essential in the indictment was already contained in the prophetic anathemas of Nietzsche's *Thoughts Out of*

3. Let us borrow this expression from Raymond Aron, who used it as a title for his essay on Dilthey, Rickert, Simmel and Max Weber (1938; second edition, 1950).

4. W. H. Walsh, *An Introduction to the Philosophy of History* (London, 1951), p. 12. [*Naturphilosophie* was an expression of German Romantic Idealism, considering Nature as an emanation from God. It is best represented by the German philosopher Friedrich W. Schelling. Cf. also E. Becher, *Naturphilosophie* (1914) (Translator's Note)].

5. H. Peyre, *Louis Ménard* (New Haven, 1932), p. 240.

Season (1874). The new feeling of being crushed beneath the burden of history which this expressed resulted in further strengthening the theme of scepticism with regard to its conclusions. This is a theme that was traditional in Western thought and was eloquently set forth in Tolstoy's epilogue in *War and Peace* (1869), making his whole novel an experimental refutation of historical dogmatism.

All of this was a very natural reaction (the history of culture is made of such *corsi e ricorsi*), following upon the sheer inflation of history's value during the nineteenth century. In the course of a few generations, beginning with Niebuhr, Champollion and Ranke, disciplines devoted to the elaboration of the knowledge of the past had undergone a prodigious development. Surely it is not surprising that this knowledge gradually penetrated every sphere of thought. The "sense of history" became one of the characteristic traits of the Western mind. In those days, the historian was king and all culture was somehow subject to his judgments and decrees. It was for him to say how the *Iliad* ought to be read, and what a nation really was (historic boundaries, hereditary enemy, traditional mission). It was the historian who would know whether Jesus was God. Under the combined influence of idealism and positivism, the ideology of Progress was installed as the fundamental category. Christendom was dismissed as an anachronism and Christians were regarded as a timid minority; no one ever supposed that they were necessarily irreducible. "Modern" thought was mistress of all it surveyed.

In one fell swoop the historian replaced the philosopher as guide and counsellor. Knowing the secrets of the past, it was the historian who, as a genealogist, provided mankind with proofs of its nobility and mapped the triumphal high-road of its destiny. "Without God, the future was spread out in disorder."[6] The historian alone was in a position to provide a

6. A. Chamson, *L'Homme contre l'histoire* (1927), p. 8.

rational basis for utopia by showing that it was firmly rooted and in some sense already developing in the distant past. Auguste Comte, with naïve emphasis, even felt justified in saying, "The doctrine which sufficiently accounts for the whole of the past will inevitably, as a result of this single achievement, preside over the mind of the future."[7]

However, these were excessive claims, and confidence was badly misplaced. The day came when man began to doubt the oracle which he had so complacently invoked, and he felt burdened by this jumble that was proving to be useless and uncertain. Suddenly, history became an "object of hatred" (Nietzsche) or of utter derision. In an exhortation on this very subject to a group of students, I remember having borrowed my text from the prophet Isaiah: *Concepimus, et quasi parturivimus, et peperimus spiritum....* "We have conceived, and been as it were in labor, and have brought forth wind" (26:18).

I wrote that in 1938. The situation has only become worse since then. The decline of confidence in history appears as one of the manifestations of the crisis of truth, one of the gravest symptoms of our troubled time—even more serious than the "decline of freedom" (D. Halévy), for this is a wound that penetrates to the very depths of being.

We all remember the atrocious words of Hitler in *Mein Kampf*: "A colossal lie bears within itself a power that banishes doubts. . . . A clever and persevering propaganda will finally lead people to believe that heaven is really no better than hell, and that the most wretched existence is, on the contrary, a paradise. . . . For the most brazen lie always leaves traces, even if it has been reduced to nothing." These ravings of a prisoner and madman, *aegri somnia,* * have been actually realized in the ordinary practice of political life during the course of our own generation. Contempt for historical truth

7. *Discours sur l'esprit positif* (1844), p. 73 (éd. Schleicher).

*"A sick man's idle dreams" (Horace).

is openly proclaimed everywhere. I say *everywhere*, for while
the examples that come spontaneously to mind are those of
the totalitarian countries (as, for instance, the burning of the
Reichstag and the massacre of Katyn, which were both used
advantageously by those who were guilty), the Western de-
mocracies are not without sin. We need only think of the
unverified calumnies used by political "witch-hunters" in the
United States in the fifties, or the stammered lies that are the
"official denials" made by the government in France. This is
a practice that has become so normal that people finally consider such lies simply as figures of speech or as a matter of
etiquette!

Is there any place left for history in this disordered world?
It has become hardly more than a play of masks in the property storeroom of the comedians of Propaganda. We are fortunate indeed if they do not go so far as to fabricate completely a history which they know to be false. At best they
discern in the knowledge of the past a collection of pictorial
anecdotes and certain parallels or precedents that can be usefully invoked.

In France, for instance, during the Pétain régime anyone
could exalt the would-be "National Revolution" simply by
mentioning Thrasybulus and the resurgence of Athens after
its defeat in 404 B.C. On the other hand, if someone wished
to dishonour the hypocritical government that was established
in power under the complacent eye of the conqueror he could
speak in terms of the tyranny of the *Thirty* and the infamy of
the "oligarchs."[8] This was diminishing history to the naïve
conception of it held by the rhetoricians of antiquity (for
whom history was merely a collection of *exempla* for the use
of any orator in need of something to say). But the facility of
such a procedure deprives it of all seriousness. Thus, the ad-

8. Title of the little book published clandestinely by J. Isaac (Editions
de Minuit, 1942).

vocates of the Oder-Neisse boundary invoke the "example" of Boleslas the Valiant and of Poland in the time of the Piast dynasty; but as the western boundary of the Slavs has ranged from the mouth of the Elbe (about the fifth century) to Stalingrad (for a brief time in 1942), whatever may be the intermediate line at which the policy of force stabilizes this frontier for the time being, we shall find the "precedent" and "justification" for it!

Consequently, the endeavor by which our critical philosophy attempts to establish history's validity upon rational bases now appears not only as a justification of the technique which we profess, but also as a participation in the struggle for the defense of culture and the preservation of our civilization. But there is much more involved, for if "scientific" history has somehow become suspect or contemptible to many, still there has never been a time when there was so much readiness to discuss History and its interpretation and "meaning." It has become a vital principle and an axiom of government. (In the unrelenting use that is made of it, the very concept acquires an inhuman character that recalls to mind the fascination and oppression that the idea of Destiny exercised upon the minds of the ancients.) This need to understand and know—and no longer merely to doubt—corresponds in our day to the profound exigencies that gradually came to light during the period between the two World Wars. The growing awareness of the multiplicity of civilizations, their relativity and essential fragility, had posed a problem to the generation of 1918 (Spengler, Valéry, Ferrero, Toynbee, Sorokin, who were all asking, "Where have we arrived? Are we witnessing the Decline of the West? Is there any possibility of resurgence?"). This problem was superseded gradually by a question that was even more anxious and more profound: "Granted that civilizations are born and mature and perish, are we on earth merely to build—and then destroy—these civilizations that are but temporary structures, *machinas tran-situras*,[9] like a generation of termites building their galleried termitaria that will be destroyed and then reconstructed in the heedless permanence of the species?[10] Must we resign ourselves to this ignoble prospect, or on the contrary, should we recognize some value, fruitfulness and meaning in this recurrently triumphant and heart-breaking pilgrimage of mankind down through the duration of its history?"

Whole civilizations have, in fact, ignored this problem. But once it is conceived as possible it can no longer be evaded and must necessarily be resolved—even if negatively, as some of the ahistorical philosophies of the absurd or of despair are inclined to formulate it. The modern revival of the philosophy —or theology—of history should not therefore surprise us. But we ought to be concerned about the naïve dogmatism and the dauntless and crude assurance still apparent in these philosophers. We find them speculating on History conceived as a pure object in a manner that is wholly independent of the problem of knowledge. In practice they are continually referring to the results (or the supposed results) of our historical science, without adequate concern for the conditions of elaboration which determine their validity and the limits of that validity. The indifference of so many of our contemporaries with regard to the preliminary question posed by critical reflection is really astonishing: "*What* do you know about this history that you mention so glibly, and *how* do you know it?"

Behavior of this kind is so strange that it requires some explanation. Personally, I perceive an effect of the swing of the pendulum which seems to govern the development of

9. St. Augustine, *Sermon 362*, 7: "Architectus aedificat per machinas transituras domum manentem."

10. L. Frobenius, *Le destin des civilisations* (1932), French translation, pp. 1–3.

2

thought. There was a "Back to Kant" movement at the end of
the nineteenth century, especially in Germany, as a reaction
against the excesses of that Hegelian tyranny which only a
Kierkegaard dared to oppose in his day. And we are now
witnessing a revival of Hegel's influence, and more particularly his philosophy of history. (But in this respect we must
incriminate Marxism. Under the diffuse and often debased
form that has so profoundly penetrated the common mentality
of our generation it has largely contributed to posing the
problem of history once again in terms of the year 1848 or
even 1830.) We must denounce the anachronistic character of
this influence, which is philosophically retrograde; and this
is all the more essential because Hegelian dogmatism, as the
central issue and aim, was itself particularly vulnerable.

Hegel witnessed the first flowering of a really scientific
history. He was the contemporary of Niebuhr and Ranke,[11]
whom we venerate as the initiators and first masters of the
present form of our science. Hegel was very familiar with
Niebuhr's work and often referred to it; but strangely enough
it was always to reject and criticize it, covering it with facile
sarcasm.[12] He retained only the weakest features of Niebuhr's
History of Rome: those hypotheses rather hastily devised
upon the ruins of tradition, which were actually *a priori* in-
ventions of fancy. He did not notice all that was really new
in this systematic application of critical methods to history.

Hegel was nevertheless too great a thinker to be unaware
of the problem's existence. He even defined it in terms that

11. Niebuhr's *History of Rome* began to appear in 1811; Ranke's
History of the Latin and Germanic Peoples from 1494 to 1535, which
was his first book, is dated 1824; the famous *Lessons on the Philosophy
of History*, published after Hegel's death, were given between 1822 and
1831.

12. *Vorlesungen* . . . , edited by Lasson (*Werke*, vol. IX), pp. 7, 8
(n. 1), 176, 665, 690, 697.

have never been surpassed for their precision,[13] only to brush it aside backhandedly at the same moment. Contrasted with Niebuhr he appears to us (as did St. Augustine with regard to St. Jerome) like a philosopher who is eager to reach conclusions and to dogmatize, unable to endure the long delays required by the subalternation of the sciences (if I may be allowed to use such a scholastic term). It is rather disconcerting to note the ease with which he eliminates the problem ("reason governs the world, universal history is rational, etc.") and rushes blindly ahead to construct a "philosophical" history, using materials whose contradictory and resistant nature he had not investigated.[14]

Such indifference—already questionable in anyone writing between 1822 and 1831—is simply intolerable today. We need not remind the neo-Hegelians that with each new stage thought must surmount the preceding stage, and not merely abolish it. Recalling to mind the suggested resemblance of the swing of the pendulum, we may say that the progress of thought requires a spiral movement rather than one that is purely circular. It is not permissible to feign unawareness of the problem raised by the critical philosophy of history and the solutions which, since Hegel's day, it has meanwhile been

13. *Ibid.*, p. 7: "We could suggest, as the first condition, that the historical must be accurately perceived, but such general terms as "accurately" and "perceived" are ambiguous. The average historian believes that he, too, is purely receptive, and always open to whatever is *given*, but his thinking process is not passive. He imposes his own categories and sees this datum through them." This could not be better expressed!

14. To cite only one example, the chapter of the *Vorlesungen* devoted to Byzantine history (op. cit., 768–774), naïvely reflects the Voltairean prejudices of Gibbon, referring to "the thousand-year series of crimes, marked by weakness and vileness, wholly characterless, presenting a picture that is successively the most frightful and the least interesting." On this shaky foundation, powerful "Reason" soars aloft and, of course, discovers profound motivations in this imaginary history, resulting consequently in new misunderstandings (pp. 770–771).

proposing. For such a philosophy is not merely something to be promised or improvised. With regard to essentials, it is already very largely constituted. Our frontispiece was designed to express for the reader's instruction (and amusement!) the origin of this school of thought, together with its mainstreams and their reciprocal connections. Its principal source is represented by the work of Wilhelm Dilthey (1833–1911), which was fruitful in so many ways.

Although his basic work was the *Einleitung in die Geisteswissenschaft* (1883), we shall remember the date (1875) of his article, *Ueber das Studium der Geschichte,* as symbolic. In this we already find the distinction made between the natural sciences and the mental sciences[15] which was the point of departure of the whole later development of his doctrine. This was the year following Nietzsche's *Thoughts Out of Season,* but we must not suppose that in Dilthey we see nothing more than a response to Nietzsche's challenge. Regardless of their points of agreement (as for instance the repudiation of idolized scientism, and life as the supreme category), their thought did not develop on the same level. Far from beginning with a protest against history, Dilthey on the contrary expressed his admiration for the greatness of its achievements. In a speech given on the occasion of his seventieth birthday he paid magnificent homage to the great historians of the first part of the nineteenth century: Böckh, Grimm, Mommsen, Ritter and Ranke.[16] Theirs was a greatness that seemed as unquestionable to him as the validity of Newton's physics to Kant, and that inspired his project to develop the theory of this practical work that was so fruitful.

Nowadays, Dilthey is quite forgotten in Germany. But this always happens when an idea, having exercised a great and lasting attraction, is finally considered out of date and thus

15. French translation in *Le monde de l'esprit,* vol. I, p. 58.
16. *Ges. Schriften,* vol. V, pp. 7, 9.

no longer useful because it has been profoundly assimilated. His influence was indeed extremely profound.[17] This notably accounts for the attention devoted to problems of history (and the very way in which such problems were posed) which we find in the "Back to Kant" philosophers like Windelband, Rickert and Simmel. Even in Dilthey himself, so conscious of his opposition to Hegel, the reference to Kant is quite obvious. He always regarded his undertaking as the elaboration of a *Critique of Historical Reason*[18] and therefore as an extension or a transposed equivalent of the *Critique of Pure Reason*. But we would be diminishing the scope of his endeavor, and that of his successors, if we identified the critical philosophy of history too exclusively with this particular moment in the history of German philosophy and made of it a matter peculiar to the "neo-Kantian school of Heidelberg."[19] In their work there is a whole series of observations and conclusions which are solidly established, and their validity is in no way bound up with the system into which their authors had inserted them. This need not surprise us, for the philosophy of the sciences is applied logic (on which our theory of history is dependent) and benefits to a rather considerable degree from the same privilege of technical invariance which we readily recognize, although likewise to a limited degree, in formal logic: the *Organon* is not entirely relative to the validity of the Aristotelian system!

Moreover, the school of thought inaugurated by Dilthey, whose legacy we are attempting to reassemble, went far

17. Even outside of Germany. For example, in Spain, J. Ortega y Gasset, in the second edition of his *Historia come sistema* (2nd ed., 1942), commented: "Dilthey, the man to whom we owe the most regarding the concept of life, and in my opinion, the most important thinker of the second half of the nineteenth century."

18. *Ges. Schriften*, vol. V, p. 9, and *Introduction aux Sciences de l'Esprit*, *Ges. Schr.*, vol. I, p. 116.

19. L. Goldmann, *Sciences humaines et philosophie*, p. 26.

beyond the school that was strictly neo-Kantian. Whatever may be the bond of relationship connecting it with Rickert, we could not possibly identify it with a man like Max Weber whose theoretical work represents an essential contribution to the construction of our critical philosophy, for Weber was also (and particularly) an economist and sociologist. We shall likewise have to integrate a considerable contribution provided by phenomenology, for even though the context of the problematical questions was wholly different, men like Husserl, Jaspers, and especially Heidegger, also encountered the problem of the elaboration of historical knowledge. The first two of these men met it when the development of the crisis in Europe had confronted them, in their turn, with the problem of history's meaning, a problem that was very real indeed at the time[20]—and in Heidegger's case in a way that was perhaps more central in the analysis of man's ontological situation, which reveals his essential "temporality" and "historicalness."

However original the method and orientation of these philosophers may be, their thinking on this point was not unaffected by the pervading influence of Dilthey. Heidegger, for instance, felt obliged to pay homage to this influence in *Sein und Zeit*.[21]

In France (I refer especially to the milieu of the professional historians) it seemed that this powerful movement was quite unknown for a long while. But let us be more exact about this. Some echo of it reached us through the efforts

20. P. Ricoeur, "Husserl et le sens de l'histoire" (based upon the largely unpublished works of the years 1935–1939), *Revue de Métaphysique et de Morale*, vol. LIV, 1949, pp. 281–316 (which lays stress on everything in Husserl's earlier writing that seemed to exclude any "variation of phenomenology in the direction of a philosophy of history"; K. Jaspers, *Origin and Goal of History* (1953).

21. *Sein und Zeit*, §77.

of the *Revue de Synthèse Historique*. But the positivist prejudices dominating the clique grouped around Henri Berr simply
nullified this remarkable and serious attempt to inform.

When I arrived at the Sorbonne in November 1925, I was
welcomed by the elderly Seignobos, whose voice was feeble
but still full of conviction. (Lucien Febvre and Marc Bloch
were still exiled in Strasbourg.[22]) Positivism was still the official
philosophy of historians. We had hardly done more than
make an instinctive and almost visceral repudiation of it when
it began to be formulated in the light of Bergson. We had
not yet gone beyond the point that Péguy had reached in 1914.
Péguy, alas, had not returned to his little shop, and had not
been able to write that *Véronique* which was to be the positive counterpart of his bitter *Clio*. We had to wait until 1938
when, with the resounding theses of Raymond Aron,[23] the
critical philosophy of history was finally integrated into
French culture. No matter how personal his position may be,
Aron took his place in extending the line of descent from
Dilthey, Rickert and Weber. It was the merit of Eric Dardel's
brilliant little book[24]— which was too brilliant perhaps—that
it let us hear a voice more directly inspired by Heidegger.

Regardless of how extensive it may have been, Dilthey's
influence was nevertheless not universal. After emerging from
the national economic self-sufficiency in which we had remained enclosed for such a long time, we began to discover
one another and think as Europeans. For its part, Great Britain revealed to us a line of thinkers who were concerned about
this same problem—an original line having its remote source

22. I was unable to be either their associate or their pupil: whence
the jarring distance which united me to the students of the *Annales*.

23. Including (1) *Introduction to the Philosophy of History* (1961) and
(2) *La philosophie critique de l'histoire, essai sur une théorie allemande
de l'histoire*.

24. *L'histoire, science du concret* (1946).

in the empiricism of Hume.[25] This was represented about
1830–50 by the curious group of "Anglican liberals" that included Thomas Arnold, Whately, etc.,[26] and closer to us, by
F. H. Bradley. His philosophical career began with the essay,
The Presuppositions of Critical History[27] written in 1874, a
date which is even more symbolic. Important too are his successors, notably Michael B. Oakeshott[28] and more particularly
R. G. Collingwood, of singular mind and rather eccentric,
who was well known to historians as an authority on the
archeology of Roman Britain, but whose philosophical
thought[29] also deserves the most attentive consideration.

Collingwood, however, was not exclusively connected with
this line of British thinkers for he expressly placed himself
within Benedetto Croce's sphere of influence. We all know
that the old Neapolitan sophist, who was also a historian by
profession and a philosopher as well, accorded considerable
attention to the theoretical problems of history. This interest
stretched from his first treatise, *L'histoire ramenée au concept général de l'art* (1893)[30] to the work of his old age,
History: Its Theory and Practice (1938), and included his
Logic as the Science of Pure Concept (1904) and *Teoria e
storia della storiografia*, written in 1912–13.

In the opinion of foreigners, the obtrusive personality
of Croce has often seemed to sum up the whole activity of
Italian speculative thought. But this is a superficial and unfair

25. Cf. his essay on *Miracles* in the *Enquiry Concerning Human
Understanding* (1748).

26. On these Oxford theologians and historians (whom Mill called the
"Germano-Coleridgean school"), cf. M. D. Forbes, *The Liberal Anglican
Idea of History* (Cambridge, 1952).

27. Republished in *Collected Essays*, vol. I, pp. 1–70.

28. *Experience and Its Modes* (Cambridge, 1933), Chap. III.

29. Regarding the subject that interests us, cf. especially his posthumous
book, *The Idea of History* (Oxford, 1946), and prior to that, his *Autobiography* (Oxford, 1939).

30. Cf. *Primi Saggi*, pp. 3–41.

judgment, especially with reference to our subject, as so many proofs have recently attested.[31]

Whatever may be the originality of each of these thinkers, the variety of positions they have taken and the still open character of the controversy (which I am not forgetting for a moment), on examination the contribution of these three-quarters of a century clearly reveals a certain convergence in the way that the problem is posed and in the solutions that are suggested. Beginning with an analysis of the logical servitudes lying heavily upon the elaboration of historical knowledge, a specific critical philosophy of history has definitely come into existence. At least a certain set of basic principles may now be considered as established—in the same sense, for instance, that the theory of experimentation in the sciences of nature has been solidly established, let us say since J. S. Mill and Claude Bernard.

This is why it seemed to me that the moment has come to take a systematic inventory of it. Of course, I am not claiming that I have extracted an illusory *philosophia perennis* of historical thought on the basis of these various endeavors. The account that is to follow will itself also be a formulation inspired by a personal point of view. But I felt that if I restricted myself to fundamental problems, and to solutions of a very general kind, it might be possible to set forth a reasonable and balanced synopsis.

I have been less concerned to be original than to assemble, filter, verify and identify everything which (under more or less different forms) was being repeated everywhere, over and

31. Cf. for instance, *Il problema della storia, Atti dell' VIII. Convegno di studi filosofici cristiani* (Gallarate), Brescia, 1953. My American readers will perhaps be surprised to find no reference here to the well known work of M. Mandelbaum, *The Problem of Historical Knowledge* (New York, 1938). This book, valuable because of the analyses included in its documentary section, seems, in my opinion, to be *the bravest if least successful attempt to give an "Answer to Relativism."*

over again. I shall express my point of view in a calm and moderate tone, for down to the present day the philosophy of history has only too often been presented in an aggressive and polemical manner (and I am not excluding my own previous writings on the subject from this criticism). No doubt there were tyrannies to be overthrown and gates to be broken down, but the way is open now. I shall seek neither the pathetic nor the paradoxical: both have been greatly misused. Existentialism, for example, has made excessive pathos quite fashionable, endangering the very seriousness of thought. I am too faithful to the humanist tradition to want philosophy to dispense with the Muses, but the philosophical Muse must be a virgin, strictly austere in manner, who will not make ill use of "make-up."

In publishing this book I am fulfilling an idea formed more than twenty-five years ago, which has accompanied me continuously since I made my start in the historian's profession. During these years circumstances led me to write a series of articles which were hardly more than successive outlines of my idea. There was no question of reprinting them, of course, but I have carefully salvaged anything in them which I felt might be useful. I give the list of these articles here only to spare the reader the effort of reading them again:

1) *Tristesse de l'historien* (concerning the theses of R. Aron), *Esprit*, April, 1939, pp. 11-47.

2) *Bergson et l'histoire*, in the posthumous homage to *Henri Bergson*, published in 1941 by Éditions de la Baconnière, pp. 213-221. (This was reprinted in the "Cahiers du Rhône.")

3) *Qu'est-ce que l'histoire?* in the collection *Le sens chrétien de l'histoire*, Vol. 4 of "Rencontres," Lyon, 1942, published by Editions de l'Abeille (and since then, by Éditions du Cerf, Paris), pp. 9-34.

4) *L'histoire et l'éducation*, an address delivered at the University of Lyons, published in the *Annales de l'Université de Lyon* for the years 1941–42, Lyons, 1943, pp. 26–36.

5) *De la philosophie à l'histoire*, in the homage to *Étienne Gilson, philosophe de la chrétienté*, Vol. 30 of "Rencontres," Paris, 1949, Éditions du Cerf, pp. 71–86.

6) *De la logique de l'histoire à une éthique de l'historien*, in the issue devoted to the problems of history, *Revue de Métaphysique et de Morale*, July-October, 1949, pp. 248-272 of Volume 54.

7) Report on the *History of Civilization, I. Antiquité*, presented to the Tenth International Congress of Historical Sciences, Paris, 1950, and published in the Proceedings of the Congress, Vol. I, Éditions A. Colin, Paris, pp. 248–272.

8) *D'une théorie de la civilisation à la théologie de l'histoire* (on the work of Arnold J. Toynbee), *Esprit*, July, 1952, pp. 112–129.

9) *Philosophie critique de l'histoire et "sens de l'histoire"* in *L'homme et l'histoire*, Proceedings of the Sixth Congress of the French-Speaking Philosophical Societies, Strasbourg, 1952, published by the Presses Universitaires de France, pp. 3–10.

10) *La méthodologie historique: orientations actuelles* (in regard to recent works), *Revue historique*, April-June, 1953, Vol. 209, pp. 256-270.

Finally, this project might never have resulted in anything at all if Mgr. L. De Raeymaeker, president of the *Institut Supérieur de Philosophie* at Louvain University, had not provided the chance to carry it out by inviting me to accept the Cardinal Mercier professorship for the year 1953. I must thank all those who heard me lecture at Louvain (and with them our colleagues of the Centre National de Recherches de Logique, in Brussels) for their most considerate reception. My book has profited greatly from the comments and criticisms which they expressed to me with such genuine friendliness.

Nor shall I ever forget my former students at the École Normale and the Sorbonne and the frequent discussions I held with them that were so helpful, especially Alain Touraine, Dom Jean Becquet, Father Pierre Blet, Odette Laffoucrière, Abbé Jean Sainsaulieu, Pierre Vidal-Naquet, Dr. Jean-Marie Harl, Violette Méjan. I owe special thanks to Jean-François Suter and Maurice Crubellier, who read my manuscript and helped me prepare it for publication.

CHAPTER I

History as Knowledge

We shall begin with a definition and then ask the question: *What is history?* Obviously, this is merely a pedagogical device. It would certainly be naïve to imagine that any definition which was speculatively elaborated and therefore posed *a priori* could possibly express the very essence, the *quid sit,* of history. The philosophy of the sciences does not proceed in that manner but has its point of departure in something given, some particular discipline already constituted. By applying itself to analysis of the rational procedures of the specialists, it discerns the logical structure of their method. Long before philosophy attempted to provide a theoretical basis for the various sciences, these had generally been evolving out of an empirical tradition. Geometry, for instance, originated in the surveying of land, and experimental medicine emerged from the tradition and lore of the "healers."

Sociology is no exception but rather a further proof of this rule. Its development was impeded far more than it was favored by the amassing of methodological speculations which Auguste Comte and Durkheim employed to explain its origins.

Similarly, we must recognize that history exists. At our point of departure we shall make no claim that we can define the best history that anyone could possibly conceive. Instead, we shall simply ascertain the existence of our object, which is that part of human culture that is the concern of a specialized body of technicians, the professional historians. Our *datum* is the method which competent specialists recognize as valid. The real existence of such a datum is unquestionable.

It is certainly a fact that professional historians are in possession of a vigorous methodological tradition. For us men of
Western civilization it begins with Herodotus and Thucydides,
continuing (let us say) down to Fernand Braudel, whose work
is regarded by other historians as among the best that any
young scholar has produced. We who belong to the profession are quite aware of all those who may be called our
peers, and we know those among the historians of the past or
the present whose work may be considered as valid. There
are men who are regarded as "authorities," so to speak, and
also others who are suspected of rather irregular procedure.
As a first step (and quite properly at the start of our study)
we shall not attempt to do more than indicate roughly the
scope of this existent tradition. With regard to its limits we
must admit that they are still largely indistinct.

Our methodological tradition has been constantly subject
to change. Herodotus, for example, now seems less like the
"Father of History" than an elderly grandfather lapsing into
second childhood; the veneration we profess for the example
he set us is not without a protective smile. And although
beginning with Thucydides or Polybius we recognize something essential in our method of work, we readily agree that
authentic scientific history was not fully constituted until the
nineteenth century when the rigor of critical methods, carefully and exactly developed by the great scholars of the seventeenth and eighteenth centuries, was extended from the
domain of the auxiliary sciences (numismatics, paleography,
etc.) to the structure of history itself. Strictly speaking, our
tradition was definitively established by B. G. Niebuhr, and
even more surely by Leopold von Ranke.

There is the same marginal indistinctness in the history
that is being taught and written today. It is doubtless true that
the experts within the profession are generally in agreement
in judging the validity of their studies and research, but this

consensus is not without a certain amount of dissonance, and is even sometimes openly opposed. The specialists, in their excessive strictness, may be only too ready to disqualify the "amateur," but voices can be heard loudly condemning the narrowness of the "official science." As a matter of fact the field of history, in which historians are at work, is occupied by a body of inquirers deployed in a fan-shaped manner. At one extremity there are the meticulous scholars busily engaged in "manicuring" documents for publication (who are often suspected of being merely philologists and not real historians). They are more like laboratory assistants who have yet to become true scholars. At the other end are exalted minds, obsessed by immense syntheses embracing enormous periods of history and evolution from eagle-winged perspectives. We contemplate them from below with a certain amount of anxiety, suspect as they are of going far beyond the level of history (but this time by way of ascent).

For the moment, let us tolerate this flexibility in the demarcation of boundaries. Let us grant to personal taste, or rather to everyone's particular bent, the right to place value upon or to disqualify any particular aspect of this multiform method. We find some historians, for instance, condemning biography as a mode that is fundamentally anti- or ahistorical,[1] while to the contrary, others[2] insist that it is almost the highest form of history, regarding it as a comprehensive view of a whole period or even a whole civilization somehow focused in one of its greatest sons.

Disputing the authority which Croce's theory of history was being accorded because of his experiences as a historian, I had occasion to write the following comments:

Croce's historical work oscillates between two forms: simple

1. Collingwood, *Idea*, p. 304; Aron, *Introduction*, pp. 81–82.

2. Dilthey, for example, whose major historical works are biographical: *Life of Schleiermacher*, I (1870); *Histoire de la jeunesse de Hegel* (1906).

local history (*The Neapolitan Revolution of 1799, The Theater in Naples from the Renaissance to the End of the 18th Century*) and the great synthesis which towers over the facts, "conceiving" them but never really working directly upon the sources (*The History of Italy, 1871-1915; The History of Europe in the 19th Century*). May I dare to suggest that the axis of real history passes between the two? But everyone will determine this axis in his own way, and I know very well that my theory may meet with the objection that it comes from a historian of antiquity, a historian of culture who is too exclusively oriented toward problems of a spiritual or religious kind, and that it would have been differently conceived if I had taken contemporary history and its economic or social problems as the areas of experience.[3] Let us accept these diverse points of view provisionally while rejecting the exclusive claims of any of them, and let us try to lay hold of history as it exists in its complex reality and full variety as set forth in the works of historians.

We can disregard the constantly repeated attempts of the theorists who seek to demonstrate the possibility, necessity and urgency of a history that is different from that of the historians: a "history" that would be more scientific, more abstract. It would attempt for example to discern the more general laws of human behavior according as the latter is manifested in empirical history (contingency, necessity, etc.)—such as Henri Berr's "scientific synthesis,"[4] the "theoretical history" of P. Vendryès,[5] and the *"theoretische Geschiedenis"* of J. M.

3. This was Georges Bidault's objection, made during a memorable discussion at the Société Lyonnaise de Philosophie on June 18, 1942.

4. *La synthèse en histoire, son rapport avec l'histoire générale* (1911; 2nd edition, 1953).

5. *De la probabilité en histoire, l'exemple de l'expédition d'Égypte* (1952).

Romein.[6] Even if we assume that these disciplines eventually prove to be as fruitful as their founders anticipate, they will not abolish the traditional history whose existence they must postulate. Our critical philosophy will continue to be both necessary and legitimate.

Let us ask the question once again: What is history? In reply, I would say that *history is the knowledge of man's past*. The practical usefulness of this definition is that it sums up briefly the substance of the discussions and the comments which it inspired. But we must explain this more fully.

We shall use the term *knowledge* rather than the "narration of the human past"[7] or "a literary work whose purpose is to relate the past."[8] Doubtless a historical study will normally culminate in a written work (and we shall examine this problem in our conclusion), but such a requirement is a practical matter pertaining to the historian's social mission. Actually, of course, a completely elaborated history already exists in the mind of the historian before he has begun writing a word of it; whatever the reciprocal influences of these two types of activity may be, they are logically distinct and separate.

We shall use the term *knowledge* rather than "research" or "study"—although "enquiry" is the principal meaning of the Greek word ἰστορία—for this would be confusing the end with the means. After all, if it were not attainable we would not be pursuing it. History is delimited by the truth that it can elaborate, and when we say *knowledge* we mean true and valid knowledge. Consequently, history is the very opposite

6. *Theoretische Geschiedenis* (Gröningen, 1946). With regard to this conception, which is much more comprehensive than the preceding two, see the report of J. H. Nota, *Actes* du XIe Congrès international de Philosophie (Brussells, 1953), vol. 8, pp. 10–14.

7. O. Philippe, *L'homme et l'histoire* (*Actes* du Congrès de Strasbourg, 1952), p. 36.

8. R. Jolivet, *ibid.*, p. 11.

3

of anything that is a false description of the past, or one that
is distorted and untrue to the facts. It is unlike conceptions
of utopia or imaginary history of the kind that was written by
Walter Pater.[9] It differs from myth, popular traditions and the
pedagogical legends of a past that is depicted in "patriotic"
imagery, which in their pride great modern nations inculcate
in the minds of their future citizens as early as the primary
grades of the elementary school.[10]

No doubt this truth to be sought in historical knowledge
is an ideal. And the further our analysis progresses, the more
apparent it will be that the ideal is not easily attainable. History must be at least the result of the most rigorous and most
systematic effort to approach it. A concise definition of history
as "the *scientifically elaborated* knowledge of the past" would
perhaps be satisfactory if the very notion of science were not
itself ambiguous.

The Platonist would be amazed that the word "science"
could be used with reference to knowledge that is so slightly
rational and so largely a matter of opinion, pertaining as it
does to δόξα. The Aristotelian (from whom there can be no
"science" unless it is general) will be quite bewildered when
he finds history described—with some exaggeration, as we
shall see—as a "science of the concrete" (Dardel), or as a
science of "the particular" (Rickert). Apparently we shall have
to speak Greek to make ourselves understood. Consequently
we must say specifically that when we use the word "science"
with reference to history it is not the Greek word for knowledge— ἐπιστήμη—that we have in mind, but rather the idea
of τέχνη, an art or technical method. In other words, as

9. *Imaginary Portraits* (1888), not to mention *Marius the Epicurean*
or *Gaston de Latour.*

10. In R. Minder's fine book, *Allemagnes et Allemands* (1948), will
be found a comparative analysis of the antithetical stylizations ("sticho-
mythy"), which elementary instruction in France and Germany have
accorded to the same historical personages: Charlemagne, etc.

opposed to the ordinary knowledge of daily experience, we have reference to an elaborate knowledge set forth in terms of a systematic and rigorous method which has proved to be productive of the *optimum* measure of truth.

We use the expression *"knowledge of the past"* even when it is a matter of wholly contemporary history. We need only mention the traffic policeman who makes a report concerning an accident which he has just witnessed a moment before. This is an example of an elementary historical act. We always mean the knowledge of *man's past*. Whatever that past may have been, we make no prejudgments. We especially reject the preliminary demands or exigencies which the philosopher of history might wish to impose on us, for the logician and philosopher of the sciences has no worse enemy than one who affirms or pretends to know what constitutes the essence of the past. We simply deny having knowledge of any such thing. We accept in its full complexity everything that was part of man's past—everything that we may be able to learn regarding it.

Accordingly, we speak of *man's past*, and reject any addition or specification that may possibly have originated in certain mental reservations.

Why, for instance, would anyone refer to the past "of men living in *society*"?[11] This is pointless. Since Aristotle we have known that man is an animal living in organized society. (The historian of eremitical life is surprised to learn that the flight to the desert does not really separate man from society: before God, the contemplative takes all of humanity upon himself.) Perhaps it is meant to be suggestive. But I cannot see why anyone would want to exclude from history the most personal aspects of the story of the past, for these are perhaps the most precious of all. Similarly, why should anyone specify

11. Ch. Seignobos, "Lettre à F. Lot" (1941), *Revue historique*, vol. 210 (1953), p. 4.

"the *facts* of man's past"?[12] This is unnecessary if "facts" merely signify reality as contrasted with what is only fantasy or imagination. It is utterly suspect if this is simply a furtive attempt to exclude ideas, values and the spirit. Moreover, we shall find nothing less clear than this notion of "fact" in the subject matter of history.

The only element that is perhaps still ambiguous in our definition is our use of the expression *"man's* past." By this we mean human activity that can be directly comprehended and interiorly perceived, including actions, thoughts and feelings; and also all the works of man, the material or spiritual creations of his societies and civilizations, all the works through which we are able to reach their creator. In short, we have reference to the past of man insofar as he is truly human: man already becomes man, in contrast to the biological past covering the evolution of the human species. This is no longer studied by history but by human paleontology, which is a branch of biology.

We shall have occasion to give further thought to this distinction between the two pasts of mankind that pertain to biological evolution and to history. However, we can already find practical use for such a distinction by devoting some thought to the status of the border-line discipline that is called "prehistory." It is not only a border-line discipline, but a highly complex one. This is often the case with the particular sciences since they are entities of a practical order which have no logical unity. Prehistory is a mixture in both its object and its methods.

In the prehistorian's field of study there is a whole area pertaining to paleontology. When he examines the remains of human skeletons, he analyzes their physical characteristics. He concentrates for instance on the size of the cranial brainpan or the erect posture that seems to be more or less verified.

12. *Loc. cit.* (and previously, H. Berr, *La synthèse en histoire*, p. 1).

His observations may lead him to adopt certain hypotheses about the psychic character of these remote races, but I find nothing in them that is specifically historical. Paleontology applies methods to the study of the past which are utilized for the study of the present by ethnology (as contrasted with ethnography, which is properly the study of "primitive" civilizations). Both the object and the methods are definitely dependent on biology.

However, the same prehistorian studies objects that bear the marks or traces of man's voluntary action (these objects are called *artifacts*). When he tries through them to gain understanding of the material or spiritual techniques (magic, religion) and to some extent of the feelings or ideas of their authors, he is really doing something that pertains to archeology, which is a branch of history. In this sense prehistory becomes real history in the full meaning of the term.

When Norbert Casteret, for example, discovered in the grotto of Montespan[13] a small clay image representing a quadruped adorned with the skull of a bear cub, an image that was pierced by iron-tipped spears in several places, he encountered no difficulty in reconstructing the rite of "sympathetic" magic in which prehistoric hunters had participated. Eskimos of our own time have also practiced this same rite.

We understand this type of behavior interiorly. Direct comprehension of this kind is something quite different from that of the physicist who "understands" the disintegration of the atom. It is our interior knowledge of man and his potentialities that enables us to understand these prehistoric hunters. In this sense they are quite historical. As a matter of fact, we regard as "artifacts" only those objects which appear *to us* as possessing intelligible traces of man's action. We hesitate whenever we are confronted with doubtful examples.

13. P. Charlus, in *Seizième semaine de Synthèse: À la recherche de la mentalité préhistorique* (1950, publ. 1953), pp. 147–148, 151.

In certain paleolithic strata in China, for instance, some stones have been found which had been split into pieces by fire, but there has been reluctance to admit that human action was the cause. Could they not be the result of some accidental phenomenon? Again, in the case of certain markings drawn or painted during the neolithic period there is some question whether they are merely decorative. If they are significative, might they not represent a crude attempt at writing?

We cannot exclude the possibility that investigators may have overlooked precious objects simply because they failed to recognize man's own trace in them. We shall show that the extent and scope of historical knowledge is always in direct proportion to the personal learning of the historian. This fact is already apparent in prehistory. Here ethnography increases our awareness of the variety of human techniques and is the instrument of learning that makes the historian more capable with regard to the object.

For anyone who has studied similar objects among the Eskimos of Alaska, the supposed Magdalenian "staffs of command" really prove to be "arrow-straighteners" (producing rectilinear arrows out of small branches that were curved or bent). Certain neolithic "message-sticks" were perhaps used in libations like the "moustache-cups" of the Ainu of northern Japan.[14]

The knowledge of man's past (which is the knowledge of man or men of yesterday, yesteryear, and long ago) by the man of today (the man of later times, who is the historian) is a definition which asserts that the reality of history is to be found in the relationship thus established by the historian's

14. A. Leroi-Gourhan, *La civilisation du renne* (1936), pp. 58, 60, 63; G. Montandon, *La civilisation Aïnou* (1937), pp. 52–59.

line of thought. We can suggest the following formula by way of illustration:

$$h = \frac{P}{p}$$

In mathematics the magnitude of the relationship is something other than each of the terms placed in relation. This formula simply indicates the fact that history is similarly the relation and conjunction established by the historian's initiative between two levels of humanity: the past lived by the men of other times, and the present in which the effort to recapture that past is undertaken for the benefit of living men and for men who will follow after. *Omne simile claudicat* : the comparison is not perfect. In a mathematical relationship the two terms possess a proper reality; in history, these two levels are only perceptible within the knowledge that unites them. We cannot isolate an object (which is the past) from the subject (the historian) except by a formal distinction.

Nothing is more significant with regard to this matter than the remarkable ambiguity that speech maintains. Language is not happy in uniting these two levels—the metonymy that is by turns irritating and instructive allows us to use the same word, history, to designate either the relationship itself or its numerator. No doubt it it legitimate to distinguish the two concepts in our thinking (and the development of our analysis will require it at every moment). But once the distinction is made we shall certainly have to adopt some suitable form of expression. More than one has been suggested or tried.

The simplest, if not the most practical, consists in contrasting historical reality and historical knowledge (rather than objective and subjective history). Hegel once expressed himself in Latin to make himself better understood, distinguishing *res gestae*—the deeds and exploits themselves—from the *historia rerum gestarum.* In German, the attempt has often been made to utilize the doublets of vocabulary, that is, a word of Germanic origin and another word borrowed from French, similar in meaning, to signify specially each of the two uses[15]: *Geschichte* on the one hand, and *Historie* on the other. In Italian, or at least in the very personal vocabulary of Benedetto Croce, the same distinction is achieved by the two words *storia/storiografia.* This is open to our objection that historical knowledge exists even if, or when, it is not yet written. In French, the most ingenious combination was suggested by Henry Corbin[16]: *Histoire* and *histoire.* Both words are spelled alike but the use of the capital letter indicates the real past that was lived by men of flesh and blood. The small letter signifies the lowly representation which the historian's labor seeks to recompose—expressing quite clearly the pejorative value attached to the poor scribblings and notes of the professors of history which have been the objects of so much sarcasm from Hegel to Péguy. A combination of this kind is unfortunately inapplicable in the English language for *History* may (without an article) be found at the beginning of a sentence, thus usurping the capital letter regardless of the meaning intended.[17]

Nevertheless—and this is what really matters—apart from the occasions when the logician's mind voluntarily fastens upon this distinction, the genius of a language (expressing the implicit wisdom of whole nations, as is often the case) simply

15. Cf. Kant, *"The Natural Principle of the Political Order considered in connection with the Idea of a Universal Cosmopolitical History,"* (1784); Cassirer (ed.), *Works,* vol. IV, p. 165.

16. In his French translation of sections 46–76 of *Sein und Zeit,* and found in M. Heidegger, *Qu'est-ce que la métaphysique?* (1938), pp. 115–208 (see p. 175, n. 1); regarding E. Dardel's preference, see *L'histoire, science du concret.*

17. G. J. Renier, *History, Its Purpose and Method* (London, 1950), p. 81.

refuses to confirm or adopt it. The reader need only listen to himself speaking. He will note that in his own mouth the word *history* is used by turns in both senses. And contrary to what is frequently supposed, this does not mean that English or French are poor in general vocabulary or technical terms. The distinction indicated in German by the use of *Geschichte/Historie* was very artificial. *Historie* is not a truly living word in German, and *Geschichte* is moreover constantly used in the sense of "historical knowledge or literature." We have explicit and authoritative declarations on the subject ranging from Hegel[18] to Heidegger.[19] This is a very general situation. In all of our cultural languages, whether English, Spanish, Italian, Dutch or Russian, we find the same ambiguity. With regard to Italian, I was surprised to make the interesting discovery that Benedetto Croce himself acknowledged this fact![20]

We must not pass lightly from the formal distinction to the real distinction, from the critical to the ontological. Actually, there has been excessive use, and even misuse, of antitheses like *Geschichte/Historie, Kultur/Zivilisation,*[21] *Community/ Society, Priest/Prophet, Apollo/Dionysus,* etc. Antithesis is a rather crude instrument of analysis that contrasts two opposite poles between which reality is reclassified but also becomes decomposed. But in this instance, and for our purposes, the

18. *Vorlesungen* on the philosophy of history (Éditions Lasson, *Werke,* vol. 8), pp. 144–145: "In our language [German!] *Geschichte* combines the objective aspect and the subjective aspect, and denotes the *historiam rerum gestarum* as well as the *res gestas* themselves. . . . "

19. *Sein und Zeit,* §73, Corbin's translation (French), p. 178.

20. Cf. *Noterelle polemiche* (1894), in *Primi Saggi,* p. 46, n. 3.

21. This is also very artificial. The meaning of the contrasted terms has certainly changed from W. von Humboldt (1836) to F. Tönnies (1887) and Max Weber (1912). See A. L Kroeber and C. Kluckhohn, *Culture, a Critical Review of Concepts and Definitions* (Papers of the Peabody Museum, vol. 47, no. 1, 1952).

only reality that language has ever designated is an awareness
of the human past that is obtained intellectually by the efforts
of the historian. It is not to be found at one or the other of
two poles, but in the relationship or synthesis which the initiative and active intervention of the conscious subject establishes
between the present and the past.

Of course, since it is defined as knowledge (and we have
specifically called it authentic knowledge), history presupposes
an object. It makes a definite claim that it reaches the past
that was "really" lived by humanity. But regarding this past
we can neither say nor do anything except to postulate its
existence as necessary (insofar as knowledge about it has not
been elaborated) in the empirical and logical conditions which
our critical philosophy will attempt to analyze. Let us continue, in Dilthey's manner, to express ourselves in terms
borrowed from Kant. (To avoid being accused of "neo-Kan-
tianism" we must stress that we use such terms only in a
metaphorical sense, transposing the vocabulary from the trans-
cendental to the empirical.) We shall say that the object of
history somehow presents itself to us, ontologically, as "noumenon." It exists, indeed, for otherwise the very notion of
historical knowledge would be absurd. But we cannot describe it, for the moment that it is apprehended it is as knowledge that this occurs. And in this same moment it undergoes
a complete metamorphosis, as though being reshaped by the
categories of the conscious subject. But rather than continue
this dependence on metaphors, let us say more plainly that
the change takes place as the result of the logical and technical
servitudes which are imperative in scientific history.

To make a distinction we must avoid designating the past
(prior to the elaboration of our knowledge of it) by the same
word—history—which we use with reference to historical
knowledge (even if a capital letter is meant to signify the
difference). Nor will any other word of the same root or the

same meaning do. Sooner or later the ambiguity or ordinary speech will again be insinuated in the mind, and the validity of the distinction will be diminished. Since apparently we must choose a word, I suggest that we decide upon the *Evolution* of humanity—in preference to "development" or "genesis"—although even this term is not without its disadvantages.

As the word evolution has been used in biology it designates the complicated network of causal relations, deployed in time, which link the living creature to his direct antecedents. It is quite legitimate to apply by analogy the same expression to the time—incomparably shorter and nearer to us —that *homo sapiens* has lived since the emergence of his type.

The difference in scale between the two durations and the distinct nature of the phenomena observed do not oppose any insurmountable obstacle to the suggested semantic extension. Our analogous transposition retains only the fundamental notion of the initial concept: the present state of a living creature is explained by the heritage of his past. As the horse's cannon bones are the result of the gradual contraction of the metatarsus of its tertiary ancestors, the Frenchmen of today have likewise been produced by the years that followed the Liberation and the interval between 1940-1945, the period between the two World Wars and 1914-1918—and similarly all the way back to Julius Caesar, Vercingetorix, the Gauls, the neolithic cultivators, and still further back. Even if modern Frenchmen knew nothing about their ancestors (assuming that there had been no attempt to obtain historical knowledge), the behavior of French citizens with regard to taxation and the attitude of French Catholics toward collections for the Church find explanation in the mental habits inherited from those ancestors and contracted under the absolute monarchy, or as the result of the Concordat of 1515.

Like the representative of a biological species, the man of a particular society or civilization is the son of his past, including *all* of his past. It is especially in this sense that we have the right to speak of the heredity of acquired characteristics! The most innovating revolutions do not succeed in abolishing all of this heritage. Accordingly, anyone who is at all familiar with the history of Russia will easily perceive that this same Soviet Union which aims to be wholly Marxist owes many of the features of its civilization to its mother, Czarist Russia, and to the Byzantine antecedents of the latter. Readiness to justify recourse to police terror may be mentioned by way of example.

Let us be doubly careful. It is normal for a discipline to borrow a concept from one of its neighbors. In a symmetrical way, biology likes to speak of "historical" phenomena when it studies, for instance, the effects of a particular glacial period on the distribution of botanical or animal species in some given area. But it must be firmly emphasized that when utilized in a sphere of experience different from the one for which it has been elaborated, every scientific concept gradually loses some of its validity. The new usage has only analogical and therefore limited character.

For my part, I am very sensitive to the misuse that could be made of the idea of biological "evolution" by transposing it without modification to the sphere of "history." Historical evolution is not, purely and simply, a new and final phase of biological evolution. We shall have occasion to consider this matter further.

However, this "past that was really lived," this evolution of humanity, is not history. History is not merely a copy of this evolution, as might have been supposed in any pre-Kantian theory of knowledge. The human past becomes something else by coming to life again in the historian's mind. It is dependent on another mode of being. In analyzing the nature of history, there has been an excessive misuse of the famous formulas of Ranke or Michelet: "to show purely and simply how things occurred" (*wie es eigentlich gewesen*), and the "integral resurrection of the past." These phrases become more meaningful when they are read in their context instead of being passed from hand to hand like a coin that becomes a little more worn and corroded each passing day.[22]

Similarly, I regard as extremely unsatisfactory that other formula which R. G. Collingwood finally decided upon in his search for a truly rational theory of history: *History as re-enactment of past experience.*

It must be stated forcefully that the historian is not under-taking the task of restoring, reviving or resurrecting the past, even if such a thing were conceivable without contradiction. These are merely metaphorical expressions. It is true that in a sense he brings back into existence in the present time something which (having become the past) had ceased to exist. But in becoming "history," and in being known, the past is not simply reproduced as it had been when it was the present. Of course there are innumerable transformations (transpositions, deformations, selections) which it must under-go because of the manipulations whereby our intellect elabo-rates its historical knowledge; but it should suffice for the moment to emphasize that the past summed up in history will consequently be affected by a specific qualification: it is known as something that is definitely *past*. When it was "real," it was something quite different for its actors, the men who experienced it. For them it was the present: the moment of application of a teeming conflux of forces that were making the unforeseeable present rise out of the uncertain future; in which everything was in movement, in a process of becoming,

22. Cf. Th. von Laue, *Leopold Ranke, The Formative Years* (Princeton Studies in History, vol. 4, 1950), pp. 25–26; O. A. Haac, *Les principes inspirateurs de Michelet* (1951), pp. 73–80: for the context, see *Geschichte der romanischen und germanischen Völker, Sämtl. Werke*, vol. 33, p. 7; *Histoire de France*, vol. 1, pp. 4, 11, 21–22, 31.

in fieri. Discovered again as the past—even if it be only yesterday or a moment ago—the flow of life has by then already crossed the threshold of the irrevocable. It is something that used to be, or has already occurred; something *geschehen* (the *dagewesenes Dasein* of Heidegger), grammatically expressed by the "perfect" tense. This is a very elementary observation but one whose consequences will prove to be profound and far-reaching. For the moment, however, let us simply single out three of them:

a) Far from making himself the "contemporary" of his object (as has been only too often asserted) the historian perceives and places it in perspective in the background of the past. He knows it as something that is past—that is, the very act of knowing this object recognizes both the fact evoked as having-once-been-present, and the distance (more or less remote) now separating us from it.

It is not true, as Proust wrote toward the end of *The Past Recaptured,* that "memory, by bringing the past into the present without modification, exactly as it was at the moment when it was the present, abolishes precisely the great dimension of time." Proust was better inspired when, on the last page of his book, he mentions his awareness that he is "perched" on the "dizzy summit" of his past. "I felt a dizziness in seeing so many years below me, and yet within me, as if I were looking down from high places . . . as if men were perched on living stilts that were constantly growing taller. . . ."

It seems that in this very ability to perceive with equal acuteness both the reality of the past and its remoteness there is to be found the sense of history, properly so-called. We note the absence of this perception in artists of the Middle Ages or the Renaissance who painted persons of classical or Christian antiquity wearing the clothing of men and women of the fourteenth or fifteenth centuries. I know St. Paul in a different way than the men of his day—as St. Luke, for instance, knew him—even if our knowledge is the same in content. St. Luke may possibly have known neither more facts, nor more specific or certain facts than are known to me. But because I know St. Paul as a man of the first century A.D., I see him from the perspective of these nineteen hundred years that separate us. I see him as quite different from myself because of all that has happened in the time that has elapsed. I chose this example purposely (rather than saying that I do not know Caesar as Cicero knew him) because, as a Christian, I feel and know myself to be in communion with St. Paul in all that he himself considered as essential to his thought. I profess to share and understand his faith in Christ. Nevertheless, as a historian I listen to his teaching with a sharp awareness of the specific differences that separate him from a churchman of today—but here again I am simply assuming the equal quality of the theological content. With regard to this point, I had a controversy with the American exegete, Edgar J. Goodspeed. In his modernized translation of the New Testament, he renders the salutation χαίρετε as *Good Morning!* (Mt. 28:9), or as *Goodbye!* (Phil. 4:4). In my opinion, this is to betray the author and mislead the reader. It leaves him with the impression that St. Matthew or St. Paul wrote like Americans of the twentieth century. In fact, they wrote like Greeks of the first, making use of a language to greet one another in which they did not mumble some unintelligible phrase such as "how d'y'do?" or "'bye 'bye!" like the Anglo-Saxons of today, but said very clearly, "Rejoice!" They were perfectly aware of this meaning of χαῖρε, χαίρετε, as the passage in Philippians 4:4 plainly indicates: "Rejoice in the Lord always; again I say, rejoice." It is quite inept to transcribe this verse as "Goodbye . . . again I say, Goodbye!"[23]

23. E. Goodspeed, *Problems of New Testament Translation* (Chicago, 1945), pp. 45–46, 174–175.

b) But this interval which separates us from the object in the past is not a complete void. All during the intermediate time, the events studied—whether actions, thoughts or feelings—have produced their fruit, entailing consequences and deploying their potentialities. We cannot separate our knowledge of them from what we may know about these after-effects.

Let us take this occasion to note how rich our theoretical analysis is proving to be in its practical consequences. The Rule of the Epilogue, as I like to call it, can be attributed to this fact. Every historical study that does not follow its object "from the beginning down to our own day" must begin with an introduction which indicates the antecedents of the phenomenon that is studied. It must also include an epilogue that aims to answer the question: What happened afterward? The study must not begin and end abruptly, like the movie-screen that is lighted at the start of the film only to be darkened suddenly at the end.

We cannot set forth the story of Martin Luther without recalling the condition of Catholic piety and nominalist theology at the end of the fifteenth century. Nor can we relate the history of religion in France during the seventeenth century without showing how it prepared the way for the explosion of the Regency and the triumphant irreligion of the eighteenth century.

Like all the rules of historical method, this one must be applied with care and proportion. Later developments must not be unduly projected onto the preceding situation, making Plato, for example, responsible for the scepticism of the New Academy, or St. Augustine to blame for Jansenius. But the very effort that leads me to prove that Jansenism is a spurious development of Augustinian doctrine is immensely helpful to me in gaining a better understanding of Augustine.

c) Finally, when it belonged to the present this past was like the present which we are experiencing at this moment: something obscure, confused, multiform and unintelligible; a thick network of causes and effects; an infinitely complex field of forces which the consciousness of man, whether he is an actor or a witness, is necessarily unable to perceive in its authentic reality. (After all, there is no privileged observation post, at least not on this earth.) We can cite the example— classic since Stendhal and Tolstoy[24]— of the Napoleonic wars; the Waterloo of the *Chartreuse,* or better yet, the Austerlitz and Borodino of *War and Peace.* (Napoleon himself, in Tolstoy's opinion, was quite as undone as Prince Andrew or Peter Bezoukhov.)

The historian could never be satisfied with such a fragmentary and superficial view. He wants and seeks much more knowledge about things over a considerably "longer" period of time than any of the contemporaries of the period had known, or ever could have known. Not that he claims to find the same exactness in detail, or the same concrete richness as that of real experience itself. That would be impossible, as he knows. Besides, it does not interest him in the highest degree. The knowledge of the past that the historian wants to elaborate aims at intelligibility. It must rise above the dust of small facts, those molecules whose agitation in disorder built the present. What the historian desires is to provide an ordered view, discerning in the main lines the orientations that can be recognized and understood, together with the chains of causal or final relations, and the various meanings and values.

History must succeed in casting upon the past that overall

24. He was profoundly influenced by Stendhal's example: cf. I. Berlin, *Lev Tolstoy's Historical Scepticism,* Oxford Slavonic Papers, vol. 2 (1951), pp. 17–54.

and rational glance which comprises, grasps and, in a sense, explains the total view which we despair of achieving with regard to our own time. This reminds us of the appeal to Clio which Péguy enjoyed attributing to Hugo's pen in *Châtiments*, the waiting upon history which we hope some day will enable men to know what we did not know because so many essential data escape our information and experience. It may especially help us understand all the things that we were unable to perceive or recognize in the heat of our struggles as we were swept along in the flow of forces that we could not contemplate from above. They could not be perceived as long as the forces in action had not revealed themselves in the fulfillment of all their effects, or for as long as the process of change and development had not been fully realized or completed. We must not be too hasty in comparing the historian to the playwright or the novelist. It must always be carefully emphasized that intelligibility has to be *true* and certainly never imaginary, finding its ground and proof in the "reality" of man's past. But if we keep this clearly in mind it is correct to say[25] that history must try to elaborate a kind of knowledge that is quite as intelligible as the writings of Shakespeare or Balzac.

We may find it useful to mention here a distinction dear to Croce. He liked to contrast real history with the simple chronicle (Sorokin uses the American expression: *newsreel*), or the report of the annalist: a narrative which relates the past faithfully but meaninglessly, in all the disorder of direct experience. This is the defect that we often criticize in local or regional history. This often considers itself to be both scrupulous and exhaustive. It feels duty-bound to report a thousand little facts with meticulous care, sparing us none of the details—not even a chamber-pot emptied on the head

25. W. H. Walsh, *Introduction to Philosophy of History*, p. 33.

of a passer-by on the sixteenth of August, 1610 (National Archives, Z^2 3265, f° 99^V° : "a full pot of big and little faeces, filthy and disgusting"[26]).

This is not yet history because the mind of the historian has not devoted enough effort to conceive clearly the raw material of the datum, or to make it conceivable in the sense of being understandable.

Before proceeding to an analysis of the profound transformation—the transmutation—which the process of elaborating historical knowledge produces in the noumenal past, we must again lay stress upon the immediate consequences which the simple ascertainment of its reality will entail in our method, and notably in whatever pertains to the criticism of the sources. It is naïve to imagine that testimony will be more valuable to the historian simply because it adheres more closely to the event. This is taken for granted by the classic theory[27] of the "critique of exactitude." Was the witness in a favorable position for observation? Did he take the trouble to observe carefully? Was he not perhaps the victim of hallucination, illusion or prejudice? Was the observed fact or event really observable at all?

The critique is valid if there is question of establishing the materiality of an occurrence that can be objectified, as for instance the circumstances of an automobile accident. The most reliable document will certainly be the police report drawn up at the scene immediately after the event which records the statements of a number of independent witnesses. But this is neither the only task of the historian nor the most essential. Far more than merely ascertaining the facts, it is important that he understand them. Furthermore, the events

26. F. Lehoux, *Le bourg de Saint-Germain-des-Prés, depuis ses origines jusqu'à la fin de la guerre de Cent ans* (1951), p. 129.

27. Ch.-V. Langlois and Ch. Seignobos, *Introduction aux études historiques* (1898), pp. 145–150.

of interest to him are often more subtle in essence than the material observations. As L. Massignon has pointed out in a justly famous essay,[28] the content of a moment of mystical illumination is more *precisely* known (because more profoundly understood) by the considerations which the hero—after a lapse of ten years and enlightened by all the subsequent enrichment of his spiritual experience—has developed regarding the matter—much more than by the little memo that is roughly scribbled during the extraordinary night.

We need only compare the notes of Pascal with the *Confessions* of St. Augustine, so profoundly elaborated and consequently so revealing, which a myopic criticism thought itself capable of disqualifying.

28. *L'expérience mystique et les modes de stylisation littéraire,* Le Roseau d'or, Chroniques, 4 (1927), pp. 141–176.

CHAPTER II

History and the Historian Are Inseparable

When it is stripped of polemical excesses and paradoxical formulations, the critical philosophy of history consists essentially in revealing the decisive role which the active participation of the historian (including both his mind and personality) must necessarily assume in the elaboration of historical knowledge. We shall no longer say, "history, alas, is inseparable from the historian."[1]

Gide's remark comes to mind: "So much the worse!" said Ménalque. "I prefer believing that if something does not exist, it is because it could not exist." However, neither *alas* nor *So much the worse!* can be called philosophical categories.

We can only acknowledge the simple fact—without surprise or feelings of anger—as inscribed in the very structure of reality. We must frankly recognize the actual situation imposed on the historian by the conditions of knowledge, including the structure of the mind and the nature of the object. It is in terms of these necessities that we shall try to show on what conditions, and within what limits, an authentic (that is, *true*) knowledge of the human past is really accessible.

It is at this point that I part company with Raymond Aron whose point of view, in my opinion, still seems to be excessively polemical. The sub-title of his thesis is very revealing: "An essay on the limits of historical objectivity." (Is a universally valid historical science possible at all? To what extent would this be so?)[2] The real problem is the "Kantian" ques-

1. L. I. Halkin, *Initiation à la critique historique*[3] (1953), p. 86, quoting P. Valéry.
2. R. Aron, *op. cit.*, p. 10.

tion: On what conditions is historical knowledge possible? In other words, this is the problem of the truth of history, if objectivity is not to be the supreme criterion.

It has become classic—and may still be pedagogically useful —to contrast this attitude (which sufficiently defines what is proudly called the new approach to history and is a fundamental principle) with the illusions of our positivist predecessors. I do not believe it would be slanderous to say that they dreamed of bringing history into alignment with the "exact" sciences—a very revealing expression, incidentally, by which they meant physics, chemistry and biology. But their conception of these sciences was very naïve, and in fact so elementary as to be utterly false. We shall have occasion to return to this matter when we explain the distinction—no doubt essential but requiring careful precision—between the sciences of nature and sciences of the mind. Dazzled and somewhat intimidated by the undeniable triumphs of the natural sciences, the positivist theorists tried to determine the conditions with which history would have to comply in order to attain, in its turn, the honorable status of a positive science offering objective knowledge "valid for everyone." Their avowed objective was to foster "an exact science of things of the mind." That was Renan's term for it. We would have to cite his book, *The Future of Science*, to reveal fully the degree of tragic assurance with which men of 1848 committed themselves and all European scholarship generally to a course which has since proved to be merely a dead-end. If there still remains a little bitterness in our voices when we mention these men who were our teachers, I would ask my younger readers to consider the great amount of rectification which we were obliged to undertake.

If we now attempt to set forth their position in terms of a formula, using the same symbols as before we would say:

$$h = P + p$$

In their opinion, history is the Past, objectively recorded, plus, *alas!* an inevitable intervention of the present of the historian. It is something like the personal equation of the observer in astronomy or the astigmatism of the ophthalmologist: a symbiotic datum or quantity which must be rendered as small as possible—or even made quite negligible, tending toward zero.

In this conception there seems to be a belief that both the historian and the witness before him whose report is utilized could only damage or diminish the objective integrity of truth by their personal contribution. But whether positive or negative—omissions, misunderstandings or errors in the second case; trivial considerations, and literary embroidery in the first—this contribution is always regrettable and ought to be eliminated. They would have liked to make the historian and his informers of the past purely passive instruments: a kind of recording apparatus which would simply reproduce the object, the past, with mechanical fidelity—or would photograph it precisely, as they probably said in the year 1900.

But the image would have been quite deceptive. We have since learned to recognize all that is personal and everything that is constructed and profoundly informed by the active intervention of the operator in all those images which are obtained with such objective means as a camera lens or an emulsion of silver bromide, from Nadar's *Baudelaire* to the *Images à la sauvette* of Cartier-Bresson.

Let us glance through an exemplary manual of the positivist scholar, our old companion, the work of Langlois and Seignebos. In their opinion, history is the sum total of "facts" derived from documents. History exists in the documents in a latent but real manner prior to the intervention of the historian's research. But let us follow the latter's technical procedures attentively. The historian finds the documents and then proceeds to sift and cull them. This is the task of external

criticism, a "technique of purging and piecing," which separates the good grain from the straw. The critique of interpretation concentrates on the testimony of the witnesses, whose
value is determined by a severe "internal, negative criticism
of sincerity and exactness." (Could the witness have been
mistaken? Did he perhaps want to deceive us?) Little by
little, the pure wheat of the "facts" accumulates in our notebooks and memos. The historian need only report them with
precision and fidelity, wholly concealing himself behind the
testimony and evidence regarded as valid. In short, he does
not construct history but simply discovers it. Collingwood,
who does not hide his contempt for such a conception of
"pre-fabricated historical knowledge, needing only to be
gulped down and then disgorged," calls it "history compiled
with scissors and paste."[3] The irony of his remark is fully
deserved, for nothing could be less accurate than an analysis
or enquiry that completely overlooks the actual proceedings
of the historian's mind.

Such a methodology simply resulted in debasing history to
mere erudition, and in fact it had exactly that consequence
in the case of one of its theorists who took it all seriously in
practice: Charles V. Langlois no longer dared to write history
toward the end of his career, but was content to offer his
readers merely a selection of texts. But what ingenuousness!
As if the choice of selected evidence was not already a very
considerable intervention of the author's personality, with his
particular orientations, prejudices and limitations! (See for
instance, *La connaissance de la nature et du monde d'après
les écrits français à l'usage des laïcs*, 1911, and republished in
1927 as volume 3 of *La vie en France au moyen âge du
XIIe au milieu du XIVe siècle.*)

In any case, "there is no *historical reality*, ready-made prior

3. *The Idea of History*, p. 257; cf. p. 246.

to knowledge, which need only be reproduced with fidelity."[4] History is the result of the creative effort by which the historian, as the conscious subject, establishes a relationship between the past which he evokes and the present which is his own. It is tempting at this point to make another comparison with idealism because of its insistence that knowledge receives its form, if not its entire reality, from the activity of the mind. But this time I hesitate to do it, for I am fully aware of the dangers which the misuse of such references may entail. Excessive emphasis upon the creative contribution of the historian would lead to the description of the elaboration of history as a kind of gratuitous game. In this view it is the free exercise of a story-weaving imagination lightly dallying with an anomalous collection of texts, dates, deeds and sayings, with all the freedom of a poet juggling verses to write a sonnet.[5] This kind of conception simply destroys the serious import of our discipline and the validity of its truth. It could hardly serve as an adequate description of the real activity of the historian, according to our own experience of such activity in the course of our daily task. Consequently, it is better to avoid making any comparison that is excessively far-fetched. We should try instead to express ourselves without metaphorical subterfuges. In my own opinion, and without pretense or paradox, I would not hesitate to accept the formula proposed by one of our British colleagues, Professor V. H. Galbraith of Cambridge, who said, *"History, I suppose, is the Past—so far as we know it."*[6]

Indeed, this is far better than the pride of the idealist philosopher who is convinced that he can construct reality

4. R. Aron, *op. cit.*, p. 120.

5. Cf. my discussion with Denis de Rougemont concerning his book, *L'amour et l'Occident*, in *Esprit*, September, 1939, pp. 760–768.

6. *Why We Study History* (Historical Association Publications, no. 131, 1944). I have separated the formula from the context, which is sometimes rather sceptical.

(as he says) with the resources of his mind alone, and certainly much better than the conscientious short-sightedness of the positivist scholar, satisfied with the accumulation of "facts" in his little notebooks. It seems to me that the moderation and logical preciseness of Professor Galbraith's formula more truly sums up the essential aspect of our real experience as historians. It cannot be described in terms of the quiet labor of the one or the triumphant expansion of the other. It is something much more hazardous, in the tragic sense. We emerge from it gasping and humbled, always more than half-defeated, rather like the struggle of Jacob with the Angel of Yahweh at the Jabbok ford.

We are not really alone in our work, for in the shadows we meet with a mysterious *other* (which I mentioned before as the noumenal reality of the past). It is a reality that is felt to be both dreadfully present and yet apparently resistant to our efforts. We try to lay hold of it and compel its submission, but invariably it ultimately eludes us at least in part. History is a struggle of the mind, an adventure. Like all human quests it knows only partial successes, wholly relative and never proportionate with the original ambition. As in any encounter with the baffling depths of reality, man ends up with an acute awareness of his limitations, his weakness and his humble status.

We are quite aware of the task we must be able to undertake. By dint of grappling with this baffling reality, we finally fix its position well enough to know what we would need and what we are lacking in order to know the historic past in an authentic and total way. We realize at last what kind of mind the historian must possess to become capable of such knowledge (in the sense in which an arc in geometry is capable of a given angle). He would, in fact, have to know everything—including all that was ever felt, thought and accomplished by men of the past. He would have to perceive the complexity clearly without overlooking, shattering or changing the internal relations—so delicate, multiple and interwoven—which bind together all the manifestations of human activity in the real world. It is the knowledge of these relations that makes everything understandable. However limited our experience may be, it is sufficient to reveal to us the existence of this close network of relations. It is a web in which the causes prolong the effects and the consequences cross-check each other, becoming entwined or opposed; and the most trivial "fact" (on which the whole course of a man's lifetime may hinge) is the culminating result of a complete, convergent series of reactions. Every problem in history, no matter how small, gradually and eventually demands a knowledge of universal history in its entirety.

I could cite the example, already quite classic, which was proposed by C. Morazé: the general situation when Jules Ferry became head of the French government.[7] A historian would doubtless have to know the exact conditions of his rise to power, the circumstances that brought it about, and consequently the French parliamentary situation in 1880. But instead of this let us refer more generally and more fundamentally to the political, and therefore the social and economic situation of France. The international ramifications cannot be neglected either. The whole enquiry must be carried out at new levels. But with regard to Jules Ferry, who was this man? We may describe him in terms of a particular character and personality, as the culmination in 1880 of a personal history that was already a long one. Our colleague, the psychoanalyst, might even insist on extending it back to the pre-natal stage! But was Ferry, the man, merely the product of a process of development that began at the moment of his conception? Jules Ferry was also Saint-Dié, where he was born; and he

7. *Trois essais sur Histoire et Culture* (1948), pp. 1–10.

was the Alsatian emigration, the cotton-mill workers of Mul-house, French Protestantism, etc. We could go back to the very beginnings of Christianity. But there is still another trail to explore: the industrial middle class, the collapse of agricultural prices, and a whole new chain of events and circumstances that will lead us as far back as the prehistoric clearing of the land as we study the arrangement and alloca-tion of the French countryside. In all of this we are mention-ing only the enquiries that our mind conceives as possible. But we certainly know what mere chance or accident may underlie the fact that we are aware of the possibility of each of them. It is clearly quite legitimate to postulate the existence of other causal series than those we have just suggested.

Accordingly, in extension as in comprehensiveness, the problem posed by the human past reveals a structure that is doubly and infinitely complex. Pascal's idea of the double infinite could be transposed to the object of history, but I shall not pursue the matter any further. We have already felt a sudden spell of dizziness!

If our conception of history raises a problem of such magnitude, what mind would ever be able to encompass it? We can reply immediately that such a mind exists. It is the mind of the Lord our God, יהוה, whose uncreated Wisdom "is really in itself a discerning, intelligent mind, subtle, per-ceptive, clear, trenchant, incoercible, firm and unerring, wholly adequate for everything, governing all things and penetrating all things. . . ."[8]

It is surely right and fitting that the philosopher pause to pronounce the ineffable Name with adoration, for such a moment of meditation will help to deliver him from the most dangerous temptation, always a threat to every philosophy of history, a really fatal error, the sin of immoderation: ὕβρις.

8. *Sag. Sal.*, 7, 22–23.

The historian must always remember that he is merely a man and that it is best for mortals to think as mortal men should: θνητὰ φρονεῖν.

I have been speaking as a Christian, but the formula of Euripides shows that this *truth* possesses an absolute value. Reference to Christian thought is imperative for everyone in our Western civilization. We see this, for instance, in Raymond Aron who felt constrained to say, "Only God could weigh the value of every deed, but in their place the contradictory episodes [?], and unify character and behavior. The whole idea of this absolute truth will disappear with theology."[9] As a matter of fact, however, it is not disappearing, for it is still conceivable as a possibility. But the theologian, whether Christian or pagan—or rather the philosopher—insists that it is not within man's reach.

With our young students in mind, the first principle of practical conduct which we must formulate will be an admonition: *You are not God. Never forget that you are only a man.* This reminder should not be considered as an admission of powerlessness or a call to renunciation and despair. St. Thomas, who extolled the virtue of *magnanimitas,* puts us on guard against this sinful deceit: it is merely a form of pride. The philosopher should rejoice to have given clear expression to the truth regarding our being and nature, no matter what it implies—in this instance it is the truth about the nature and capacity of the historian. Indeed, young man, you are only human. But that is no reason to give up your life-work, your own calling as a man and a historian. It may be humble and difficult, but within its limits it is most certainly fruitful and worthwhile.

Our philosophy also is only human, and can go forward only one step at a time. This fruitfulness—genuine but limited—will be demonstrated at the proper time. For the present,

9. R. Aron, *op. cit.,* p. 71.

however, the first point had to be clearly established: the fundamental disproportion between the object with which history is concerned (the noumenal, historic reality which only God can encompass and perceive) and the limited means available to historical research (the pathetic little efforts of the human mind with its methods and instruments). I remember standing on a high crag overlooking a mountain lake, watching the exertions of a fisherman. I could see the beautiful trout that he was excitedly sighting from the shore as they playfully sported and frolicked far from his much too short line. The historian often faces the same situation. His limited means do not allow him to sweep the whole extent of the lake of the past into his nets. History can only be *the Past so far as* . . . it can be encompassed by his nets. Even this is something, of course, but it is not everything. And what is still more important, it is not the same thing. History is whatever the historian succeeds in reaching in the past. But while passing through his instruments of knowledge this very past has been so re-elaborated and so worked-over that it has been made into something quite new and has become ontologically quite different. But we must now devote our serious attention to this process of transmutation.

In order to discover what history will become, we shall have to stop concentrating on its object—that indeterminate something, ἄπειρον, transcending experience—and begin instead with the historian himself, following his endeavors in the procedure that will lead him to knowledge. History will be whatever he finally succeeds in elaborating.

Let us now consult our Langlois-Seignobos manual: Book I, Chapter 1, first line. We learn that "history is constructed with documents." This is a formula we find again in the conclusion, which assures us that "history is merely the applied utilization of documents."[10] This is quite understand-

10. *Introduction aux études historiques*, pp. 1, 275.

able, but logically it is not the document that is the point of departure. After all, the historian is not a factory-worker intent upon the transformation of raw material; nor is the historical method a funnel-shaped piece of machinery into which documents in the rough state can simply be poured, with a fine and continuous fabric of knowledge emerging from the other end. Our work presupposes original activity resulting from personal initiative. History is the response (obviously elaborated by means of documents, as we shall see later) to a question which the curiosity, concern, and existential anxiety—as some would say—but in any case the inquiring mind of the historian asks of the mysterious Past. At first the past appears to him rather indistinctly, like a phantom, without shape or solidity. To lay hold of it the historian must encompass it tightly within a network of questions that leave no room for evasion, compelling it to reveal itself frankly. As long as we fail to set upon it in this way, it remains veiled and silent. Logically, the process of the elaboration of history is set in motion not by the existence of documents but by an initial step, the "posed question" inscribed in the choice, delimitation and conception of the subject.

In practice, of course, it sometimes happens that a historical study is undertaken as the result of the casual reading of some document. The goat grazes wherever it happens to be tied. How often I have heard this reason given by my colleagues when asked about their work! The proximity of some collection of records and documents, the resources of a particular library, the accidental discovery of some new monument by archeologists (a frequent occurrence in the study of Ancient History, in which documents are rare and any new material is given a welcome)—any of these may appear to be the starting-point of historical studies. But this changes nothing with regard to the logical priority of the "question" which the historian poses in the presence of the documents.

The apparently superficial analysis of Langlois and Seignobos can be explained (let us be fair!) in terms of the rather
limited conception of history that was prevalent for such a
long while. Whatever its value may have been, it held them
captive. It was limited in practice to what was called general
history. This is the study of the "great" historic events: primarily the wars and the diplomatic negotiations that prepared
the way for them or somehow ended them. It also included
the vicissitudes of internal politics, studied with reference to
men at the top: the king, his ministers, the royal court; or
else the leaders of political movements, the assemblies and
their parliamentary life. If a few natural calamities were added
to all this, such as an epidemic of the plague, we would possess
practically all that Thucydides considered useful to report
about Greece in his day; and for centuries historians were
content with that kind of outline. At the very most, since
Voltaire they have added to their account a portrayal of the
state of the sciences, letters and arts as an appendix or a
kind of digression. In these circumstances the outline was
completely delineated, the questions were all posed in advance,
and the subject's conception simply amounted to the choice
of some particular period.

But in our day a wholly different conception of history
has triumphed which is both "greater in scope and more extended in depth." This was Marc Bloch's comment.[11] It is only
fair to emphasize the part taken in France by the team of
Lucien Febvre and Marc Bloch in the victorious struggle
against the old idol of political, episodal history, which was a
kind of "historicizing history."

In any case, the reaction was very widespread and was
never restricted to any particular school of thought. Lord
Acton had already given his students the following suggestion:
"Study problems rather than periods." All during the nine-

11. *Apologie pour l'histoire, ou Métier d'historien*, p. 17.

teenth century we can see the progress of the history of civilization, *Kulturgeschichte,* in opposition to its old rival, the "history of battles."

Political history is nearly stifled by the proliferation of studies concerning "special" history. This would include for instance economic and social history, the history of ideas, points of view, *Weltanschauungen,* the history of the sciences, philosophy, religion and art. This specialization has been carried so far that perhaps it is now necessary to react against it, at least at the pedagogical level. In its excessive quest for comprehensiveness and depth, the study of history runs the risk of forsaking concrete reality and simply dissolving in abstract pipe-dreams. We must constantly remind younger historians that the history of civilization (and each special history) must be based upon a close web of names, dates and actual happenings; and that political facts—ordinarily the best documented—provide the solid background for such a sketch.

Accordingly, whenever the historian undertakes the study of a certain time or place there is no method of inquiry established *a priori* and serving somehow as a master-key, which is either obligatory for him or even available. The method or outline is something which the historian must personally decide upon. Consequently the entire later development of the study—and the knowledge itself in its final culmination—will be orientated and predetermined by the questions that were posed. I say "questions" for the sake of brevity. But when the mind elaborates a question it immediately formulates one or several possible answers. A precise question (and only a question that is precisely formulated can serve any purpose in history) presents itself in the form of a hypothesis to be verified. "Could it be true that . . . ?" No doubt in the process of verification the hypothesis will often be restated, corrected and changed until it becomes unrecognizable. But the fact remains that there was a creative effort by the historian at the start, beginning with the elaboration of a provisional description of the past.

Once again, we must be careful to rid ourselves of the dangerous phantom of idealism. Let us limit the part of autonomous "construction" which such an elaboration of the questions and their related hypotheses may entail. Apart from the fact that the validity of the hypothesis is dependent on the process of verifying its suitability in relation to the documentary data, it must certainly be obvious that historical knowledge does not begin with an absolute zero. It is by analogy with a human situation already known that we formulate a hypothetical description of the past to become known. The part or role of transposition is of little importance in this. Except in the case of a newly discovered civilization that is wholly exceptional (and what could ever be really known about it?), the historian ordinarily knows in general which questions can possibly be asked. He knows what are the sentiments, ideas, reactions and technical achievements that can be attributed to the men of a particular time and place. His initial hypotheses will be all the more fruitful if they contain the least possible extrapolation.

We must now consider the idea of progress within the homogeneous development of the study. Whenever historians approach some new field of study, it is almost impossible for them to avoid committing the frightful sin of anachronism. They do not yet know what questions to pose and the mind does not have access to analytical instruments of sufficient precision to construct a satisfactory set of questions.

That is why I would not, for instance, throw stones at Michelet for having made of Abelard a free-thinker, an apostle of rationalism challenging the "Scholastic obscurantists." The categories inherited from the *Aufklärung* did not provide this romantic liberal with the mental equipment necessary for an understanding of Christian thought of the twelfth century.

If we are more successful in this respect today it is because of the progress achieved and the efforts continuously put forth from Michelet himself to Etienne Gilson.

It must be kept in mind that knowledge of an historical object may be dangerously distorted or diminished by the crude or narrow point of view by which it was approached at the start. An example of a badly formulated question is evident in the controversy that lasted for a whole generation concerning St. Augustine. It was asked whether he was converted to Neoplatonism or Christianity in the year 386 at Milan. But P. Courcelle has since proved that Neoplatonism was the official philosophy of the Christian intellectual milieu of Milan in that era, beginning with its bishop, St. Ambrose himself.[12]

Insufficient, diminished knowledge is especially exemplified in two historical works on the little town of Gap.[13] They cover hardly more than the medieval era. Even this period is reduced to a series of monographs on the successive bishops, pertaining almost exclusively to their political quarrels with the municipality, the lord paramount, Count de Forcalquier, or with the Dauphin. We are told nothing about the history of the people of this little human cell; nothing of their economic activity, their social structure, or the development of either. Nevertheless, I did seem to catch a glimpse of a prosperous middle class transforming itself into a landed gentry, such as J. Schneider investigated so thoroughly in his book on the city of Metz.[14] Nor is there anything concerning their spiritual life, although the crisis of the Reformation was extremely serious in the region of Gap—as indeed every-

12. See especially his *Recherches sur les Confessions de saint Augustin* (1950).

13. Th. Gautier, *Histoire de la ville de Gap et du Gapençais* (1842, published by P. P. Guillaume, Gap, 1909); J. Roman, *Histoire de la ville de Gap* (1892).

14. *La ville de Metz aux XIIIe et XIVe siècles* (Nancy, 1950).

where in Dauphiné. Farel, one of the leading French Reformers, came from Gap. But we learn nothing about the place except the political events and religious wars. There are only banal comments concerning the origins of the town, although like A. Déléage's book on Burgundy[15] there could have been a systematic utilization of the toponymy represented by particular "place-names." These are attested as fully in our own day as in the medieval records. They would enable a historian, by etymological analysis, to reconstitute the successive stages of settlement of the area (and consequently of the population itself) going all the way back to the pre-Celtic clearing of the land. Moreover, by studying the hagiographic legends and investigating the distribution of titular saints of the various churches of the region, it would have been possible to reconstitute the stages of the implanting of Christianity in that part of France at the end of the era of Antiquity and the beginning of the Middle Ages.[16]

I must, however, interrupt this analysis of possibilities, which are unlimited. It must be emphasized that every period, every human environment, every historical object always presents a great number of problems and, logically speaking, is likely to raise innumerable questions. Any knowledge the historian may acquire will obviously depend on the question or questions which he chooses to investigate. And this choice will in turn be directly attributable to his personality, the orientation of his mind, the level of his learning, and finally the general philosophy which underlies his mental categories and his principles of judgment.

Let us consider a specific historical phenomenon: Christian monasticism, for example, in its beginnings in fourth century

15. *La vie rurale en Bourgogne jusqu'au début du XIe siècle* (Mâcon, 1941).

16. G. de Manteyer tried to do this, but his method was not rigorous enough. Cf. *Les origines chrétiennes de la IIe Narbonnaise* (Gap, 1924).

Egypt. This can be studied from the perspective of the history of Christianity, in so far as it represents a particular episode of that time and place. Or it can be considered as an aspect of the development of the Christian religion. We can study it from the comparative point of view of the history of religions, as one of the manifestations of the ideal of solitude, asceticism and contemplation which has found expression in so many other ways among men (Brahmanism, Jainism, Buddhism, Taoism, and perhaps even in the pre-Columbian civilizations). There is a social aspect in this phenomenon which could be stressed: the flight to the desert. Devotion to an "anchoretic" life (which means literally to "take refuge in the wilderness"), was a very common phenomenon in Greco-Roman Egypt. The desert was a favorite haunt of criminals, debtors and especially insolvent tax-payers, together with non-social individuals of every kind who were not exclusively religious men. There could also be a study of their economic function. The cenobites of St. Pachomius left their monasteries by the thousands to harvest the crops in the Nile Valley and thus earn their meager subsistence for the whole year in a few days' time. They were a kind of reserve labor force resembling the migratory farm workers of California who were described in Steinbeck's *Grapes of Wrath*.

Each of these perspectives is intrinsically legitimate, and perhaps fruitful also. Each apprehends the reality of the past in part, or under some particular aspect. But we shall delay our examination of the umbilical cord that binds each of them to the historian's individuality, and the resulting consequences for the validity of the knowledge obtained. In our attempt to outline the virtues of the historian gradually, we shall for the moment simply lay stress on the fact that the copiousness of historical knowledge will depend directly on the skilfulness and ingenuity with which the initial questions are posed. It is this which conditions the general orientation of all sub-

sequent research. The great historian will be one who, within
his own system of thought, is able to pose the historical problem or question in the richest and most fruitful manner. No
matter how extensive his learning may be, or his broad-
mindedness either, he will recognize the limitations that form
necessarily imposes, and will readily see what question would
be worth asking of the past. The value of history (and by this
I mean its human interest as well as its validity) is therefore
strictly dependent on the ability of the historian. As Pascal
said, "In proportion as we possess greater ingenuity, we find
that there are more original men," or in other words, greater
treasures to be retrieved in man's past.

Consider, for example, the singularly enriched vision of
Hellenic civilization which the genius (as well as the vast
erudition) of the great Rostovtseff opened up to us.[17] We now
see it as the admirable maturity of ancient civilization—"that
long summer under the perpetual sunlight of the south." No
longer is it depicted as decadent. This was the evaluation of
a certain narrow kind of humanism utterly obsessed with the
idea of a Golden Age, and the desire of romantic history,
which was almost uniquely concerned about evidences of
originality, creativity and initial spontaneity. All this led the
romantic historians to become primarily interested in the
"archaic" aspects of "youth" of an art, an idea or a whole
civilization.

17. *The Social and Economic History of the Hellenistic World* (3 vol.,
Oxford, 1942).

CHAPTER III

History Is Compiled with Documents

Once the question has been posed an answer must be found, and at this stage the document becomes necessary. The historian is not a necromancer as some have imagined! He does not evoke the ghost of the past by incantations. We are unable to reach the past directly. We do so only through intelligible vestiges left behind—insofar as these vestiges have subsisted, and to the extent that we have discovered them and are capable of interpreting them. More than ever we must insist upon the qualification: *insofar as*. It is here that we encounter the primary and most burdensome of the technical servitudes that weigh so heavily upon the elaboration of history.

This has not been sufficiently emphasized by philosophers, perhaps because our critical philosophy originated with Dilthey in a period of euphoria in which the science of history, intoxicated by its triumphs, tended to forget its limitations. It is nevertheless important to give some thought to the matter, for here we find one of the major causes for the real distinction, previously indicated, between the noumenal experience of humanity and our written history. With regard to this I must mention Spengler's unpleasant attack against Ranke.[1] As a good technician, Ranke wrote in the preface of his *Weltgeschichte* (a universal history): "History begins only when monuments become intelligible and there are documents worthy of credence." Spengler burst into invective, asking, "Is life only a fact when we mention it in books?" He had no trouble in showing that there *must have been* events of

1. *Decline of the West,* II, Chap. i, §11.

capital importance about which, for lack of documentation, we shall never know anything at all. This enabled him to direct his sarcasm toward the shortsighted old scholars who could see no farther than their notes and memos, and he triumphantly brandished A. Meyer's formula: "Whatever is now or ever has been active, is historical." Yet this is a subtle fallacy based upon the ambiguous fact already mentioned: that history is indeed "whatever has been active," the real past which was really lived by men of flesh and blood on this solid earth, but only insofar as we know it. And we can only know it if it has bequeathed documents to us. Now, since the existence and preservation of documents are due to the interaction of a whole series of forces which were not ordained in view of the needs of an eventual historian (this is what is really symbolized by the irrational word "chance"), it follows that we shall never know all that this past has been, nor even all that we are capable of wanting to know. It is quite as ridiculous to be surprised or irritated by this fact as to inveigh against an automobile because it has run out of gasoline. History is compiled with documents, as the automobile engine operates with motor fuel.

Many of the problems which the historian might raise, or the questions which he actually poses with reference to the past, must remain unresolved and unanswered for lack of adequate documentation.

It is not the most interesting questions that are always the best documented. For example, when we study first-century Palestine we find more about the love affairs of Herod than the date of Christ's birth, and more about the *ius gladii* of the Procurator of Judea than the religious beliefs of Pontius Pilate.

Even when some kind of passive cooperation is established between the heroes of the past and their future historians, when Darius or Shapuhr had their burial or triumphal figures carved on the rock of Naksh-i-Rustum, or when modern governments organize and maintain a bureau of records, the pre-established harmony is not perfect. It is not always what we would like to know about them that we are actually told.

Documents that have been preserved are not always those that we would like to have, or what we really need. (Experience almost suggests that it might be better to say that they never are!) Either there are none at all, or not enough. This is generally the case in Ancient History in which we work most often from literary sources that are always too incomplete, and in any case are second- or third-hand versions. Titus Livius, for instance, did not use original documents in compiling his history, but was content to re-write the narratives of his predecessors, Polybius or Valerius Antias. The few primary sources which we possess are represented by the archeological documents, including inscriptions and papyri discovered in the course of excavations and therefore in pursuance of an arbitrary selection.

Until the recent discoveries at Dura and in the desert of Juda, we hardly possessed any manuscripts except the Egyptian papyri. And this was a rather random selection due to the aridity of the region. It distorted our knowledge of the Hellenistic or Roman world, for Egypt was a country that was very different from other lands. Nothing happened there exactly as it did elsewhere, and it was not a country where the most important events took place. We need only recall the very eccentric place so long occupied by Egypt in the history of Christianity.

Some evil genius seems to have taken pleasure in depriving us of the information we sought. How often we found a papyrus that was torn at the very line where it was beginning to be worth reading! Consider, for example, J. Carcopino, attempting to determine the exact date of the death of Attalus III of Pergamos.[2] (The ideas we form regarding the respective

2. *Autour des Gracques, études critiques* (1928), pp. 37–38.

merit of the two Gracchi actually depend on our knowing at what moment in the year 133 the event took place.) Carcopino did find two pertinent inscriptions. But one refers to a local calendar which we are unable to translate, and the other uses the Roman Calendar—but unfortunately the stone is broken at the very point that would give the date. We read only: *the . . . . th day of the month of . . . . ember.*

Often the documents are too numerous. This is normal in contemporary history in which the inquirer succumbs beneath the burden of accumulated records that are only too carefully preserved. Really interesting problems become unapproachable because they would require almost endless investigation, or at least research not in proportion with the hoped-for results. This means limiting ourselves to specimen-monographs, or else dooming whole teams of inquirers to a monotonous and thankless task. And what society will provide these research scholars?

We may study, for instance, the Reign of Terror in northern France and Pas-de-Calais, federalism in Haute Garonne, the sale of emigrants' property in the district of Rouen, conscription in Charente, provisions and supplies in Yonne and especially in the district of Auxerre.[3]

One of the best subjects which the history of the French Revolution offers us is the remarkable pedagogical innovation exemplified in the central schools. Stendhal was educated at the school in Grenoble. One of my former pupils has given us an excellent monograph concerning the school in Lyons. His interesting findings quite naturally made the whole subject seem attractive, but a hundred central schools had existed and of these fifty had already been studied in a more or less satisfactory manner. In order to know something about each of the others it would have required an average of one year's

3. See the monographs of L. Jacob, M. Albert, M. Bouloiseau, G. Vallée, C. Porée.

work, considering the conditions imposed upon the inquirer by our society. Would the importance of the subject warrant the dedication of the inquirer's entire life?

Up to this point I have cited examples in which the pertinence of the document was rather obvious. This simplified the research procedures. But whenever a more subtle question arises, the answer will be provided by the convergence of a thousand scattered clues. Who will guide the explorer in this labyrinth?

We can present these factual observations in a more strictly logical form. Following Charles Morazé's example, we previously made mention of the double infinite that the structure of the historical object reveals to analytical inquiry. This entails heuristic consequences. The historian ought to know *everything,* and indeed that is what he would like. *Everything*—including the most precise facts. The inquiry rapidly reaches a point of extreme exigency: the solution of a problem finally depends on the date, for example, when a decision was made by some particular individual; or an important move was made which must be pin-pointed almost to the month, the day and the hour. The probability that such exactness was correctly recorded by preserved testimony tends toward zero very rapidly. *Everything*—the infinitely complex network of causes and effects which converge at the precise moment in man's past which we would like to know about. But who could ever be capable of examining fully the immense documentary material needed for an investigation that is really thorough?

Here we discover one of the narrowest and most rigid limits within which historical knowledge is confined. Its possibility, exactness, interest and value are determined (prior to any inquiry) by the brutal fact, wholly external, of the existence or absence of documentation that has been preserved concerning each of the questions which the inquirer intends to examine.

But that is not all! Insofar as the documents exist, one must still gain mastery over them. Here again the personal traits of the historian will intervene, including his intellectual qualifications, his technical training, his ingenuity and general learning. To complete our sketch, let us add some finishing touches. The great historian will not only be one who is best able to pose the questions. There are chimerical minds that are quite clever in raising insoluble problems—which is a sheer waste of time. But he will also be quite capable of elaborating a practical outline of study leading to the discovery and appearance of the most numerous, reliable and revealing documents. This quest for documents, or heuristic procedure as it is called, is a whole art in itself.

Our predecessors generally took an over-simplified view of the matter. Langlois-Seignobos, for instance, tell us: "The number of documents that exist, if not all those that are already known, is a given quantity. In spite of all the precautions that are taken, time is constantly diminishing it. Nor will it ever be increased." (This clearly proves that neither of these two authors was an archeologist!) And they go on to say, "The historian has only a limited supply of documents at his disposal. . . . etc."[4] At the end of his life this same Seignobos commented, "Except for the chance discovery of objects, and efforts directed toward collectors of family papers or private collections, 'heuristic methods' are actually limited to bibliographical usage."[5]

The real situation, however, is much more complex. Any set of documents represents an inexhaustible source of information, for there is an unlimited number of different questions to which the documents can provide the answers, provided

4. *Introduction aux études historiques,* p. 275.
5. "Lettre à F. Lot" (1941), *Revue historique,* vol. 210 (1953), p. 5.

that the questioning is properly done. The historian's originality will often consist in discovering the direction in which any particular set of documents, no matter how well exploited previously, can lead to information about a wholly new question.

The *Collations* of John Cassian, which were written as though coming from the Fathers of the Desert in order to set forth their teachings on Egyptian monasticism, have been subjected to the most thorough examination and criticism, and it was decided with considerable regret that his testimony was not very reliable. Yet one day an English historian, the Rev. Owen Chadwick,[6] decided that this document was primarily a direct source of information concerning the theological and spiritual climate dominant in monastic centers of Provence in the years 425–430 A.D., and that Cassian had formulated his own teaching while attributing it pseudonymously to his Egyptian teachers as Plato had attributed his own doctrine to Socrates.

In the library of the École Normale there is a copy of Herodotus which some former student covered with notes regarding the religious beliefs of Herodotus the man, (that is, his conception of the jealousy of the gods, etc.). I recall seeing it in the hands of my companion, the late Charles Lecoeur, who found it all very amusing. In his opinion as a sociologist the interesting thing about the testimony of Herodotus was his reporting, as a historian, the various aspects of collective psychology, the more or less archaic customs, and the "prelogical" kind of thinking that was done. All of this was much more significant than what Herodotus thought about such matters.

The choice of documents that can be useful in studying a particular question is not therefore a purely mechanical

6. *John Cassian, A Study in Primitive Monasticism* (Cambridge, 1950), and my review in *L'Antiquité classique,* 1952, pp. 240–243.

operation, and the talent of the inquirer finds a real occasion for exercise in this respect. To begin with, the heuristic method is definitely an "art" in the ancient meaning of the term *ars* (τέχνη), which entails traditional rules and regulations, working instruments and special skills. No one can be a historian by improvisation. The writings of amateurs, in which so much sincere effort is expended (often quite uselessly) are sufficient proof of this fact. It is essential to learn about the existence and nature of the various kinds of historical sources, and also to know how to make good use of them. It would be futile to try to depict the main lines of such a technical preparation, for our historical discipline has had to adapt its method of research to the extremely diverse conditions of the periods and aspects which it studies in the past. The historians of Pharaonic Egypt, Greek philosophy, feudal society, baroque art, or the capitalistic economy, do not use the same kind of documentation, or consequently the same collections or the same methods of research.

The exploration of the "bibliography" of any subject being studied is closely connected with the search for sources. When we undertake a historical work we must read whatever has already been written on the same subject, or on related matters —and in a general way the whole field of interest. This is necessary first of all to avoid doing something quite useless (how many amateurs, through ignorance, imagine that they are discovering America!); then, more especially, in order to guide the heuristic quest and learn from our predecessors the kinds of sources in which there is really some chance of finding something worthwhile. This procedure requires tact and care. If the beginner allows himself to be too readily influenced by established tradition, he runs the risk of seeing the past through the spectacles of others, and may lose the sense and direction of the original and fruitful problem or question that he was personally capable of posing.

Heuristic investigation is also an art in the modern meaning of the term. The documentary sources at our disposal may be quite perfected in some respects. But since their compilers did not have in mind (and could not even have conceived as possible) all the questions which the documents themselves suggest to us, they do not provide us with the means of discovering such questions. Often the existence of the documentation only becomes evident when the historian, as the first to become interested in a particular problem, requires it and looks for it—somehow bringing about its appearance by means of ingenious procedures specifically devised for this very purpose.

One of my collaborators, Abbé J. Sainsaulieu, undertook an extensive investigation of eremitic life in France, having discovered both the interest and existence of this subject which had until then been largely overlooked by historians. But the published inventories of the archives, no matter how satisfactory in other respects, had failed to foresee the need for an index entry under *Hermits*. The archivists who were consulted invariably replied that the subject was an unknown phenomenon, or at least exotic, archaic or purely adventitious. Consequently, Abbé Sainsaulieu decided to produce a "guide for research," a dependable procedure for learning about the hermits, a real *methodus ad eremitas inveniendos*. He suggested the following method:

a) Begin with the toponymy. Using topographical dictionaries and ancient large-scale maps, look up such place-names as the Hermitage (chapel, farm, hamlet), the Hermits' Woods, the Fountain of the Recluse. b) On the spot, try to identify the archeological remains, including the hermits' cells transformed into chapels or storerooms. These are often recognizable by their Gothic aperture facing the location of the altar. c) Among the records and archives, the basic document from the sixteenth to the nineteenth century is the death certificate. This is to be found in the parish register, and is normally followed in the same year by the report of the taking of the habit or the installation of a recluse, etc.[7] As a result, within three years the existence of more than five thousand hermits or hermitages had been pin-pointed in time and place.

However, the ingenuity of the historian will not only become apparent in the art of discovering documents. It is not sufficient to know where and how to locate them. One must also, and especially, know *which* documents to look for. In this respect, some thought must be given to the whole idea of documentation and historical sources, for concerning this standard or prevailing theory does not provide an adequately comprehensive definition. As long as an inquiry is limited to the merely elementary level of what we called "episodal history" it is quite easy to decide what a pertinent document would be. But the matter becomes much more complex (and especially more uncertain) when over and beyond the material verification of the reality of a precise "fact" (that is, an external manifestation of human activity) we investigate all the particulars and details, the causes and effects. This is especially true when we seek the significance and value of them for those who took part actively, and for their contemporaries and ourselves as well.

And now, returning to the matter of eremitical life, we may conclude that as long as it is simply a question of ascertaining the existence of a hermit or recluse at some particular time or place, the pertinence of a document will be easily recognizable. Is it dated? Is it associated with some particular locality? Does it mention a hermit? But suppose we want to rise above this heap of isolated facts in order to encompass the problems which the hermit's existence has raised. These are problems

7. Cf. the pamphlet, *Enquête sur l'érémitisme,* published (1950) by the Bibliothèque d'Histoire des Religions, Sorbonne, Paris.

which, as always, are infinitely varied: religious, psychological, social—and among religious problems some that pertain to canon law, doctrine and spirituality. Here we must envisage an inquiry that embraces many other sources of information than the archival records would provide. We would turn to folklore (proverbs and ballads); the plastic arts (Abbé Sainsaulieu has taught us to distinguish carefully the images of hermits from those of monks or pilgrims); and to literature—medieval epics, and even tales and stories like those of Molière and (indeed!) of Claudel. We would also refer to the history of law, noting the many diocesan regulations and the statutory laws of royal courts regarding the civil status of the hermit. Our inquiry would cover the whole history of civilization, for every advance and preferment of hermits actually reflected the great thought currents that excited or troubled men in those days.

Any source of information is a "document" in the broad sense, if the historian's mind can extract something from it to increase our knowledge of the human past considered with reference to the question that has been posed regarding it. It is obviously impossible to say where the documentation begins or ends. Step by step the concept itself becomes enlarged until it finally includes texts, monuments and observations of every kind.

When we study with Marc Bloch[8] or Roger Dion[9] the history of the agrarian arrangements in France we must note the open field and the practice of triennial rotation. The countryside viewed from an aeroplane or examined on a large-scale map is a historical document insofar as we are able to perceive something more than the effects of natural laws alone (geology, climatology, botany), and recognize the intervention of man.

8. *Les caractères originaux de l'histoire rurale française* (1931; 2nd edition, 1952).
9. *Essai sur la formation du paysage rural français* (Tours, 1934).

6

It was this truth that led Lucien Febvre[10] to say, "No doubt history is compiled with written documents . . . when there are any. But it can, and must, be compiled with anything that the historian's ingenuity will enable him to utilize." And so it is with words—or with signs and symbols, with landscapes and roof tiles,[11] the shapes of the fields and the weeds that grow there. And with eclipses of the moon and harness collars,[12] geological surveys of rock formations and the chemical analysis of metal swords.[13]

In short, anything in the subsisting heritage of the past which can be regarded as a clue revealing something of the presence, activity, sentiments and mentality of mankind in the past will enter into our documentation. Defined in this way, documentation appears as a function of two independent variables. Since it is the past it is represented by the material of all kinds which has come down to us. It is incumbent on the historian, with his personal initiative and talent, to make full use of his technical instruments and his knowledge. But primarily he must use whatever he possesses within himself, employing his intelligence, his openness of mind and any learning that he has acquired.

The French historians of my generation were required to make a series of studies that afforded us an acquaintance with geography and a real liking for it. We are very conscious of the fruitfulness which the study of environmental conditions

10. *Combats pour l'histoire*, p. 428.

11. This refers to the distribution of flat and hollow kinds of roof tiles in France, mentioned in *Histoire de la Nation française*, by G. Hanotaux (vol. I, 1920, pp. 438–444. See Roof Map of J. Brunhes in this book).

12. Comte Lefebvre des Noëttes, *L'attelage, le cheval de selle à travers les âges* (1931; the 2nd edition of this book which was originally published in 1924 under the title: *La force animale à travers les âges*).

13. E. Salin, *Rhin et Orient*, vol. II, *Le fer à l'époque mérovingienne, technique et archéologique* (1943); *La civilisation mérovingienne, d'après les sépultures, les textes et le laboratoire* (1949–1952).

makes possible for research that is properly historical. L. Robert, the great epigraphist and author of *Études Anatoliennes,*[14] has this to say about it: "It is not paradoxical to insist on the value and advantage for our studies to spend whole days in travel, even when we fail to find a single inscription to be copied. On the high plateaus and grazing lands, inside the dark tent of a mountaineer who hospitably offers us yogurt and cream, trudging through immense pine forests standing solitary and silent, or near a spring at the edge of the trail—even if we find no dedication to the nymphs, we may be sure that the nymphs are there. They are really present among the plane-trees and the oleander, giving new courage to men and beasts as they did for centuries to Carians and Greeks who stopped there and prayed to them while they rested." I am merely giving an abridgement of all this, although the whole page ought to be quoted. It is quite evident that one must first have acquired some geographical familiarity with this area before there can be any possibility of conceiving the idea of seeking a source of information concerning Asia Minor in ancient times.

We can readily understand why the English author Robert Graves made our "colleague," the Emperor Claudius, burst forth with the remark, "History is an old man's game!" According as the historian acquires a wider range of knowledge and a broader human experience, together with an increasing awareness of the unlimited potentialities inherent in man's activity and in his mind and heart (*accedet homo ad cor altum. . . .* Man shall come to a full heart),[15] the more he will begin to see the unsuspected possibilities of documentation. Quite naturally Pascal's formula, "In proportion as we possess greater ingenuity . . ." comes to mind again, and

14. *Acts of the Second International Congress of Greek and Latin Epigraphy (Paris, 1952)*, published in Paris, 1953, pp. 11–12.

15. Psalm 63:7 (Vulgate).

for good reason too. The broadening of our ideas of documentation progresses conjointly with the deepening of our conception of history. The narrow conception of the "topical text" was suitable perhaps for a "historicizing" history, strictly episodal. But there is a history that now confronts the past with questions that are always newer, more varied, more extensive or more penetrating. And there is a corresponding inquiry that is enlarged and extended in every direction, encompassing the vestiges and remains of every kind which this multiform and inexhaustible past may have left us.

The principle is now established beyond dispute. Consequently it seems especially fitting for us to indicate the limits of the useful interval or area within which it may be applied. But let us resist the universal recourse to paradox. Collingwood, for instance, went so far as to say, "everything in the world is potential evidence for any subject whatever."[16] This is true, provided that the potential coefficient is not overlooked. Theoretically, there is no limit imposed on possible connections or relations. But in reality it is not true that for any particular subject one can always find sufficient documentary material "somewhere," or that all the documents in the assembled material will be equally relevant.

In a moment of high enthusiasm I once wrote the following comment: "We do not understand the metaphorical significance of 'illumination' in the theory of knowledge of a Neoplatonist like St. Augustine until we have known what the light of the Mediterranean[17] can be in the splendor of a morning in spring." There is some truth in this, of course. But perhaps it should also be said that it is even more necessary for the historian to locate precisely the immediate sources of Augus-

16. *The Idea of History,* p. 280.

17. "Un historien en Sardaigne," in the *Revue de Géographie de Lyon,* vol. 26 (1951), p. 141.

tinian doctrine in some particular passage of the *Enneads* of Plotinus or in the Prologue of St. John's Gospel.

Lucien Febvre argues controversially against the restrictive factor which he finds in the formula attributed to Fustel de Coulanges: "History is compiled with texts."[18] He is quite right in insisting upon innumerable other sources of documentation. Yet perhaps we ought to inform his younger readers that while history is not compiled with texts exclusively it is nevertheless compiled especially with them, and nothing can ever substitute for their precision. Consider, for example, Holbein's admirable portrait of Henry VIII which hangs in the Hall of Christ Church. Certainly no text could ever teach us so many profound and detailed truths about the extremely complex personality and character of this king. However, it is only by referring to documentary texts that we can know for sure that it really is the portrait of Henry VIII. The same painting, considered as a source of historical information, would not be as significant if it were merely the portrait of someone unknown.

Finally, we must point out that this new intervention of the historian's mind (together with his capability and ingenuity in selecting documents) imposes still another limitation on historical knowledge. It is not enough that documents have escaped destruction. The historian must also succeed in retrieving them. Even when someone regards a document in the narrow and restricted way that we have criticized (as *the* pertinent record), or even when it is a matter of a well-known kind of evidence fully provided with means of access (texts of classical authors, Latin inscriptions, medieval registers of charters and titles, diplomatic documentation—all of which abound in publications, indexed catalogues and guide-books of every kind), the historian can never be certain he has not overlooked some essential document or record, no matter how

18. *Combats pour l'histoire*, pp. 4–5, 71, 428 . . .

methodical, careful and thorough his searching has been. *A fortiori*, if we now conceive the problem of documentation in the generalized form that we have given it, who could ever pretend to have exhausted all the possible sources of knowledge, neglecting not a single possible category of new information? Logically speaking, we must certainly agree that no historical study or research can give us the assurance of having exhausted all the existing documentary material.

If we turn our attention to practical aspects at this point, I would remind the apprentice historian: θνητὰ φρονεῖν —think as a mortal—because you are only a man, not a god. Learn how to get the most out of each day, and do not waste your efforts. There are, as we noted, insoluble problems in the sense that they would require a colossal task of documentation yet result in something that is still uncertain or perhaps even lacking in interest altogether. Other questions are premature until certain preliminary endeavors have been completed, including for instance, collections or publications of sources. There will be a great temptation—and many succumb!—to prefer questions that are merely trivial (although well-documentated) rather than the really human and deep problems whose solution would require an uncertain heuristic investigation. This antinomy is not easily surmountable. The condition imposed on the historian, as a special instance of man's condition in general, is not wholly secure or tranquil. To conclude, I would now like to mention the matter of production. Imagine, for example, a steel mill in which, by using some particular process, they now succeed in extracting perhaps 80% of the metal contained in the ore, at a cost of so much per treated ton. If it were necessary to increase the cost tenfold or a hundredfold in order to raise the yield from 80% to 85%, what engineer would accept the responsibility for such a decision? The situation is often analogous in the search for historical documentation. There comes a time when all the conceivable procedures of inquiry have nearly exhausted their efficacy. To increase the supply of collected documents the search would have to be indefinitely prolonged and require immensely greater efforts—and all for the sake of a very small yield. Reason then gives us the practical counsel to put a stop to our quest.

Pursuing our outline of the historian's task, we find him confronting a file of collected documents. He reaches for the first of these which, for instance, may be the funeral inscription long known as the *Laudatio Thuriae*.[19] (Let us imagine that he is studying Roman life in the early years of our era.) Objectively, this document appears to be a mass of little segments of straight lines adjoining a few half-circles. There are also (less numerous) full circles, all put together in an uneven regular way, in parallel lines. The whole thing is engraved upon the original marble and traced with ink upon the paper of a reproduction sheet or a publication. But this would be a paradoxical description, because the document does not consist of that material reality itself. It is a document only insofar as the combination of straight and curved markings appears to the historian's mind as constituting the lines of a particular kind of writing (the symbol and vector of thought) utilizing a known alphabet—in this case, the alphabet of Latin capitals—to symbolize a language (the classical Latin which he knows very well). In short, it is a document to the degree in which the historian is capable of *understanding* something in it.

We have just used the key word. From the moment that contact is first made with the material object which is the document, the elaboration of historical knowledge shows us the fundamental logical operation in action: this is the process

19. *C.I.L.*, VI, 1527, republished with a brilliant commentary by M. Durry under the title: *Éloge funèbre d'une matrone romaine* (Paris, Coll. "Budé," 1950).

of understanding, *das Verstehen*. All the rest of our analytical study will continue to manifest this operation at each successive level of the historian's endeavor.

Considered empirically, the understanding of history apparently consists in the interpretation of meaningful symbols, like the inscription we mentioned or such clues as the ashes of a home and hearth, or finger prints. Through the immediate reality of these remains we succeed in perceiving something about man in former times. This includes his activity and behavior, his ideas and inner self, or sometimes simply his presence—anything indicating that man has passed this way.

Among these clues and traces not all have necessarily had their origin in the activity or intervention of man. The bed of solidified mud or layer of ashes and lava covering Herculaneum or Pompeii constitute a historical "document" quite as truly as the famous letter of Pliny the Younger to Tacitus regarding the eruption of Vesuvius in 79 A.D. Or let us suppose that a cow has suddenly crossed a busy highway along which it was wandering and had caused an automobile accident. The cow's hoof marks would be as important in the investigation as the report of a witness.

Knowledge of the human past is not exclusively limited to the strictly human data of that past. Man does not live in isolation, as though in a diving-bell. He is inseparable from the "environment" in which he is merged—a very complex environment, physically, chemically, biologically and humanly. Man's historical knowledge will integrate the natural phenomena which, as a part of his environment, have played a role in his past: the plague in Athens during the Peloponnesian War, the cold weather that enabled the Vandals and Alani to cross the frozen Rhine near Cologne on the first of January, 407 A.D.

We should note that in our daily life the experience of the present provides the same association of natural phenomena with those that are strictly human. For example, right in front of me in the street some pedestrian slips on a banana peel. He falls and then picks himself up, grumbling crossly and rubbing his knee. In my awareness of this incident there are two different phases or aspects: a) proceeding from the effects back to their cause, I reconstitute the chain of observed phenomena by using my implicit or positive knowledge of the laws of biology and mechanics. The totality of forces applied at a particular moment to the right heel of the pedestrian admitted a horizontal resultant force. b) Interpreting the expressive signs and gestures that are manifestations of the victim's pain and indignation, I understand the sensations that he is experiencing.

History is not only concerned with whatever is specifically human in man's past. To conclude from the presence of fingerprints to the fact that "a man has passed this way" is no different from interpreting the prints or traces of an animal —or more generally, of any mobile body animated by a particular movement. However, it may happen that this mobile body belonged to a murderer. The purely physical fact of his presence at a specific place and particular time will be included in the synthetical kind of knowledge which history constitutes, together with the properly human significations of his deed. Obviously, it is the understanding of both these factors which confers on historical knowledge its specific character.

If we try to account for this understanding process satisfactorily, we cannot make use of any transposition of the methods of the sciences of nature. Properly speaking, the historian does not proceed by way of deduction or induction. The point of departure must instead be the ordinary or common knowledge which we use in our daily life. From the perspective of the theory of knowledge, history as the encounter with the "other" seems to be closely related to the comprehension of the Other in our experience of the present. Together with this it enters into the more general category of man's knowledge of man (in which both are rejoined by knowledge of the self). The problem of the understanding of history leads therefore to a more general problem of which the solution is presupposed.

I shall not make the absurd attempt to improvise briefly a solution of the difficult questions that arise from the possibility of self-transcendence, or the encounter with the Other, or the mutual influences of minds and personalities. These are questions seriously investigated by modern thought from Hegel[20] down to the present day.[21] For my part, it is sufficient to observe that no serious thinker can avoid giving some kind of answer, even if it be the lazy and facile solution of pragmatism.[22] Only solipsism, a paradoxical position which has probably never been seriously adopted, will refuse to admit the genuineness of the encounter with the Other. Every theory of knowledge that is conscious of its duties must integrate the fact of "intersubjectivity." (If need be, it will pose the "we" as the fundamental datum, and then call it undemonstrable.) But it must somehow account for it and prove that this fact, accepted by the common mentality, is not illusory.

I shall therefore leave the task of formulating an answer to this general question of the knowledge of the Other to gnosiology, properly so-called. Since I am now concerned with the theory of historical knowledge alone, I need only

20. J. Hyppolite, *Genèse et structure de la Phénoménologie de l'esprit de Hegel* (Paris, 1946), pp. 311–316.

21. We are familiar with the role accorded the plurality of conscious minds in the philosophy of Husserl or the *Mitsein* of Heidegger's philosophy. Mention should also be made of the fine contributions of M. Nédoncelle in *La réciprocité des consciences* (1942), or those of M. Chastaing, *L'existence d'autrui* (1951). Also see F. J. J. Buytendijk, *Phénoménologie de la rencontre* (French translation, 1952).

22. Cf. G. J. Renier, *History, Its Purpose and Method* (London, 1950), pp. 146–154.

account for the comprehension of documents pertaining to the past. I shall do this by showing that from a logical point of view it is no different from the understanding of the symbols and traces that make knowledge of other men possible in our experience of the present. The following examples will illustrate my point: a) understanding the words spoken to us by a friend who is present; b) understanding a note that the same friend, in our absence, has just scribbled on our table which records the message he would have spoken in the same words if he had found us at home; c) understanding a letter which he wrote to us, not just a moment before but yesterday, or a year ago, or ten years ago; d) and then, skipping over the intermediary degrees, understanding the *Confessions* of Saint Augustine.

Or consider these differences, for instance: a) understanding a letter forwarded to us by a friend which some person, a mutual friend, had written to him; b) once again omitting the intermediary steps, understanding a letter of St. Jerome to St. Augustine. Do I not know both of them as if they were friends of mine, and certainly much more intimately than some of my present acquaintances? Finally: understanding any document whatsoever, emanating from another human being.

I have no intention of repeating here the old fallacies inherited from the Megarians (with their captious quibbling). Whenever a transition is imperceptible or the dividing-line wavers between two species we cannot always gradually blend or combine the two extremes, as for instance the "language" of the ant with that of the "poet."[23]

This gradation simply serves to indicate that, logically speaking, there is nothing unique in our understanding with regard to the past. It is definitely the same process that takes

23. P. Ricoeur, criticizing the thesis of M. Chastaing in *Esprit* (February, 1954), p. 291.

place in our understanding of other men in the present, and particularly in the understanding of articulated language. (Most frequently, and in the best examples, the document under consideration is a "text" of some kind or other.)

I would suggest that my readers refer to the classics of the psychology of language (Janet, Delacroix, Piaget) in which the revealing fact will be found that the normal or pathological behavior which is examined by these authors is precisely the same, psychologically and gnosiologically, as that of the historian struggling with documents of the past. We are told how the understanding of any word that we hear takes place in the present, and how an interpretation is then formed in our mind. We learn how it is specified, verified and corrected. Now the historian's task is accomplished by following the same procedure. It is apparently paradoxical and could perhaps be defined as a vicious circle. As a matter of fact, the most suitable geometrical image is rather that of the helix, and even the conical helix which becomes wider with every turn of the spiral. This paradox was elucidated long ago by Saint Augustine in his *De Magistro*.

I should like to offer a definition in Platonic terminology as the dialectics of the Same and the Other. In order to understand a document (but more broadly, another person) this Other must pertain quite largely to the category of the Same. I must already know the meaning of the words (that is, the symbols) of the language used. This requires a previous knowledge of the realities themselves which are symbolized by the words or signs. We need an illustrated dictionary in order to understand the meaning of words designating certain objects or instruments of specialized usage. Generally speaking, nothing is harder than to try to make the technical terms of a "special vocabulary" (for example, shop-talk or professional jargon) in any way understandable to someone who knows nothing about the trade or technique in question. We

only understand another person by his resemblance to ourselves, our acquired experience and our own mental climate
or world. We can only understand whatever is already our own
in large measure, and in some fraternal relation to ourselves.
If the Other were completely dissimilar and totally alien it is
difficult to see how any understanding would be possible at
all.

Admitting this, there can be no knowledge of other men
unless I meet them half-way. I must forget for a moment what
I am, personally, and emerge out of myself in order to be
open toward these others. Although it may be a very pedantic
subterfuge, I would suggest borrowing the concept of ἐποχή
(*Ausschaltung, Suspension*) from contemporary phenomenology. Of course we must make the necessary transpositions
in applying it to the self with its preoccupations (which I
called existential urgency—but not, however, as Husserl applied it to the natural world). Indeed, the encounter with others
presupposes and requires that we place ourselves "in abey-
ance," as if in parentheses. We must forget for the moment
whatever we are, so that we may be openly receptive to
Otherness.

I must interrupt this analysis to continue the outline of our
treatise on the virtues of the historian. He must be capable
of real self-effacement to an eminent degree (and quite
naturally). But this is not possible for everyone. In the course
of our lives all of us have met men who seem quite incapable
of becoming open or attentive toward others. We say that they
do not listen when others speak to them. Such men would
make very bad historians.

Sometimes this is due to shallow-mindedness, and in such
cases there is a lack of intelligence. We should not call this
egoism, however, because real egocentricity is more cunning.
Quite frequently, of course, they are men who are over-
whelmed by the burden of their preoccupations so that some-

how they deny themselves the luxury of being wholly open to life and other men. This kind of personality is often found among philosophers, and this accounts for the temperamental incompatibility often noticed between them and historians. The real philosopher, it will often be said, is the man obsessed by a problem that challenges him as something inevitable. He would immediately feel unfaithful to his vocation if—only for a moment—he were to stop working on the problem, even within the perspective of his own dialectics. Digging ever deeper in his mine of reflection, he soon becomes incapable of lifting his head to look elsewhere in order to understand some thought or idea foreign to his own. This explains the "dialogue of deaf men" which is so often characteristic of any discussion carried on by philosophers! On the other hand the historian is one who willingly suspends his own thinking—but need I say that men of this type can also be found among philosophers themselves, including some who are very eminent? He does not refuse to take the long, roundabout way in which he will be quite out of his element. He knows what a broadening of the self this circuitous route will procure, proceeding by way of the discovery of other men. We will mention this again in the course of our study.

However, let us go on with our analysis. How is this roundabout method or this self-transcending displacement to be realized? Understanding the meaning of the words (or symbols)—and consequently entering into the thoughts or feelings that inspired them—represents two successive stages of the circular movement, or better yet two spirals of the helix. In the remarks addressed to me by another man, there are words and phrases that I know very well and could have used myself. These expressions evoke in my mind certain sensations, impressions or ideas that could have been my own. Accordingly, I understand quite effortlessly. The other person is so much like myself that we are really of one mind. On other occasions, the expressions used may surprise me, and I tell myself, "That is something I would never have thought of. . . . I have never come upon anything just like that in my own experience." However, it contains enough elements in common with the general content of my acquired experience to enable me to construct a hypothesis of analogy regarding its possible or intended meaning. (Here I use the word "analogy" in the strict sense of the Thomistic concept of the analogy of attribution.)

In possession of this hypothesis, I turn my attention to the other person again; I replace my interpretation in the context; I try to determine its suitability. If it does not prove wholly satisfactory when put to the test, I make another attempt to correct it and try once again to verify it. The process can be simple or complex. It may be automatic and therefore unconscious, or on the other hand, slowed down by the difficulty, it may then take place with my full awareness.

Ordinary experience gives us a thousand examples of such a process in our daily life. How often we interrupt someone to say to him, "I'm not quite following you. . . . What exactly do you mean?" Or else we say, "If I understand you correctly, you believe that . . ." and we proceed to offer our hypothesis for verification. Obviously, this is a very favorable situation— and it is very different from that of the historian. But the difficulties which the historian must surmount are also encountered in the experience of the present. What is the difference between understanding the familiar conversation of a friend, whom we may properly interrupt at will to ask for necessary explanations or verifications, and listening to a lecturer or teacher whom we cannot interrogate regarding his remarks because of necessary deference or tradition? Here again we see that the "past" character of the historical object introduces nothing that is specifically new in the process of understanding.

Let us turn once more to the previously chosen example of

the *Laudatio Thuriae*. I understand this text because it is written in classical Latin, that is, with the great precision in the written language that was used in the aristocratic circles of Rome in the time of Caesar and Augustus. This is a language exemplified by abundant literature taught in our schools. And I learned it, having been a good student! The vocabulary and style of the funeral oration does not baffle the humanist who is familiar with the writings of Cicero and Livy. The sentiments and ideas expressed by this man of antiquity (a widower speaking in praise of his dead wife) are not too surprising. He expresses broadly human reactions that are often but little different from those that might be manifested in analogous circumstances by someone living today. Doubtless there are some aspects that are less luminous. The sentiments of this Roman of the first century are not entirely those which I can personally share by sympathy. As a Christian, for instance, I am surprised by his wholly Hellenistic indifference to the religious question. As a citizen of a *Welfare State*, I find difficulty in understanding the place afforded to questions of inheritance and patrimony in the conjugal life of those wealthy property-owners. Furthermore, since my personal education has been conditioned by the state of modern science, it is not easy for me to grope my way through the maze of juridical riddles posed by the indefinite allusions of this particular text to criminal or civil trials conducted by the subtle procedures of Roman law. Struggling with these difficulties, I try to formulate hypotheses. I extrapolate my human experience and theoretical knowledge in an effort to get a clearer understanding of the expressions and context of the document.

The hypotheses will be all the more precise (and will have greater chances of being exact) if they are based upon the solid ground of similarity existing between other men and myself. According as the degree of Otherness increases, and the category of Sameness diminishes (as happens insofar as the document is derived from a more remote past or a more distant and alien environment) the more difficult, uncertain and partial our understanding will be. The language will not be as well known, the realities evoked by the signs and symbols will belong to a less familiar order, and they will therefore be less readily conceivable.

However, while difficulties may rapidly increase in the understanding of the past, the mechanism or process employed is not technically different from the one which we take for granted in our daily life. Do we not face similar difficulties whenever some original artist suddenly attracts attention or when a writer gives new meaning to our tribal words and expressions? The philosopher is a typical example. By definition, he is someone who has cast a new look upon knowledge, existence, the universe or man. He brings us a message that is always hard to communicate precisely insofar as it contains a factor of novelty radically heterogeneous to our common culture.

This accounts for the inextricable difficulties of philosophical language, which sometimes attempts to utilize all the resources of common speech (and there are philosophers like Plato, and more recently Bergson, who have done this with incomparable skill). Their language includes rhetorical figures of speech and thought in order to suggest: *Quel che la parola non ha detto e non dice* (what the words so far had not been able to say, and in fact do not say). Consequently we are never quite sure that we have understood, or we wonder if we have been duped by the skill itself or by some metaphor or imagery. At other times the philosopher takes the risk of elaborating a technical language replete with neologisms which disgusts the reader because of its abstruse jargon and, even

7

worse, because it substitutes for the glimpse of reality a mere game of abstractions and empty phantoms.[24]

Whatever method is used, the understanding of a philosophical "document" is always difficult and somehow precarious. We are rather shocked by the lack of understanding that we find in Kant's contemporaries with regard to his philosophy. We may already have noted the emphatic but singularly deformed echo which the reading of Heidegger awakened in the mind of Jean-Paul Sartre.

Whether we are confronting some contemporary text presenting special difficulties or a historical document derived from the remote past, the process of understanding is entirely analogous. I shall refer my readers to the psychologists of language once again. I have in mind especially the experiments of Piaget with children of eleven to twelve. "If we slip an unknown word into a sentence, the unknown word is understood in terms of the general context."[25] But this is exactly how we proceed as classical philologists or historians of antiquity when we try to increase our knowledge of the vocabulary of dead languages.

I have attempted to show, for instance,[26] that the word μελογραφία, which according to its etymology was being translated as the recording of music, or "musical dictation," had instead the meaning of "sung lyrical poetry." I laid emphasis upon the homogeneity of the context of documents which included this word, especially inscriptions concerning scholastic competitions, and the epigram of Apollodorus the grammarian: "Homer, elegy, tragic muse, μελογραφία."

This process of understanding is not infallible. Mistakes

24. We have limited ourselves to only a few brief remarks. The problem has been examined with considerable competence by Y. Belaval in *Les philosophes et leur langage* (1952).

25. H. Delacroix, *Le langage et la pensée* (1924), p. 462.

26. *L'Antiquité classique*, vol. XV (1946), pp. 289–296.

occur which a fuller experience and more carefully analyzed approximation will enable us to correct later on, at least in some happy instances. Here again we find a perfect analogy between our early introduction to common speech and the understanding of the past.

"The child understands most words differently than the adult. First hearing them in some particular phrasal usage, he frequently misunderstands them."[27] I once knew a boy of nineteen, a jewelry-worker, for whom the adjective "local" meant pornographic! He had only encountered this word on music-hall placards advertising a "Spectacular Local Revue." It happened to be a spectacle that was indeed quite undressed.

The most competent orientalists do not proceed differently when they attempt to translate some little-known language like the archaic Phoenician of the texts of Ras-Shamra, written in cuneiform symbols. For example, in the word written with the three consonants *T.R.KH.*, they first recognized the name of Abraham's father, Thare or Terah, and according to the context they made a lunar god of him. Then they believed that they had reached a better understanding of the passage and decided that it was the equivalent of the Akkadian *tirhatu,* which means "dowry" or something like it (being the price to be paid to the father-in-law for obtaining a bride). Other hypotheses soon followed. It was suggested that it meant a "precious stone" or a "chalice for divination," or that it was the name of an animal.[28]

I should like to remind anyone who is astonished by these variations, and may be inclined to reach sceptical conclusions —perhaps even supposing that the "mental age" of the historian was equivalent to a retarded adolescent's—that this

27. M. Cohen, "Persistance du langage enfantin," in the *Journal de Psychologie,* 1933, p. 391.

28. D De Langhe, *Les textes de Ras-Shamra Ugarit et leurs rapports avec le milieu biblique de l'Ancien Testament* (1945), vol. II, pp. 504–519.

method of understanding the dialectics of Sameness with Otherness is not only applicable to the relatively elementary case of the language of daily life. The element of Sameness must necessarily prevail over Otherness in order to understand fully. Whatever may be the exact meaning of *T. R. KH.*, if the tablets of Ras-Shamra have on the whole been quite rapidly and unquestionably translated, it is because their vocabulary is related to western Semitic speech and is even very similar to Hebrew, a lingual group and a particular language that are both very well known. But the method also accounts for the first experience of any mode of expression, even the most complex—as for instance, artistic expression. Music provides a good example of this. A lover of music whose ear has been exclusively accustomed to the classical and romantic repertory and who then hears something from Schönberg or Pierre Boulez for the first time is often quite as perplexed as the archeologist in the presence of an unknown language. It is absolute nonsense for him.

How can we ever succeed in broadening our taste and understanding in this area if not, once again, by familiarity, habit, and the patient confrontation of analogies and likenesses, and by adaptation to the context. This also presupposes, and even requires, an open mind. There are people of such narrow taste, whose refusal to consider anything different is so unyielding, that they will never understand anything in the new forms that art may be led to assume. It requires a willingness to be enriched and to come forth from the self. This is a mental structure analogous to that which has been found necessary for the understanding of documents in the study of history.

"To alternate tension and relaxation; to let come what may and allow everything to reach maturity; to be mistaken and then undeceived, agreeing no longer to take for granted whatever had been supposed; to begin again only to become weary once more; and to follow along externally before proceeding to the truth with all one's soul—this is the art to which I apply myself." This is a philosopher's comment,[29] and he is trying to describe the understanding of some difficult author. We need not change a single word of his analysis in order to apply it to the lover of art in the presence of a style, whether plastic or musical, which perplexes him at the first encounter. Or it is directly applicable to the historian confronting the witnesses of the past.

29. Y. Belaval, *op. cit.*, p. 154.

CHAPTER IV

The Conditions and Means of Comprehension

We must now give some thought to the subjective conditions which make possible yet somehow limit our ability to understand. The historian appears to us as a man who can transcend himself through *epokhè,* a real self-suspension in order to be outgoing in his encounter with the Other. We can give this virtue a name: it is called sympathy.

In saying this, I seem to hear our old positivist teachers turning over in their graves. What a complete reversal of perspective! When we read their manuals we get the impression that in their opinion the primary virtue of the historian ought to be the critical spirit. Every document and every witness should be approached with suspicion. Methodical distrust is the form that the Cartesian principle of methodical doubt will take when applied to history. And this will be the point of departure of all real science. It will be asked systematically in the presence of any document whether the witness was perhaps mistaken, or was he deliberately trying to deceive us?[1]

But our image of the historian must be quite different. He certainly should not confront the witnesses of the past with an attitude that is surly, fussy, or peevish, like some unpleasant policeman for whom anyone summoned to court is suspect, *a priori,* and regarded as guilty until there is proof to the contrary. Any such exaggeration of the critical spirit, far from being a qualification, would be a radical vice for the historian. It would make him practically incapable of recognizing the

1. Langlois-Seignobos, *Introduction aux études historiques,* p. 131, etc.

real significance, import or value of the documents that he is studying. Such an attitude is as dangerous in the study of history as is the fear of being duped in daily life. This is an affectation that Stendhal liked to attribute to the characters of his novels (. . . "I always assume that the person speaking to me wants to deceive me . . .").

If understanding is really that dialectical relationship of the *Same* with the *Other* which we have described, it presupposes the existence of a broad basis of fraternal communion between the subject and the object, between historian and document. (Let us also say, more precisely, that it is presupposed between the historian and the man who is revealed through the document as by a sign or symbol.) How can we understand unless we have that attitude of mind which makes us connatural with others? It is this that enables us to feel their passions and re-conceive their ideas in the very light in which they were experienced—in short, it permits us to commune with them. Even the word "sympathy" is insufficient in this respect. Between the historian and his object a friendship must be formed, or how else can the historian understand? According to St. Augustine's splendid formula, "we cannot know anyone except through friendship," *et nemo nisi per amicitiam cognoscitur*.[2]

A conception of this kind certainly does not eliminate the critical spirit. The tendency to sympathy which is realized in friendship is developed within the fundamental category that led us to define history as knowledge, or rather as a conquest of authentic knowledge of the truth about the past. I want to know and understand the past—and first of all the documents that concern it—in their real nature. I want to love that friend who is an existing Other, but certainly not as someone of the same name who is merely a creature of my mind, a phantom complacently nourished by my own imagination.

2. *On Eighty-three Various Questions*, 71, 5.

Both in real life and in history genuine friendship presupposes truth. Nothing could be more open to question than the conception of friendship attributed to Péguy by the writers Jean and Jerome Tharaud. According to them, he loved and cherished an ideal image which he thought he perceived in his friends. He was quite ready to reject them whenever he noticed that they did not embody sufficiently the archetype which he wanted them to represent. But a sincere attachment does not destroy the sense of reality. I can somehow rejoice even when I discover the limitations or defects of someone I love. This very contact (sometimes quite harsh) with an existent person is a confirmation of his reality and his essential alterity. Since he is not identical with my imagination, it can only mean that he is not the fruit of any complacent illusion. If we are really able to love, this experience of alterity and self-transcendence will enable us to surmount all disillusion.

The critical spirit and sympathy are not inherently contradictory. But we cannot say that these virtues can always be easily reconciled or combined, or that they are both equally represented in the mind of every scholar. However, the elaboration of history is the fruit of collective effort: the excesses of the one somehow correct the deficiencies of the other. It is advantageous to the progress of our science that a demanding criticism—or even one that is unjust—serve to rouse a somnolent sympathy that is tending to yield to complacency or facileness.

But when we examine closely the real contribution of these various phases of research, it certainly seems that it is always sympathy, the source and condition of understanding, which represents the constructive phase. Criticism demolishes the provisional edifice of imperfect knowledge and suggests requirements that are useful in the later reconstruction, but of itself it contributes little. For example, Lucien Febvre (in his brilliant monograph on *Martin Luther*) showed how the historical account of the great Reformer had definitively benefited from the aggressive and angry destruction of his image by Fr. Denifle. But this was primarily an indirect benefit which consisted in the destruction of the complacent image that had prevailed in Lutheran hagiography and emphasized its disagreement with the real data of our documents. If Denifle made a positive contribution to our growing knowledge of Luther, however, it was not because of his criticism. On the contrary, it was rather to the extent that his personal competence as a medievalist and his own experience as a Catholic belonging to a Religious Order (and as a theologian) led this Dominican of the nineteenth century to sympathize with the Augustinian of the fifteenth, in spite of himself.

There is another misconception that needs correcting. Our fathers believed that the historian found the opportunity for his finest achievements in the exercise of the critical spirit. The symbolical equation: $h = P + p$ was considered true of the document before it was applied to the historian. It seemed that documents could contain nothing but a little truth mixed with many errors which the incompetence or deceitfulness of the witnesses or the transmitting agents had added to the objective recording of the facts. The historian was consequently, and above all, the critic who would not allow himself to be taken by surprise: he was quite clever in discovering an interpolation, unmasking a forger, or retracting an undeserved or usurped ascription. In the long run this accounted for the historian's unpleasant tendency to lay stress in a sneering manner on the meannesses and weaknesses of others. It accounts for his haughty and scornful attitude and an inability to be open and receptive, or to say "yes"—or even to recognize authentic human values wherever they exist. This explains Péguy's invective in *L'argent* and especially in *L'argent suite* (so pertinent and profound beneath the passionate excesses of his style) against the history produced by critics who could only deny, diminish or destroy: critics who discovered only liars and puppets everywhere, but never any heroes or saints.

This reminds us of Péguy's angry reaction to the book review (so ingenuously full of praise) which his adversary, Charles V. Langlois, had written in the *Revue Critique* regarding Charles Babut's *Saint Martin*: "the author shows, as if it were as clear as day, that Saint Martin was a kind of dubious and detestable lout . . ." This book can certainly now serve as an example of the critical attitude of mind culminating in the inability to understand. What was left of it after its double execution by the Bollandist, H. Delehaye, and our own Camille Jullian?

But today we believe that our experience as historians, far from allowing such pride, requires of us and even develops within us a constant and profound humility. History is an encounter with others and we shall show that for anyone whose soul is neither narrow nor base it often reveals a greatness that confounds us. Men of the past, whom we discover in history, were frequently much greater than we are. But before we reach this point and as soon as we have entered upon the preliminary phase of the task (which is the initial dialogue with the document) our attitude will be determined by a concern to be attentive and somehow receptive to the object, and primarily to the document that reveals it. Certainly there must be none of the cold formality of the examining magistrate when he says, "The accused will rise!" The healthy fear that we ought to feel is not so much that we may be deceived, but rather that we may be mistaken, or be quite unable to understand. It is no easy matter to understand a document: to know what it represents and what it is saying or all that it means. How many times has it happened that a critic thought he had discovered some oversight or error only to learn that further research proves, to his shame, that he was unable to understand!

I shall not attempt to beat a *mea culpa* on my neighbor's breast. When I was a young man I wrote a whole chapter trying to show that Saint Augustine was unable to write well. This judgment merely revealed my incompetence as a young barbarian, both ignorant and presumptuous.[3] When I was a little better informed about classical rhetoric (that subtle and refined technique of which St. Augustine was an incomparable master) I realized that what I had regarded as decadent unskilfulness was really the refinement of an art so perfectly sure of itself that it avoided quick impressions and was not reluctant to take the risk of deformed expression. With greater discernment I gradually perceived the vain pride of up-to-dateness, that pride of the barbarian who scorns whatever he does not know—and I understood a little better.

Every new demand that we make on the historian marks out still another boundary in history as a consequence. In order to know something about an era in the past, it is not only necessary that meaningful documents about it must subsist. There must also be a historian capable of locating them, and especially one who can understand them. This may seem like a truism, but experience shows that the mention of anything so obvious is not entirely in vain. It is difficult for the layman to imagine the blindness of the positivists regarding this matter. They were always most concerned about the strictly technical requirements of historical research. They insisted, for instance, that before studying the history of Armenia one should first learn the Armenian language. But for a long time they were singularly unconcerned about the indirect exigencies which are no less severe. In order to know his object, the historian's personal learning and the very

3. I am citing my own *Retractatio* (1949), with reference to *Saint Augustin et la fin de la culture antique* (1938), pp. 665–666.

THE CONDITIONS AND MEANS OF COMPREHENSION 109

structure of his mind must include psychological affinities that will enable him to imagine, feel and understand the sentiments, ideas and behavior of men of the past whom he will encounter in the documents before him. The history of art requires an esthetic sensitivity that is quite extensive and flexible. The history of Christianity demands that one have at least a feeling for the religious phenomenon's essence, an awareness of spiritual values. For sheer lack of understanding, how many books on history give us the impression of being like a painting done by someone born blind, or like music contemplated by a deaf man!

For example, there is a ponderous book on Serbia and its Orthodox Church.[4] The author, who was obviously insensible to religious values, limited his subject with a perfectly clear conscience to the study of the political aspects and factors of the religious life of the Serbian people. And he did this to such an extent that we witness the strange performance of an invisible actor! He depicted Orthodox monks as being merely guerilla-fighters sniping at Turks—but *why* were there any monks at all?

The value of historical knowledge is directly attributable to the interior resources, the openness of mind and the quality of soul of the historian who has compiled it. As professional men we are too prone to forget this. We are so proud of our technical competence, distorted though we are by our years of specialization and by the superhuman effort that we often had to put forth to acquire it.

The public, on the other hand, is very sensitive to this matter. I am referring, of course, to our real public, which is the society for which we are working. Think of the disappointed reception accorded our productions, with the comments about our "academic history, official science and pure erudition," and the indifference and contempt which we feel as some-

4. J. Mousset, *La Serbie et son Église*, 1830–1904 (1939).

thing unjust. All these arise from the contrast (excessively apparent in our writings and other labors) between a technical exigence carried to the point of scrupulosity and a general philosophy concerning man, life and its problems, that is hardly worthy of a third-class journalist. There is also our childish disregard for the great problems weighing heavily upon the mind and conscience of our time. A sufficiently alert attentiveness would have readily recognized these in the life of those men of the past whom we are supposed to be discovering again. The historian must also and primarily be a man who is fully human—open to everything human—rather than a stunted bookworm restricted to libraries and memo files!

According to his ability, the historian must therefore make an effort to understand his document. Here again we confront the idea of *epokhè*, the effacement of the self. The attitude of submission to the object which we have already defined implies that one forget for the moment even the very question that led to selecting the document. We must listen to it, allowing it to speak. We must give it a chance to reveal itself for what it really is. We cannot know in advance everything it may be able to say to us. If we are too hasty in imposing a questionnaire, formulated *a priori,* this would be the surest way to waste or distort its testimony. The Baconian metaphor has been used excessively: "subject the document to torture, and make it spit out the information." But this is surely mistaken procedure. We must never treat it in a brusque manner, for the problem is to perceive in all of its exactness and nuances the precise scope and import of its signification. We must never be in a hurry; the historian should know how to make use of long delays. As a matter of fact, how many times *escam quaerens margaritam repperit!* Seeking food we find a pearl! We do not always find what we are looking for, but sometimes we discover in a document something we had not dared to expect.

One day in Cairo I was glancing through the *Papyrus Maspero,* hoping to find information concerning the administration of a Byzantine convent in Alexandria. I discovered the origins of the Roman diaconate, vainly sought for a long time —a curious and interesting ecclesiastical institution of the medieval era which still survives in the "titles" of our Cardinal Deacons.

In our encounter with Otherness in historical documents we must proceed as in daily life. Is it a good way to become acquainted with a new friend—or a document—if we subject either to a whole series of questions concerning our interests of the moment? Certainly not, for we must be open to the Other, quite forgetting ourselves. We must try to perceive the inner essence as something different and other than we are . . .

No doubt these considerations will seem elementary. But they serve the purpose of throwing new light on the traditional theory concerning the preliminary work to be done with documents. If we consult the manuals of methodology that are used in the study of history,[5] we will generally find a procedural outline presented according to the following schema:

A. External criticism.

1. *With regard to authenticity:*

Is the "text" that we are examining actually what the author had written? Are we in possession of the original document itself, or a copy? Is there perhaps only a copy of some previous version; and in the latter case, is it faithful or incorrect? The critique of restoration is sometimes linked with this phase, described as a critical "expurgation and

5. The presentation has not greatly varied from Droysen's *Grundriss* first edition, 1867), and Bernheim's *Lehrbuch* (1889), to P. Harsin's *Comment on écrit l'histoire* (Liége, 1933, 5th ed., 1949), including, of course, Langlois and Seignobos (1898).

renovation" which aims to reconstitute an original document that has disappeared. However, all of this really pertains to a very different and more demanding aspect of the historian's task.

2. *With regard to the source:*

This requires an analysis of the intrinsic aspects—going so far as to consider the water-mark or filigree of the paper, if necessary—and a comparison with the evidence provided by other documents. Through this technique they attempt to answer the following questions: who wrote this document? when? where? how? (that is, the form of the document), and by what means has it come down to us?

B.   Internal criticism.

1. *Critical interpretation:*

What the author actually said, and what he intended to say.

2. *Critique of credibility:*

This is a negative critical approach, concerned with honesty, competence and precision. An attempt is made to determine the value of the testimony. In this respect, the well-known questions arise: Could the author have been mistaken? Did he want to deceive us, or was he perhaps compelled to do so? In connection with the consideration of his competence, there is also the problem of sources. Was he an "eye-witness"? Or did he derive his information from previous witnesses? If his sources have been preserved, the document holds no further interest. If they have been lost, the "search for sources" (*Quellenforschung*) soon becomes disappointing.

In spite of its systematic and logical appearance, this schema does not really possess the comprehensiveness which it claims. It is only applicable to the "historicizing" kind of history that puts its emphasis on events in the narrative style and uses primarily textual, literary sources.

Actually, this procedural method was particularly commended by specialists of the political or ecclesiastical history of the Middle Ages of western Europe. This is a field in which the documentation is encumbered with second-hand chronicles, forged charters and decretals, and lives of the saints that are outrageously antedated.

On the basis of this conception, historical research concentrates on proving the reality of the "facts," that is, the objectively verifiable human activity. The ideal document is consequently the original version of an official report established on-the-spot by reliable and competent eye-witnesses. Any document encountered is qualified as good or bad according as it approaches this ideal testimony to a greater or lesser degree. But as we have already indicated, this can no longer be regarded as history's unique ambition or purpose, nor even its greatest. We have learned how to utilize many kinds of documents in many other ways, and to question them much more skilfully and variously.

On the other hand, we must not confuse the empirical division of the various technical operations with the logical analysis of the rational inferences implied by these operations. This is the problem that we must now examine. If the question is posed in its full extent, it can then be said that the whole "critical" problem (that is, the entire series of operations to which the document is subjected by the historian before making use of it for the elaboration of knowledge of the past) is ultimately a matter of determining the nature or essence of this document. We must make an attempt to know exactly what it is, in itself and of itself. Rather than the idea of a critical examination that is basically negative (establishing what the document is *not*, and merely stating that it is not a forgery or is not deceptive), I consider it advantageous to

8

substitute the positive idea of *comprehension* of the document. This kind of approach attempts to determine what the document really is, and in fact succeeds in doing so.

There is no need to emphasize that its real "substance" will often prove to be something quite different than first appeared, and perhaps wholly different than its author himself intended. This effort of positive comprehension easily combines whatever was validly elaborated in both the external and internal criticism. We then realize that one particular document *is* an original, while another is an immediate or mediate copy, whether faithful, inaccurate or forged. It *is* authentic, pseudepigraphic or apocryphal. It *is* veracious, pretentious or perfidiously deceptive.

However, there is no point in allowing ourselves to be confined within the categories of a questionnaire devised for episodal history. As a matter of fact, our effort of comprehension will culminate in conclusions that are much more fully nuanced. Knowledge of the real nature of the document teaches us to read it as it should be read, and to avoid looking for things that it does not contain or studying it from a distorting point of view.

Consider, for instance, the interpretation of the canonical gospels. How much time has been wasted by "criticism" in investigating the credibility of the testimony which these gospels contain concerning the events of Jesus' life! The founders of *Formgeschichte* were still too subject to the tradition established in the nineteenth century to be able to infer all the conclusions that follow from the very fruitful principles which they had the merit to develop and set forth. And we ourselves are only beginning to realize that it is necessary, first of all, to understand what a gospel really is. It must be kept in mind that it is not a collection of official or certified reports about certain events, presented with varying degrees of exactness or bias, which have been more or less faithfully transmitted to us. It was never the intention of the author to provide documentation for eventual use by "historicizing" historians, but something quite different indeed. Within the existential perspective of ecclesiastical catechesis, he wanted to convey to his readers the knowledge of Christ that is necessary for salvation. In order to elaborate this portrait of Jesus, he may have resorted to a considerable manipulation of sources. We may perhaps find this perplexing because of the author's unconcern about chronology, for instance, but it would be naïve to call it falsification or deception. It would be even more naïve to imagine that this testimony can be analytically dissected, and by separating the wheat from the chaff somehow isolate a pure nucleus of authentic "facts." The gospels are not direct testimony concerning the life of Christ, but rather a primary document of incomparable value regarding the primitive Christian community. We can only approach Jesus through the image of himself that was formed by his disciples, but this does not mean that the image is misleading—although it may not be the one that the episodal historian would prefer. It would give us a great deal of satisfaction, for example, to know the date—to the day, month and year—of Christ's birth and passion. But this was a question that left the first Christians completely indifferent.

The deepening of the preliminary inquiry will necessarily lead to positive conclusions. Since it exists, the document possesses a certain "substance" which must be discerned through comprehension and sympathetic fellow-feeling.

I can easily transpose to historical knowledge and its documents what St. Augustine said somewhere[6] about sensible knowledge and material objects: we cannot say that a document, in its real substance, is ever "deceptive." It may mislead the historian because he is credulous or careless. This is especially so if he takes it for something that it really is not.

6. *De vera religione*, 33 (62).

But in such a case it is the wrong hypothesis that is the source of the error and not the substance of the document itself. If we are mistaken, it is not *ex eo quod est,* but rather *ex eo quod non est.* Not by what the document is, but by what it is *not!*

The best example to consider is a *forgery.* According to the prevailing theory, it would seem that once a document has been recognized as a forgery, it should simply be thrown into the waste basket. On the contrary, it should only be withdrawn from the historical file where it was accorded a place of importance—provisionally and unduly—and instead be placed in the file of the forger. Thus it becomes a positive document, because it happens but rarely that any forgery was simply a "gratuitous" act.

The cartulary of the abbey of Saint-Germain-des-Prés contains three charters,[7] one from Charlemagne, the second from Louis the Pious, and the third from Charles the Bald. By all the evidence all three are forgeries. The proof,[8] based upon analysis of the paleographic, documentary and sigillographic script, leaves no room for doubt. Obviously, these "documents" must not be used for studying the history of the Carolingian period. But all three are by the same hand. And it is the very hand that drew up a fourth grant[9]—in this instantce authentic. Here at the request of Abbot Hubert Henry I, in 1058, making reference to the first forgery (*inspecto privilegio Karoli magni*), confirmed the grant supposedly accorded by Charlemagne. We must add these three forgeries to our file on this matter because they throw much light on it in many respects. They not only reveal to us the

7. R. Poupardin, *Recueil des chartes de l'abbaye de Saint-Germain-des Prés,* vol. I, p. 25, no. 17; p. 41, no. 27; p. 53, no. 33.

8. In addition to Poupardin's arguments, cf. also M. Prou, *Comptes rendus de l'Académie des Inscriptions,* 1922, pp. 125–130.

9. Poupardin, *Recueil . . .* vol. I, p. 101, no. 63.

procedures employed to obtain concessions from King Henry but also teach us something about the juridical principles of the Capetian dynasty (especially regarding the importance of a Carolingian precedent), and the moral conceptions prevalent among those who were associated with the Abbot of St. Germain. They even reveal the kind of historical knowledge that was possessed in those days. It is amusing to note the extent of success achieved in acting out the role of Carolingians!

A forgery is certainly a falsehood, but the informed historian is enabled to understand this "perfect crime" through fellow-feeling. He need not be duped himself (and, need we add, does not have to omit a more severe moral judgment as well). He can utilize the very truth which the act of falsification conceals within itself.

Comprehension of the document, as we said, is actualized through the dialectics of Sameness with Otherness. We must mention this again if only to explain more fully, though in passing, a notion which till now has continued to be rather controversial. This is the conception of history as knowledge of the particular.

It is no doubt true that historical knowledge aspires to perceive "that which will never be seen twice." There is no real recurrence or repetition in the evolution of humanity, and each historical event bears its own incommunicable difference within itself. Historical knowledge discerns the particular as such in the same mode or manner that is done by divine knowledge (all allowance being made, of course, and within the limits of the analogy).

This accounts for the contrasting difference so easily established between history and the sciences of nature. The natural sciences try to reach a knowledge of whatever is common by general laws. Physics, for instance, is not interested in *this* apple fallen from *that* apple tree on the head of the individual

whose name is Isaac Newton, but in motive power, of which
the motion itself corresponds to the equation:

$$e = \tfrac{1}{2} \, gt^2$$

This contrast must be nuanced, however, as Rickert already
had the merit to insist: antithesis is an oratorical device which
should be repudiated as something that is frequently very
crude. *Natura non facit saltum.* There are no gaps in nature!

As a matter of fact, historical knowledge also makes use of
laws—psychological, for instance, and the knowledge of man
in general—in order to know some individual man in particular. On the other hand, the sciences of nature, for their part,
likewise study particular facts in their own fields of interest.
In meteorology, for example, they observe a particular cyclone
in the area of the Caribbean Sea to forecast its particular
trajectory and havoc. Such a phenomenon is so particular
that they even give it a name, as soldiers do for a landing
operation. In geology, they refer to *the* Alpine folding, and to
the Riss glacier or to *the* glaciation of Würm. These are phenomena which, by a partial but real analogy, are frequently
described as "historical."

Inversely, however, we must stress the fact that this comprehension of the particular, that is to say of the Other as
such, is knowledge of the analogical type. It is constructed
with elements which, if not universal, are at least very general.
If this were not so, we would slip into irrationality. I understand a document in the way that I understand a word or
expression in the language of daily life: to the extent that it
does not present itself to my mind as though meant for one
person only. Every historical document possesses a certain
uniqueness, at least numerically (the same, for instance, as
identical gold coins which, in quantity, constitute a treasure
and thus confer importance and special significance upon
such a discovery). On the other hand, the document must be

similar in one or another of its aspects (or we may say more precisely that it must be analogous) to other documents already known. It is only knowable in terms of this analogy.

The deciphering of an unknown language is a case in point. Champollion was able to understand Pharaonic Egyptian because he knew Coptic, a language derived from it. On the other hand, Etruscan still resists our efforts because no one has succeeded in relating it to any known language. A script that is still undeciphered, like that of the Indus River civilization, or Minoan hieroglyphs, possesses at least enough traits in common with written alphabets that we know quite well to enable us to recognize that it is some kind of writing. But consider, instead, the Peruvian *quipu*, that mnemonic device consisting of a cluster of small cords provided with one or several knots tied according to various patterns. If we had not known about its use and purpose through the direct experience of ethnography, we would not even be aware that it represents a kind of writing. This is because it is so completely different from all other known systems used in the noting or recording of thought.

In fact, the more nearly a document resembles a quite homogeneous group of similar documents that are already well known, the more easily and unerringly will its interpretation become possible. Here again it is a question of understanding *what* it really is, that is, its *quid sit*. This accounts for the strength and practical usefulness of the specialized disciplines. We call these the auxiliary sciences of history, including archeology, numismatics, epigraphy, paleography, diplomatics and sigillography. All are dependent upon the systematic comparison of a certain kind or category of documents. They observe the constants in analogical subject matter and formulate rules, or rather laws, based upon this element of generality which particular examples will reveal when compared in this way.

We must perhaps introduce a little more exactness in our
terminology. I am not including all the disciplines whose
knowledge proves useful to the historian when I refer to the
auxiliary sciences of history. As we said before, the historian
really ought to know everything. This includes the sciences
of nature because of their interferent effect on man's history,
and especially the human sciences of psychology, sociology,
political economy, etc. There is not one of them which, at
some time or other, does not have its particular contribution
to make. The whole idea of auxiliary sciences can become too
vague to serve any purpose.

The use of the more limited conception that we suggest
will itself require several precautions. This is because the
"disciplines," as we noted with regard to prehistory, are
entities of an empirical kind that often dissolve when analyzed.
We need only consider philology, a pretentious term covering a multitude of interests. And I cannot regard it wholly
as an auxiliary science. Linguistics is now conceived as the
historical study of languages and their development. This is
certainly an integral part of history as such, and in the same
sense as the history of philosophy or the history of art. In
my opinion, the only part of philology that can still be called
an auxiliary science is that which pertains to textual criticism.

Anyone who examines the real auxiliary disciplines themselves from a logical point of view will find that they are
complex conglomerates. Epigraphy affords a good example,
although we must be more specific because it includes many
varieties. Let us say, more exactly, Latin epigraphy, or the
knowledge of the general laws common to all Latin, pagan
and ancient inscriptions. This can be separated into three
elements: archeology (the study of the monuments on which
the inscriptions are engraved or attached); paleography (deciphering and dating texts according to the kind of writing);
and diplomatics (the study of formularies).

It can be interesting to observe the method employed by these auxiliary sciences in a particular instance, and the full range and scope of the method. I can find a good example of this in Roman epigraphy, the discipline that I have just mentioned:

This is a copy, preserved in a manuscript dated 1521,[10] showing an inscription[11] which was discovered at Saintes Maries de la Mer in Camargue, in southern France. It was believed that this text lent documentary support to the famous legends whose popularity and gradual multiplication in Provence can be followed from the end of the eleventh century. These tell of the miraculous arrival there of a whole group of biblical persons: the risen Lazarus, the two sisters Martha and Mary (Magdalene), among others, and especially the two holy women, Mary, the mother of James, and the mother of Salome.[12] The basilica which now bears their names also preserves their purported relics. These relics were exhumed in 1448 in the course of excavations undertaken for this very

10. Arles, *Bibl. Mun.*, ms. 113 (le "Livre Noir"), p. 24.
11. x.C.I.L., XII, 120*=4101.
12. Mark 15:40 (cf. Mt 27:56); 16:1.

purpose beneath the floor of the crypt. The writer of the manuscript claims, although no doubt mistakenly,[13] that the finding of the relics was facilitated by the reading of the inscription which he interpreted (reading from right to left, and in defiance of the spelling) as follows: *Sub (h)umo muri/ cava/ara*(sic) *bas(ili)ce a(l)tiori/M(arias) Iacobi (et) S(alome) v(idebis)*. "Dig under the ground of the altar wall of the upper basilica: you will see the Marys, James and Salome."

I shall not astonish my readers by saying that this interpretation is unacceptable, but we must still see why this is so. It contains nothing contradictory, and is not impossible *a priori*. Is it perhaps simply improbable? That is what we must prove. And we are familiar with documents that require an interpretation that is quite as far-fetched. Consider, for instance, the reverse side of a gold piece[14] that is kept in the Bardo Museum of Tunis:

It bears the following inscription in Latin capitals (arranged in a circle): D S E T E R N S D S M A G N S O, and in the

13. No mention is made of the inscription in the official account of the excavations made in 1448. This documented report is preserved in the Departmental Archives of Bouches-du-Rhône (B 1192), published by M. Chaillan, *Les Saintes Maries de la Mer, recherches archéologiques et historiques* (Aix, 1926), pp. 77–142.

14. Unpublished. This is the kind of coin described by H. Lavoix under notation no. 109 in his *Catalogue des Monnaies musulmanes de la Bibliothèque Nationale, Khalifes orientaux* (1887), p. 35.

center, horizontally: R T E R C N. This is a coin minted in
Carthage at the beginning of the Arabian occupation. The text
is Latin, but of Moslem inspiration, and should be understood
as follows: *D(eu)s   eter(nu)s,   D(eu)s   magn(u)s,   D(eu)s*
o/(m)n(ium) cre(a)t(o)r, with the horizontal line reading from
right to left. Surely this is quite as remarkable and unexpected
as the document of Provence.

If the inscription were unique in its particularity, it is difficult to see how it would be possible to interpret it with any
certainty. But the final formula V S L M (which the pattern-
drawer faithfully reproduced although his hypothesis actually
required V S I M) is one of the combinations of initial letters
which we very often encounter engraved at the end of a
Latin inscription. We possess thousands and thousands of
such inscriptions, coming from all parts of the Roman world.
Consequently, we must exclude the possibility that there is
question here of some particular allusion to the two Marys
of the gospel. It is simply a formula of common usage. Sometimes, indeed, it appears in a less elliptical abbreviation as
VOT SOL LIB MER, or even with all the letters: *Votum*
Solvit Libens Merito, the pagan equivalent of the *ex voto*
formula commonly used today.

In this instance, therefore, we have a simple votive inscription. But inscribed or dedicated to whom? A minimum
acquaintance with the paleography of Roman inscriptions is
sufficient to reveal the words: "to the Majestic Junos." The
copy cleverly reproduced the "ligature" of the two letters
—N I—and the abbreviation of the second word was also
quite customary[15]: *Iunonibus/Aug(ustis).* We know that
Iunones was one of the names used in Latin for the protective

15 So ordinary that it diverts us from noting the superfluous markings
of the second letter which could suggest a ligature of *Avac* or *Anac*
(as F. Benoit supposed, cf. *Mémoires de l'Institut historique de Provence,*
vol. 5, 1928, p. 16).

divinities of Celtic (or pre-Celtic) origin, analogous to the *Matres*.[16]

An examination of the form of the monument (which is obviously a pagan votive altar—our museums possess a large number of similar objects) will confirm this interpretation archeologically. And finally, let us resort to diplomatics in continuing our investigation. The uniform pattern of votive dedications leads us to note on line 3 (after the name of the divinities in the dative case) still another name in the nominative. This identifies the author of this votive offering. It was a woman who, in accordance with classical Roman onomastic custom, bore a gentilitial name. The latter could not be clearly copied[17] because of the stone's condition, but there was also a *cognomen* which was apparently *Barbara,* a very common name.

No epigraphist or informed historian would question this interpretation. Nevertheless, we must explain what is meant when we say that it is "certain." It is not a matter of mathematical certitude obtained by way of rational deduction. Nor is it the empirical certitude procured by experimental verification. Although in this particular case we have an example of one of the most assured conclusions that historical research can attain, it is still only a logically probable conclusion. This

16. We know that the Romans had assimilated the divinities of the conquered "barbarians" to those of the classical Pantheon. At Rome, Juno was the feminine equivalent of the *Genius,* the popular tutelar deity, and consequently any protective goddesses could be called *Iunones* without difficulty. This fact is attested by many documents, ranging from the Narbonnaise to the Norique. See for instance K. Prümm, *Religionsgeschichtliches Handbuch für den Raum der altchristlichen Umwelt* (Freiburg, 1943), p. 777.

17. O. Hirschfeld found a copy (unrelated to the one we mentioned) in a Vatican manuscript, showing the same inscription and, concordant in general, manifesting the same hesitation and perplexity with regard to line 3: *Sitzungsberichte* of the Academy of Sciences of Vienna, vol. 107 (1884), p. 235.

is very pertinent to one of the fundamental principles of the
theory of history which has often been much to the fore from
Leibnitz to Raymond Aron (and we may retain the latter's
formula, set forth in Kantian terms): "the modality of historical judgments is possibility."[18] And yet the probability in
this instance is practically infinite.

Certainly we cannot treat the author of the manuscript as
a fool simply because he considered the text to be a cryptogram prepared by "the disciples of our Lord . . . as obscurely
as they could, on account of miscreants who were in the
region at that time, so that the Holy Women would not be
put to ruin or death." But what probability could there be in
all this? If a cryptogram is to be deciphered some day, it
must at least be apparent that it really is a cryptogram. But
the authors of this text would surely have succeeded only too
well in disguising it with the inscription to the *Iunones!* An
obstinate objector might reply that even this procedure is not
wholly impossible. (And I agree! During the Resistance period
in war-time, I happened to receive a clandestine message so
cleverly contrived that in my naïveté I only understood it in
the literal sense.) In any case, what is the degree of probability
for such an explanation?

Historical certitude is never more than a probability which
it would seem perhaps unreasonable to question—or at least
there would be insufficient reason for doing so. Like the
pragmatists, we might say that it provides a "practical satis-
factoriness."

Both in the example given and in similar conclusions
reached by the auxiliary sciences this result itself is only
obtained because of the *general* nature of the facts employed
in the reasoning process. Insofar as a document becomes more
particular and original—and from the historian's point of

18. R. Aron, *Introduction*, p. 196.

view, more interesting—the element of Otherness increases to the detriment of Sameness, and its interpretation becomes more difficult.

With regard to the inscription of the two Marys, we will find that fundamentally it does not offer much that is of real interest from the documentary point of view. Its uniqueness (apart from the name of the dedicator . . . *Barbara* . . . which, moreover, is uncertain) is hardly more than numerical. It is just one more document attesting the existence of the cult of the Majestic Junos in southern Gaul.

This needs to be emphasized because it is on the basis of the undeniable triumphs achieved since the seventeenth century by the development of the auxiliary sciences that historical dogmatism has conceived the dream of a truly "scientific" knowledge of the past with a certitude comparable to that of the sciences of nature. But the extrapolation is quite illegitimate. The comparative method on which the certitudes of our auxiliary sciences are based can only be applied to facts occurring in repetition. And the documents that are most valuable to the historian are those which enable us to reach the properly particular aspects of the reality of the past. Anything essential in their message somehow escapes the laws that are based upon the observation of certain constants. As soon as an inscription has been elucidated and explained to any degree—or in other words when it has acquired particular significance—epigraphic science no longer has much to teach us about it. For it has then become merely one literary text among many others, unique in particularity.

We can turn once again to the *Laudatio Thuriae*. There is nothing specifically epigraphic in the analysis that can be made of this long and beautiful text. (The preserved part covers eleven pages in the Durry edition.) It matters little that it was engraved in two columns on a marble plaque instead of being copied in ink on papyrus. Consequently, to which auxiliary science shall we go for an explanation or criticism? In my opinion, it does not seem very likely that literary history, by making us familiar with the development of the form and style of the funeral *laudatio* in ancient Rome, can help us assign this particular text to any tradition. In view of the mutilated condition of the preserved remnants, the historian must resort to all the resources of conjectural criticism in order to bridge the gaps. But is this also a "science"? In the inscriptions of the common type certain observable facts are evoked through repetition. Conjecture is dependent on analogies and parallels, and often finds itself rewarded by experimental verification which a new discovery occasionally represents. Nevertheless, this means proceeding at random, and the suggested complements are necessarily quite arbitrary. This has just been proved by a recent find. A new fragment of the *Laudatio* contained the end of ten lines of text which had been missing until then. Earlier scholars (including famous names among them: Mommsen, Vollmer, et al.), had tried to provide what was lacking. Actually, however, they hit the mark only one time in eight.[19]

But that is generally the case. Most frequently, in an historical study that is pursued in depth to any extent, the documents to be examined do not come under the jurisdiction or within the scope of these exacting disciplines. The effort of comprehension can hardly be divided into two distinct phases: the one external and preliminary, attempting to specify the nature of the testimony with precision; the other, more central, seeking to analyze the content. The two become inseparable, and our knowledge of the particular object then becomes dependent only on the analogy that we make available to it. And this derives from our general familiarity with all the documents derived from the same period in the past,

19. A. E. Gordon, *American Journal of Archaeology*, vol. 54 (1950), pp. 223–226; M. Durry, *Revue des Études latines*, vol. 28 (1950), pp. 81–82.

and still more generally from our empirical knowledge of man.

If it is a question of translating a document as rich in its originality and uniqueness as one of Plato's dialogues, everything is particular. If I can somehow fall back on my knowledge of Greek, I shall still need to know the habits of style and vocabulary that were typical of Plato's Greek (including, of course,[20] the smallest pecularities in the use of the particles). Or in recalling what I know of Greek literature, it is especially with reference to the unique kind of style found in a Platonic dialogue that I will have to know something about the rules and patterns.

My understanding is guided, orientated and determined in a general way by whatever I can know about Greek man of Plato's time. This includes his inner world and the ideas and conceptions that can be considered as possible for him. Finally, and above all, I must depend on whatever I know about man in general, including his thoughts and feelings.

These are all general elements that facilitate our understanding of a particular document. But it is the ingenuity and capability of the historian that must yet reveal the existence of possible analogies between the data of the document and the known or experienced facts of human nature. Every time that our theory lays stress on some new virtue needed by the historian we are imposing one more limitation on history itself. A document will be precisely understood *insofar as a historian can be found who is capable of judging its nature and scope with greater profundity.*

To conclude the preliminary examination, let us note still another limit to the validity of the historical construction. For practical reasons it is not always possible for the historian to

20. Studies undertaken by L. Campbell and W. Lutoslawski have shown that the statistical study of the use of particles made it possible to reach definite conclusions regarding the development of Plato's style and consequently the dating of the various dialogues.

have direct access to original documents in the pursuit of his task. Ancient or medieval literary works, for instance, are most often consulted by the historian in some modern edition, and not in the actual manuscripts that transmitted these works to us. Consequently, between the "noumenal" past and our own knowledge there is an interposition of a supplementary stratum of transformations resulting from human intervention. The truth of history will be dependent on the validity of operations beyond our control carried out by those who prepare the material for publication—and primarily on the value of the disciplines used for this purpose. A century and a half of experience has given us much greater concern regarding the worth and significance of disciplines and methods employed by textual criticism than was felt in the heroic times of Lachmann and Madvig. We are now fully aware of everything arbitrary, uncertain and subjective that enters into this "art" which is certainly the most conjectural of them all.

This is so true that the practical rules which we give to beginners (advising them to read a text in its best and latest critical edition, and to be capable of verifying the work of our predecessors) have only a provisional value. At a deeper level of study, a return to the manuscripts becomes necessary. If, for example, Father M. Verheijen has now given us a completely new version of the very obscure history of the monastic *Rule* attributed to St. Augustine, it is because he was not content merely to read *Letter 211* in the widely received critical edition of Goldbacher in the *Corpu*s of Vienna. He also searched for manuscripts and found some that were much older than those which Goldbacher had studied. In this way he reconstructed a history of the tradition of this text more complex than anyone could have suspected.[21]

21. M. Verheijen, *Vigiliae Christianae*, vol. 7 (1953), pp. 27–56; *Revue du Moyen-Age latin*, vol. 8 (1952), pp. 97–122; *Augustinus magister*, Actes du Congrès international augustinien (Paris, 1954), vol. 1, pp. 255–263.

9

We must insist on this because the classic theory of "external criticism" has failed to realize that the document linking us to the past is not, for instance, the text of *De Civitate Dei* as we find it in the Dombart-Kalb edition, but rather the 376 manuscripts which have been located to date. Doubtless the content of these manuscripts is no longer purely derived from St. Augustine himself. There are, moreover, the accumulated errors of the copyists, and the more or less ingenious corrections made by these same copyists or their readers. However, the "expurgated and restored" text that we receive from the hands of the philologist adds to these data still another supplementary layer of tractates. And the value of these must in every case be carefully weighed and judged. But even more than the possible or eventual errors, I am sensitive to the substantial mutation that the document undergoes in passing through the hands of those who do the editing and publishing. I have proved, for instance, by the study of the three oldest manuscripts of the *City of God,* that to read this work as St. Augustine intended one would have to disregard the divisions into chapters which was introduced by modern editors and instead consider each book as a whole, a complete development that needs no sectional division whatever.[22] It is understandable why Helm, editing the *Chronicle* of Eusebius-Jerome in the *Corpus* of Berlin, chose to put a text in uncial calligraphy arranged like the archetype of our manuscript tradition, according as he reconstructed it.

22. *Mélanges J. de Ghellinck* (Gembloux, 1951), vol. 1, pp. 235–249.

CHAPTER V

From the Document to the Past

We do not study a document for its own sake, but rather to reach the past through the document. The moment has come for us to analyze this passage from the sign to the thing signified, from the document to the past. It is by this decisive step that the essential task in the elaboration of historical knowledge is accomplished. With this purpose in mind, however, we must be careful to avoid over-simplified explanations. The analysis will require us to distinguish logical operations which, in fact, are closely related and in constant interaction.

The historian begins by posing a question to himself, as we have indicated. Then he prepares a file of documents that are pertinent to the matter. Each of them is annotated with regard to its credibility, according as this was determined by the preliminary inquiry. But this portrayal of the process is still too elementary. The increase of knowledge is achieved by that dialectical movement described as circular—or better yet as spiral—in which the historian goes successively from the object of his study to the document that is its instrument, reciprocally. The question which started the whole process in motion does not maintain its original identity, but in contact with the documentary data it is continuously changing.

Suddenly the historian realizes, for instance, that the question was preposterous and anachronistic ("the problem does not even arise"). He learns to formulate it in more precise terms, better adapted to the nature of the object. This is the advantage to be derived from a provisional self-effacement. Instead of an impatient interrogation constantly interrupting the witness to tell him, "Get back to the question!" the historian asks the document, "What are you? Help me to know you."

But this very question already implies an answer, formulated on a hypothetical basis. At each of these reconsidered starting-points—at every successive whorl of the symbolic spiral—the hypothesis is formulated anew, corrected, expanded. Consequently historical knowledge has its beginning and gradually increases. Observed empirically, this elaboration of history does not take place in two distinct and successive stages: 1) judging the value of a document, and 2) concluding from the document to the past. There is only one process, entirely homogeneous: this includes "comprehension" of the documents by familiarizing oneself with them; thinking about them seriously, and examining them over and over again. It means gradual penetration. All of this finally makes it possible to know what they really are, while also revealing the human past of which the documents have preserved a record and to which they now bear witness. The historian is the man who acquires this familiarity with the documents. It enables him ultimately to know their meaning, scope and worth with assurance, and to perceive the image of the past which they conceal and finally communicate to him.

Is this process much different from the one whereby we succeed in knowing, understanding and accepting other men in our daily life and present experience? It is by seeing other men, observing their activities and their reactions, hearing them speak and noting the many indications they give of their alterity that we gradually form a conception of the Other that is finally valid. Can we say that the situation is really different in our study of history? It is our familiarity with the documents that also enables us eventually to know the man of the past as a living man knows his friends today.

Nevertheless, we must examine more closely how this knowledge of the signified past is achieved. It is important to distinguish several possibilities, for between them all the intermediate stages can be found. The concatenation is very revealing:

a) Often the object of historical knowledge, the past which the historian attempts to perceive, is not distinct from the very nature of the document that is studied. This situation arises in the history of philosophy and more broadly the history of man's thought, as well as in the history of art and the history of those manifestations of what Dilthey called the objective mind (by a partial transposition of the Hegelian concept): the history of a language or a technique. The whole endeavor in this instance is reducible to comprehension, a matter of *Verstehen*. For example, suppose that we are in the presence of a philosophical work such as Plato's *Laws*. What does the text really mean? What is the internal coherence of the doctrine which it expresses? This provides a direct and immediate knowledge of the past that has no condition or limit other than the historian's capacity: I shall know as much about the *Laws* of Plato as I shall prove myself capable of understanding.

Similarly, there is an entire aspect of the history of art which is very well explained, although paradoxically, by B. Berenson.[1] Here the same immediacy in comprehension can be found as when we look at some picture or monument of considerable significance and try to analyze and probe its full import and meaning thoroughly.

b) Inevitably, further inquiry will soon suggest questions that some would describe as "more properly historical." We will no longer be asking, "What is the particular beauty of this painting?" but rather, "What was the intention of the

1. See notably *Aesthetics and History* (Anchor, 1954).

painter who conceived it?" Or no longer, "What does this dialogue of Plato signify by and in itself?" but instead, "What was Plato trying to say in this instance?" It may be asked, for example, if he actually commits himself to the truth of his propositions, as sometimes occurs in conversation when we interrupt the Other to say, "Are you really serious?" This question, in Plato's case, is often necessary because it is so difficult to discern in this keen mind and refined artist the exact area in which his recourse to the irony inherited from Socrates finds occasion for expression.

As a representative example of the debatable question,[2] we may ask whether the eulogy of Isocrates at the end of the *Phaedrus* was sincere or ironical. Was it perhaps sincere in Socrates' mouth at the time that Plato had him speaking, while expressing bitter regret concerning the unkept promises that Isocrates had made in his youth? Or else, in the person of Isocrates, the true-to-type orator, was Plato simply conjuring up the ideal rhetoric (according to his own conception) which young Aristotle must teach to the Academy? The field of hypotheses is not limited to these . . .

This kind of problem constantly arises. It is one thing when reading *Aucassin et Nicolette* to find a reflection of the ideal of courtly love; it is another thing to realize that the author mentioned it only to ridicule it. The answer is never simple. Who can discern the extent of Cervantes' complicity with Don Quixote?

These are difficult problems that we can never be sure of resolving fully; they can be clarified only by a greater effort of interior comprehension.

c) There is another possibility—very different from the first

2. The bibliography that I have given, "Histoire de l'éducation dans l'antiquité"[2] (1950) pp. 492–493, is no longer up to date; at least add R. Schaerer, "La question platonicienne" (Neuchâtel, 1938). (But see the English translation, Mentor Omega, 1964.)

—in which the same direct apprehension of the past in the document is achieved (although in another manner). This occurs when we turn to the document seeking, not any testimony it can provide regarding a past that is exterior to itself, but rather the expression of the past that the document represents inherently. If we read Marcellinus, for example, we may regard his book not primarily as an account of the events that marked the reigns of Constantius II, Julian the Apostate, and other emperors, but instead as a portrayal of a man of the fourth century of the Christian era—a man like Marcellinus himself, such as he appears in his way of thinking, feeling and judging. We would no longer ask what he knew (or whether there is any truth in what he claimed to know), but rather what he was. Comprehension of the written work provides us with direct knowledge of its author. This is frequently the method used to exploit our historical sources, one of the surest and most fruitful of all. It is this procedure that is used in the elaboration of the history of the mentality, sensibility, spiritual climate and *Zeitgeist* of an era or a society. It is one of the most flourishing sectors of our science.

I must again refer to the *Laudatio Thuriae*. It includes a valuable contribution to the history of love. The husband explains that his wife had voluntarily suggested divorce because their marriage had remained childless. In this respect she was complying with the old Roman tradition that regarded marriage, *Liberorum procreandorum causa*, exclusively in terms of the family. The husband, however, reacted in a very "modern" way. We may say, without anachronism, that he showed himself to be a Hellenistic man for whom the human person possesses an absolute value. Accordingly he refused to allow this sacrifice.[3]

Let us note the precautions that must be taken. (The effort of comprehension, as we said, excludes credulity in its quest

3. *C.I.L.*, VI, 1527, ii, 31–47 (ed. Durry, 99. 19–23).

for the truth of the past.) The witness may have feigned certain sentiments or emotions which in fact he never felt. He may have tried to glorify himself in his document (as often happens with authors of *Memoirs,* who do not ordinarily write disparagingly about themselves!). The truth of the conclusions obtained will be the direct task of the historian's technique, and of the skill and judiciousness with which he formulates the questions and the answers.

In the example we have cited, we must not hasten to draw conclusions regarding "men of the time of Augustus." This would be acting like the proverbial Englishman who, hardly disembarked at Calais, wrote in his notebook, "French girls are red-heads." Instead we should say, "In the time of Augustus the old ideal of ancient Rome had lost some of its hold over men, since we know of a husband who honorably refused to divorce on grounds of sterility." On the other hand, we shall not make any attempt to know whether this husband really felt the sentiments which we expressed. The historical question is, "How did this man formulate the expression of his love?"

This truth, of course, will be found within the limits that the reciprocation of conscious minds is always confined to. Even in our ordinary experience, can we ever be sure of having penetrated to the very depths of another person's mind?

d) In any case, the historian will be led gradually to pose "factual" questions regarding the past, including those "events" to which our predecessors were strongly inclined to reduce all history. Even if we reject this narrow conception of episodical history, we shall nevertheless be compelled to seek reality: past existence, and human phenomena localized in time and space. This will be necessary in every field of research, even those that are the most generally resistant to pure historical curiosity, like human thought or art. Questions are always arising in regard to documentary dating and attribution.

It is important for our understanding of a particular Platonic dialogue to determine its place in chronology, and consequently its place in the development of Plato's thought. Our interpretation of Aristotle's system requires that the whole of his writings be of his own authorship, and not in large part that of his disciple Theophrastus, as a recent hypothesis suggests.[4]

In this instance the historian must take the plunge and infer from the document to a reality that is external to it. But the reality of this particular past is naturally much more difficult to establish, and the amount of uncertainty soon increases. Positivist methodology had elaborated a very rigorous doctrine regarding this procedure. It can be summed up in the following outline:[5]

Taken by itself, no document proves the existence of a fact in such a way as to be unquestionable. Critical analysis merely results in determining the credibility that its testimony seems to deserve. On the other hand, *testis unus, testis nullus:* we cannot conclude to the reality of the fact on the basis of only one document (for all of our assertions would be affected by the coefficient of incertitude: "If we can believe our witness . . ."). Now, if we succeed in gathering together the accounts of several witnesses, all of equal authority, and if their comments concerning the same fact are strictly convergent and can be proved to be independent testimonies—and not derived from one another or from a common source—then the probability that we may properly decide in favor of

4. J. Zürcher, *Aristoteles' Werk und Geist* (Paderborn, 1952).

5. See for example Langlois-Seignobos, *Introduction*, pp. 166 ff. Positivism has not been a specifically French failing; see for example the discussion of G. J. Renier, *History, Its Purpose and Method*, p. 131, concerning A. Rhomberg (1883) and W. Bauer (1921).

their veracity becomes greater, and eventually becomes practical certitude.

We need say no more about these principles except that they are almost never really applicable. Resulting entirely from a deliberate emulation of the sciences of nature and from the avowed ambition to raise history to the dignity of an "exact science of things of the mind," the positivist theory defines the necessary conditions to assure the desired purity of knowing. But it is unable to guarantee the scope or interest of the known which will actually be accessible in these circumstances. The proposed requirements disregard the servitudes of our human condition and the situation imposed upon the historian by the capricious "chance and accident" that preside over his documentation. For the most part, none of the conditions mentioned above are ever quite realized. They would presuppose the establishing of negative and singular propositions. And this of course (as all logicians will agree) is the hardest thing in the world to achieve.

What about the independence of the witnesses? Within the limits of our information we can determine the positive relations of dependence which may exist between the documents. Or if that is impossible, we can always conclude, "Until more information is available, they *seem* to be independent." But when can we definitely say that they are? Similarly, with regard to credibility, internal criticism determines the maximum degree of credibility that (in view of our information) a document seems to deserve. But it does not determine the real degree, because we are unable to make a complete enumeration of the possible causes of error.

When I have proved that my witness really was present at the scene which he describes, and was in a favorable place to observe it, I shall never be able to know whether, by mischance, he may have blinked his eyes or sneezed at the decisive moment—as for instance when Napoleon, during his coronation, seized the crown that Pius VII was supposed to place on his head.

Is there perhaps agreement among several witnesses? But this implies that the object of their observation was really the same. And yet we know that two different men will never see exactly the same object in the same human spectacle occurring before their eyes because they are interested in different things, do not possess the same mentality, nor the same mental habits. It is extremely rare to find two testimonies that really and exactly pertain to the same group of empirically derived data—or more briefly stated, bear upon what is called the same "fact."

No doubt the fields of observation may simply cross-check one another, and this often happens. Agreement then centers upon the common element in these testimonies. But we must see that this identity can only pertain to the most external elements of reality, those which are objective or objectivisable, and then only when an agreement can be established that is based upon experimental verification. Nevertheless, this is merely a fleshless skeleton in relation to the total human reality, which alone deserves to be studied and known—a complex reality in which external deeds and visible activities are inseparable from the psychological and other factors which confer significance and import upon them.

"Caesar crossed the Rubicon" is a "historical fact," but the historian is not primarily interested because the troops led by someone named C. Julius Caesar at a given moment on the seventeenth of December in the year 50 B.C. (according to our calendar) marched from the left bank to the right bank of the little river in question, but rather because this "deed" had such political significance as to start a civil war.

It is surprising to note how the classic theory we have just set forth results in the distortion of historical reality so that it can apprehend that reality through the crude instrument of its categories. Actually, of course, it is simply an illegitimate transposition of the categories of the judicial inquiry.[6] These categories themselves correspond to an order of preoccupations that is entirely different. They have as their object something that is always quite simple and necessarily objective. It cannot be confused, except to a very small extent, with the much greater object of historical study.

To expound his own theory of history Collingwood, for example, chose to imagine a short detective story on the theme *Who Killed John Doe?*[7]

And, as a matter of fact, the police investigation which the discovery of a murder sets in motion is indeed a study that can properly be called historical. There is research, together with criticism and interpretation of documents, clues pertaining to the case in question (footprints and fingerprints), and the recorded testimony. But this is history of a very elementary kind, almost crude—because the event to be reconstituted (in this instance, a dagger stab) is so simple, factual, easily recognizable and "understandable." The appearance of the Platonic Theory of Ideas in the world of the objective mind was also an event, but one which requires special treatment. The judicial investigation is to the theory of history what whole numbers are to the modern theory of numbers, which must account not only for integers but also for fractional numbers, and for those that are algebraic, irrational, imaginary and transfinite.

Confronting the reality of the past, which must somehow be apprehended, it is less the question of existence than the question of essence which concerns the historian. Establishing the reality of an element or detail (and this, let us say once

6. As the great Bollandist, P. Peeters, has shown in his study, "Les aphorismes du droit dans la critique historique" in the *Bulletin* of the Royal Academy of Belgium, Cl. of Letters, vol. V, 23 (1946), pp. 81–116.

7. *The Idea of History*, pp. 266 ff.

again, may be a sentiment or an idea instead of a deed, or a very general phenomenon as well as an individual act) is certainly important, but it cannot be sufficient of itself. The episodical skeleton must be provided with nerves, flesh and skin—the delicate and quivering epidermis of life. It is the whole complexity of reality and mankind that is the object of history. If its object is the *human* past, it will be true insofar as it succeeds in re-discovering the reality of man in all its plentitude. If we merely reduce him to a mobile body animated by movements or activities that can be located in time and space, this is not equivalent to a real knowledge of man. The classic theory of verification by convergence can only retain their greatest common factor from the various kinds of evidence. This results in the neglect of whatever in each of them is most valuable—because most discerning and most nuanced, and therefore most real (being closer to the inexhaustible complexity of human reality).

It is best to give historical knowledge a logical structure that is rigorous without being rigid. Knowledge must be adapted to its object. Our positivist predecessors were haunted to the point of obsession by the ideal of "objectivity." They understood this quite specifically as referring to knowledge that is somehow or other mentally verifiable, a kind of knowledge that is "valid for everyone," as they liked to say. However, this amounted to nothing less than a practical denial of the very possibility of history.

Logically enough, they assumed that when we did not possess sufficient qualified convergent testimonies we merely needed to avow our ignorance: "The only correct attitude is agnosticism."[8] But since it is impossible to attain the imposed conditions in all genuinely human problems, the result was a history that conformed strictly to positivist requirements and was therefore full of blank pages.

8. Langlois-Seignobos, p. 133.

When we are confronted with a document or a witness, we will no longer be preoccupied principally by the question of whether we can contrast it with others. As a matter of fact, essentially, the testimony is almost always proven to be unique of its kind, its import, or its orientation—or whether the witness tried to mislead us, and so forth. The problem will be to know whether he understands what he is talking about (or, if there is question not of voluntary testimony but of an indication implied in the body of the document itself, whether he could clearly express it). We must know how well he understood and expressed it, to what degree of perfection, with what richness, complexity, and depth he was capable of reflecting, recording, and transmitting to us the subtle human reality that we are endeavoring to perceive.

Let us take the classic problem of Socrates: for nearly a century, in agreement with Hegel (this is another of his regrettable errors), it was accepted that the historical Socrates was that of Xenophon rather than that of Plato. Is it not obvious that this was merely a pseudonym under which Plato revealed his own philosophy? (Should we say that Plato lied and simply wished to deceive us? No, he did not write his *Dialogues* simply to supply future historians with documentary material about Socrates! When he put his doctrines into the mouth of his old master, as he did, it was a tribute paid to the man to whom he realized he owed everything.) On the contrary, it was said that it was impossible for Xenophon to distort Socrates' teaching as he had no philosophy of his own, in reality not even any personal thought to put in its place. It was a long time before it was understood (despite Schleiermacher's prophetic warning) that for those precise reasons Xenophon was perhaps incapable of understanding very much of Socrates' teaching and thus gave only the poorest reflection of it, banal to the point of caricature.

It is almost always useless to hope that we can control the

validity of our witnesses from outside. Very often the only thing we can do is to study our document carefully, forcing ourselves to penetrate more and more deeply into it, and thus formulate a judgment concerning the degree and the nature of its veracity. Then we must decide, step by step, that we will or will not have confidence in it.

Here we touch upon the very essence of historical knowledge. When it bears fully upon its object, in all the richness of human reality, it still cannot accumulate all the probability which, theoretically, could lead to a quasi-certainty. Our knowledge of the past is *what we believe to be true* from what we have understood of what the documents have preserved for us.

There is no need to be scandalized by this. It is simply a fact, and our critical philosophy need merely acknowledge it. The philosopher seeks the nature of things (and having found it, rejoices: *laetatur inventor*)[9] because, such as it is, being is always superior to non-being. Contact with reality, however crude it may be, is better than embracing a chimera.

To admit that historical knowledge results from an act of faith (for "to have confidence in" and "to have faith" is all one, as is amply proven by the Greek and Latin, πιστεύα, *credo*) does not necessarily mean that we must deny its truth or deny that it is at least possibly true. Once again let us be careful not to confound mere rigidity with strength of mind. It is a mistaken rigidity to reduce the rational to the apodictic, or to restrict the possession of truth only to those conclusions derived from deduction *more geometrico* and from experimental verification of inductive hypotheses. This is a pusillanimous search for security: through fear of making mistakes, reason is rendered powerless. Indeed an authentic philosophy which intends to let nothing escape will be the first to testify to the legitimate and necessary role that knowledge by faith plays

9. Saint Augustine, *De libero arbitrio*, II, XII (34).

in the life of man. I am impressed at hearing, across fifteen centuries, the voice of Karl Jaspers[10] echoing Saint Augustine. The Church Father set forth clearly the role played by faith in history, and showed that it reappears in many other sectors of knowledge—so much so that if we refuse to appeal to its action, life itself would become impossible, *omnino in hac vita nihil ageremus.*[11] And it is indeed true that no matter how rational a man may be or may wish to be—even the philosopher—he never ceases to resort to faith. This is as true in the most ordinary behavior of everyday life as in the strictest exercise of pure thought:

We "have confidence" in the timetable of trains furnished us by the railroads, even though they themselves warn us against the possibility of error; at the other extreme, think of the role of the axiom in mathematics, and of the unprovable character of the principles upon which a philosophy is based.

This is no exceptional type of knowledge, reserved to the very special case of theological faith.

Christians will naturally be particularly sensitive to the supreme example, which is essentially important for them. Contrary to other religions that are based only on eternal truths or mythical symbols, Christianity rests upon truths of an historical nature (the Incarnation, the Passion, the Resurrection . . .). Whoever believes in him in whom Saint Peter believed is a Christian. Thus our theory of historical knowledge may profit from all that Christian theology and, I venture to say, psychology have accumulated around the notion of "divine faith"; *mutandis mutatis,* and taking the precautions necessary to any transposition, we might say:

The act of historical faith need not be arbitrary; it includes

10. *The Philosophical Faith* (1953).

11. *Confessions,* VI, v (7): the whole passage should be reread. The clearness of the terms will be remarked in what concerns history: "(Mihi) consideranti quam innumerabilia *crederem* quae uiderem neque cum gererentur adfuissem, sicut tam multa *in historia gentium* . . ."

rational *preambula fidei*. We have made an effort to understand the documents. (As we have seen, this completely overflows the boundaries of simple external or internal "criticism," and appeals to all that we can know of that civilization which was the source of the documents, and finally to all we know of man, life, being and the void.) This effort leads us finally to a judgment of credibility founded on reason. The conscientious historian will always take care to avoid what Catholic theology terms the "fideist" error: that is, a tendency to minimize or deny the role of demonstrative reason in establishing a well-balanced faith.

This is a necessary condition, but one which is not in itself sufficient. When once it has been accepted that confidence is not credulity, and that faith is not purely arbitrary nor the effect of a willful despotism that "would subjugate" the intelligence (giving the word the full sense which Bossuet liked to give it), then it is agreed that an act of faith remains a free act—*credere non potest, nisi volens*.[12] This involves the whole man, and implies an existential decision.

We will give further consideration to this last aspect. For the moment we will limit ourselves only to the logical analysis of the historians' behavior. We must emphasize once again the fact that none of the conclusions drawn from this investigation—no historic truth, in the strictest sense of the term —is incontestable or constraining. This becomes unquestionably apparent from the ensemble of facts collected in the curious file of hypercriticism. One must have the courage to open it and study it without being shocked. In the first place it contains a series of outrageously paradoxical experiments, just as their authors wished them to be. These men (either to combat the historic scepticism engendered by too strict rationalism, or on the contrary to bring back within bounds

12. Saint Augustine, *Tractatus in Johannem*, 26, 2 (P.L., vol. 35, col. 1607).

10

the tangled dogmatism of the builders of hypotheses) have
tried in a polemic context to demonstrate in some way the
non-obligatory character of historical truths. They show that
one could with all logical strictness, and without contradicting
oneself, deny what seems most evident: question for example
the very existence of Napoleon I:

The most famous of these "experiments for seeing" are
those of R. Whately, *Historic Doubts Relative to Napoleon
Buonaparte*[13] and of J. B. Pérès, *Comme quoi Napoléon n'a
jamais existé* (As though Napoleon had never existed).[14] The
first writer (later to be the Anglican archbishop of Dublin)
was a member of that curious group of Oxford liberals whose
importance I have already mentioned. He wanted to show,
by going the limit, how excessive were Hume's rationalist
exigencies against the Gospel miracles[15]; the second (a former
Oratorian who became librarian in Agen) turned Napoleon
into a sun myth in order to ridicule Dupuis' theory, famous
in its day, on the "explanation of the fable by means of
astronomy."[16] These are not the only known cases; when
Max Müller in his own fashion took up the Dupuis hypotheses
on the solar origin of the Greek myths, an anonymous tract
circulated in Oxford among the students: *"Comme quoi M.
Max Müller n'a jamais existé."*[17] And I myself, arguing one
day against one of those amateurs who so lightly question the

13. London, 1819, often republished.

14. Agen. 1817 (or 1827); numerous editions; one of the first has the
significant title *Le nouveau Dupuis*, or *l'Imagination se jouant de la
Vérité.*

15. Whately on many occasions applies the rules formulated by Hume
in his *Essay on Miracles* (which is part of the *Enquiry concerning Human
Understanding*).

16. Title of a brochure published in 1779–1790 in the *Journal des
Savants*; his major work is *L'Origine de tous les cultes ou la religion
universelle* (1795).

17. Translated into English in the folklore magazine *Mélusine*, vol. 11,
col. 73 foll.

existence of Jesus, undertook to prove that Descartes was also a myth created out of whole cloth by the Jesuits of La Flèche, because they were anxious to draw attention to their school.

As a companion piece to this, however, there is the even more revealing instance of interpretations that are seriously advanced by their authors. These are apparently logical and coherent, and do not conflict with any absolutely rational possibility. These authors consider them to be authentic, but their colleagues, the competent technicians of history, consider them completely false, totally unacceptable, and unworthy of being more than shrugged off.

I will cite the really astonishing case of the Jesuit scholar Jean Hardouin (1646-1729), who was a very learned man and a great servant of history in many fields (numismatics, philology, etc.). We still use his big edition of *Themistus* profitably, for its commentaries, and his *Acta conciliorum* were a milestone in the progress of ecclesiastical studies. But from August 1690 he undertook to question the authenticity of the major part of Greek and Latin literature, including both the classics and Christian writings. His judgments are wildly arbitrary: he condemns the *Aeneid* but accepts the *Georgics*, as he accepts Horace's *Satires* and *Epistles* but rejects the *Odes*. All these apocrypha were supposedly invented by monks in the fourteenth century!

Insofar as it is possible to try to understand this really extraordinary case,[18] it seems that the starting point of the ridiculous construction was the naïve personal desire to deprive the wicked Jansenists of the arms furnished by Saint

18. For it is difficult to find one's way around in this enormous confused work, whose bibliography is complicated by the existence of clandestine or plagiarized publications, by protests or denials whose sincerity is doubtful, etc. See for example M. Veyssière de la Croze, *Vindiciae veterum scriptorum contra Harduinum* (Rotterdam, 1707).

Augustine. Apparently it was the authenticity of the Church Fathers that he suspected first of all. He complacently explains to us how their barely completed works, toward the middle of the fourteenth century, were used by heretics such as Wyclif, before Luther and Calvin made use of them!

Father Hardouin is not an isolated phenomenon. At about the same time, erudite Protestants who were worried by the reinforcements that Catholic argumentation found in the monuments of the Roman catacombs[19] tried to deny the Christian character of these subterranean cemeteries and to attribute their frescoes to forgers of the Middle Ages.[20]

Early in the nineteenth century a certain J. F. Müller, inspired by nationalistic pride, argued that the documents dealing with the Germanic Middle Ages had been falsified by jealous foreigners who were anxious to disprove that the Germans had been the most civilized and politically unified people of Europe![21]

It would be a simple matter to multiply the examples and to furnish more recent ones. . . .

Might we say that we reject this nonesense just as the Academy of Sciences every year rejects those communications that harmless fools send it, dealing with the erroneous value of π or the possibility of perpetual motion? No, for the cases are quite different. We cannot, properly speaking, discern true paralogisms in the theories of our hypercritics, nor oppose to them genuinely restraining evidence. Historic reason is situated at the level of the possible, of (more or less) the

19. Revealed by the posthumous work of Ant. Bosio, *Roma subterranea novissima* (Rome, 1651).

20. G. Burnett, *Letters (from) Switzerland* (Rotterdam, 1686), at least five editions in forty years; F. M. Misson, *Nouveau voyage d'Italie* (The Hague, 1691), several editions and translations into English, German, Dutch; P. Zorn, *Dissertatio historico-theologica de catacumbia* (Leipzig, 1703).

21. G. J. Renier, *History, its purpose and method*, p. 134.

probable. Our consent is asked for taking things simply at their best—testimonies that nothing prevents our believing, and that good reasons encourage us to accept. But what can we answer to someone who believes that these motives of credibility are insufficient? Mgr. Duchesne's reply to the person who called him a hypercritic is well known: "And if I reply that it is you who are the hypercritic?"

No one can be forced to have faith. From this (and every generation of historians experiences it) comes the impassioned character, the sharpness, the infinity of discussions engendered by such hypercritical hypotheses. It is impossible to agree, to force anyone to share your conviction. . . .

Beyond doubt, a kind of unanimity soon arose against poor Hardouin, beginning with the seventeenth century. Therefore it is perhaps not impossible to define by common accord what we might term the proper zone of application of historic reason, *a standard way of thinking about its subject-matter*[22] that can be qualified as normal. Unquestionably . . . and it is exactly in this sense that it seems possible to defend the validity of history against scepticism (which should be sought not in the inaccessible rigidity of the apodictic, but on the level of the "practically satisfactory"). Still, the logical conditions of such an accord must be defined.

Note first of all that if it exists, the accord is not established on the same level of critical exigence in all fields of historical research. There are tranquil zones in which testimonies are taken at their face value; in others, on the contrary, disquiet, scruple and mistrust reign. What a contrast for instance when we go from the history of the Roman Empire to that of Christian origins (yet we are in the same centuries, in the same milieu of civilization)!

The contrast can be studied in the work of a single author. Here is a worthy successor of Father Hardouin, Polydore

22. W. A. Walsh, *Introduction to Philosophy of History,* p. 96.

Hochart, an honorable professor of French secondary education, who devoted two large volumes to contesting the authenticity of the *Annales* and the *Historiae* of Tacitus.[23] According to him, these are fakes due to the pen of Poggio, the celebrated fifteenth century humanist. He sees for instance in *Annales* iii, 58, where there is the question of forbidding Jupiter's flamen to leave Italy, a reflection of the polemics of the day concerning the sojourns of the cardinals far from Rome.[24] That hypothesis met with the most complete indifference—manuals and bibliographies do not even mention it. On the other hand, this same Hochart, with equally poor reasoning, rejected Book X of the *Letters* of Pliny the Younger, containing the famous letters (X, 96–97) on the Christians of Bithynia.[25] As he touched upon a bitterly contested problem here, attention was paid him; he was quoted (even though it might be to reproach his lack of judgment) by those who went to the bottom of the question.[26]

Why? Because the question of Christianity for most of our contemporaries remains a posed, present, imperious question, placing their fundamental option on life in hazardous position. Can we really be surprised that the existential stake parallels critical exigency? In this field (in which all historical affirmation constitutes by itself a supplementary reason for believing or doubting) it is natural that the historian should advance with circumspection, figuratively speaking, testing step by step the solidity of the ground on which he sets his foot. Let us say without metaphor: he demands with particular in-

23. *De l'authenticité des Annales et des Histoires de Tacite* (1890); *Nouvelles considérations au sujet des Annales et des histoires de Tacite* (1894).

24. *Nouvelles considérations*, pp. 211 foll.

25. *Études au sujet de la persécution des Chrétiens sous Neron* (1885), pp. 79–143.

26. As for instance M. Durry's edition of Pliny the Younger, *Letters*, Book X (coll. "Budé," 1947), p. 70.

sistence their letters of credit from documents, and in each case he takes another step only after long personal debate.

But it must be emphasized that these historical conclusions which are of such great importance for religious faith themselves come from the gnoseological category of faith. This is something that positivist history, over-proud of the equivocal title of "science" which it assumes, deliberately avoids recognizing. Critical analysis, however profound it may be, will never get beyond the examination of reasons for credibility—can never reach a conclusion concerning the reality of the past—if the will to believe, to "have confidence" in the testimony of the documents, does not enter into it.

The hypercritical experience frequently confronts us with what the theologian in his field would term obstinacy in incredulity. A historian need only be stirred by some profound passion (and the moralist well knows that simple curiosity may become a formidable passion) in order to demand more and more from his documents before deciding to believe them. He will examine them with an eye that becomes more and more suspicious, and that is the end of the possibility of drawing any conclusion! Such cancerous points exist more or less everywhere in history, where discussion drags on, becomes more bitter, and bibliography accumulates with no positive benefit.

Since the epidemic spreads from time to time, doubts spring up. When a new question enters the discussion, there is a great temptation (against which we must be on guard) to succumb to scepticism and decide that "nothing is certain in history." What tends to become certain, finally, is not so much the well authenticated fact as that fact which no one has found it useful to dispute.[27] "That is why historic truth is only valid for those who desire that truth."[28]

27. As I indicated, carried away by polemic passion, in 1939: *Tristesse de l'historien*, p. 36.

28. *Ibid.*, p. 37; cf. R. Aron, *Introduction*, p. 88.

This would be exaggerating, however. Scepticism is only legitimate in reference to positivist dogmatism, whose roots go back to Kant, as we know. Unlike the rationalism of Descartes, historic facts known through personal experience and the testimony of someone else would be scientific matter for Kant. It is only with regard to such illusions that deception can exist. As a matter of fact all the preceding remarks have merely underlined the fundamental fact: historical knowledge, based on the notion of testimony, is no more than an intermediary experience of reality through an interposed body (the document). Thus it cannot be demonstrated and is not a science properly speaking, but only a knowing by faith.

Consequently, it becomes possible to determine the useful interval in which critical exigence can be exercised, as we have noted that historians effectively do. Pushing it too far is often labor lost, for the time will soon come when criticism will reveal that there is only the general principle: historic judgment is in the realm of the probable, not of the necessary. Nevertheless, things could always have happened differently and all testimony can be questioned; as is well known! Let us rather try to understand our document, see what can be known of its reality, and what can reasonably be drawn from it. Reasonably, no more than that. To him who demands more, reply as the Venetian courtesan replied to Rousseau: "Lascia le donne e studia la matematica": abandon history and limit yourself to mathematics, for this is the only field on which the geometric mind can find a legitimate ground of application and full satisfaction.

If we take up once again the striking example of the history of the origins of Christianity, how much time has been lost— as much by Christian apologetics as by its adversaries' counter-apolegetics. Both have uselessly aggravated the debate—one side attempting to make history an "evangelical demonstration," a sort of converting machine; the other side seeking to prove the illegitimacy of an adhesion through theological faith to the historic articles of the *Credo*. But Christian faith has always implied a certain specific, essential element of obscurity, "for now we see in a mirror darkly,"[29] and as for the "probability," paradoxically it appears to reason as "scandal" and "foolishness."[30]

I would like to chose this chapter by emphasizing the practical results which come from this analysis. Much could be said about the really blameworthy ignorance of too many historians in regard to those servitudes which limit the fruitfulness of historical work, the unpardonable carelessness with which they dispose of problems which they should know to be unresolvable for them and for us. We are not God; we cannot know everything. In contrast to the natural sciences where, within the limit of common experience (in the interval between the infinitely large and the infinitely small) it is always possible to increase the precision of the experiment, in history the precision increases, very rapidly, at the expense of certainty.

A good example is the conversion of Constantine, one of the major controversies for a whole generation. If we consider this question as a whole, we may take it for granted (within the limits of historical "certitude") that after Constantine's victory over Maxentius, the religious policy of the Roman Empire was definitely committed, contrary to the general tendency established by Diocletian, to a course that was favorable to Christianity, and that Constantine himself showed increasing preference for this religion, and died baptized. We may try to go a step farther and make an attempt, for instance, to date the first official indications of this pro-Christian policy with some degree of accuracy. Legislative documents and numismatic evidence will be helpful in this respect. However,

29. I Corinthians 13:12.
30. I Corinthians 1:23.

if we hope to acquire more specific information regarding the personal conversion of the Emperor himself, determining whether he actually had a vision on the night of October 27 or 28 in 312 A.D., and what he saw or thought he had seen in that moment, it is quite futile to pursue such an inquiry for lack of adequate documentation. With regard to Constantine's court, we do not possess the equivalent of the *Ephemerides* of Alexander (or Dangeau's *Journal,* among modern works), nor do we have anything on his interior life to compare to St. Augustine's *Confessions* (or Rousseau's).

We must cheerfully recognize our restrictions with regard to documents, carefully determining their scope, and know what can possibly be found in them. No matter how ingenious a historian may be, he cannot continually extrapolate the testimony of his sources, making them say things other than they were meant to say. Our limitations with regard to logic should not be forgotten either, for we must measure our own capacities and never promise more than we can accomplish. We must set a limit to our curiosity at the right moment, pursuing our tasks within the conditions and bounds in which they can really prove efficacious. Mgr. Duchesne mentions one of St. Paul's precepts that deserves careful thought: *non plus sapere quam oportet sapere sed sapere ad sobrietatem.*[31]

---

31. Preface to his *Histoire ancienne de l'Eglise,* vol. 1, p. 15 (citing Romans 12:3).

CHAPTER VI

The Use of the Concept

Through research, understanding and the use of documents, the historian's mind finds an answer to the questions by which he has discovered and encountered the past. Taking up the analysis at a higher level of abstraction, we must now specify (from the logical standpoint) how—by what means, and with which instruments—this elaboration is made. This is most important, for the entire problem of historical truth is based upon the validity of these mental operations by which the "Noumenon" is changed into knowledge, and human "reality" (which occurred in the past) into history.

The most important instrument appears to be the concept. To know (in this case, to know historically) is to substitute a system of concepts elaborated by the mind for the raw event itself—and this at the very moment the historian acquires his historical knowledge, prior to any preoccupation with formulation and literary expression intended for others. As Croce[1] clearly saw, the historian cannot grasp even the most elementary, simple and objective historical "fact" (for example, Caesar's death) without "qualifying" it. To say only that he existed is not enough, without in some way specifying *what* Caesar was. Croce analyzed this mechanism in rigorous terms, invoking the logical principle of the indissolubility of the predicate of existence and the predicate of qualification in any individual judgment.[2]

1. *Logica come scienza del concetto puro*[4], pp. 184–185; a doctrine taken up again in his later works, such as *La storia come pensiero e come azione,* English translation, p. 46.
2. Ideas elaborated by Croce in *Logica,* pp. 103–113.

But how can we qualify the past without giving it a name, a form that the mind can grasp, a face that the mind's eye can see? By means of a concept, elaborated *ad hoc* by the human mind. What an illusion to believe it possible to reach the things themselves, the past *as it really was!* It would be contradictory to claim to know, without using the logical instruments of knowledge. We can easily show this by examining the example mentioned—Caesar's assassination. What is the meaning of this episode if we "go to the facts themselves"? With a great deal of trouble, we would at best come out with an account such as this:

The Ides of March 44 B.C. at 11 a.m. At a moment t in the flow of the universe (specifiable by reference to the equinoxes and the apparent movements of the sun and moon) at a point of the terrestrial surface whose coordinates are $x°$ N. latitude and $y°$ E. longitude, within a closed rectangular space, some 300 males of the species *homo sapiens* were assembled. A new member of this same species entered the enclosure along a straight-line trajectory. At the moment $t+n$, twelve of the assembled individuals (while others present were oscillating mildly about their points of equilibrium) accelerated into high-speed trajectories which converged, at point m, with the trajectory of the newcomer. Filed steel pyramids were present at the prehensile extremities of the superior right-side appendages of these twelve, and thanks to their active strength penetrated the body of the newcomer causing traumatism and death.

Rome,

Curia,

the Senate,
Caesar.

Brutus,
Cassius, etc.

In parliamentary terms: various movements.

Daggers.

Clearly, we did not observe things directly as they really happened. We conceive them: we grasped them by means of concepts. These concepts were chosen from the many that man has elaborated for the natural sciences, for mechanics, biology, and so on. Far from enabling us to grasp the past more directly, these diagrammatically obtained concepts give us a distorted picture of human reality. In order to reflect its richness more fully and completely—without ever flattering ourselves that we have covered it entirely—we must supplement these scientific concepts with a series of specifically human ones. Not only will they enable us to grasp historical reality better, but they will give it a highly intelligible structure. These include such ideas as republic, monarchy, aristocracy, legality, dictator, Senate, *nobilitas*, conspiracy, ambition, liberty, ingratitude, despair.[3]

Our problem is to determine the validity of these concepts, their adaptability to reality, their truth—on which the truth of history depends. We must distinguish among several different cases, for a lack of this kind of distinction has too often made historical theory simplistic and inadequate. All historical instruments do not have the same logical structure, and are not equally valid. I suggest a distinction between at least five major categories:

a) First, history uses concepts having a universal ambition, that is, concepts applicable to man at any time and place. Partisans of historical relativism (and there are many among historians, whether they are aware of it or not) shrug disdainfully at this idea, as they scorn "the *cliché* of eternal Man identical to himself through the ages," an "abstract anyman, eternal, basically immutable and perpetually identical to himself."[4] Nevertheless, before examining the unusual aspects

3. The example selected by Croce is that of a sentence from Titus-Livius, XXII, XLIV, 1, which questions the concepts of: man, war, army, pursuit, road, camp, fortification, dream, reality, love, hate, fatherland, etc.

4. Cf. L. Febvre, *Combats pour l'histoire*, p. 21.

of man, the aspects particular to a given civilization, the historian must necessarily understand man purely and simply as man. Who among us can briefly conceive of the human past without calling up such universal notions as man, *homo* or *vir*, woman, life, and death.

Let us take a more refined example. If, following Thucydides, I should like to know the political or cultural history of Athens during the years immediately preceding the Peloponnesian War, I am constantly forced to mention Pericles, who is in the forefront of this history. The use of this name presupposes the notion of "personality," the idea that notwithstanding all his biological and psychological changes, there was something permanent, coherent and unified about Pericles throughout his life: a factor of intelligibility.

We say, "concepts having a universal *ambition*" so as not to jump to conclusions about their validity. We are, in fact, dealing with a heterogeneous class which must be carefully analyzed. Some of these concepts are borrowed by history from the natural sciences: Caesar, the man, was first a body having a certain mass, and as such was capable of being accelerated. Secondly, his living body was susceptible to somatic affections. Historical knowledge about Caesar should integrate everything that mechanics and biology can bring to bear on the subject. Many more concepts are made available by the "sciences of man," such as sociology, psychology, and ethics ("Nero was cruel"). The validity, the actual universality of these concepts depends of course on the validity of the sciences which elaborated them, and is relative to the degree of truth of which they are capable in their actual state of development. The proposition "Caesar was bald" uses the truly universal concept of "baldness" defined by medical science. "Nero had not rid himself of his Oedipus complex," on the other hand, derives from the discipline of psychoanalysis, whose methods and explanatory value are still being questioned . . . so that the historian's use of such concepts will have variable dependability.

Another example of this type is the aggregate of ideas on man, on human beings and humanity that the historian, consciously or not, derives from his own civilization: his language, the dominant ideas of his time (*Zeitgeist*), the ideology of his social class, the philosophy whereby he learned to think. Here the relativists' criticism has had ample subject matter, and makes a useful contribution. For just as "historicism" (everything in man is relative to his time) is a lazy philosophical conclusion and an error (and I will return to this), it is also an illegitimate reaction to a collection of well-observed facts. It is only too evident that the historian is often a prisoner of a particular viewpoint derived from—or at least suggested by —a personal mentality which is largely taken from the collective mentality of his own society and period. Unless he is careful, he will often believe that he is thinking of man in universal terms when actually he is only imagining him within a narrower framework, borrowed from the experience of his own period. The result is the anachronism; insofar as the men of the past are different from himself, the historian cannot grasp them with these imperfect instruments without deforming them. Historicism justifiably exposes the danger of naïve dogmatism which, wishing to ignore history, results in a fallacious pseudo-universalism.

One example is the French classical school of writers, who thought they were dealing only with man in general: when they speak of kings and princesses in connection with Homeric heroes, they artlessly give Agamemnon or Iphigenia characteristics learned from their own experience at the court of Louis XIV.

It is a good deal easier to indicate our predecessors' obvious mistakes than to avoid similar extrapolations ourselves. For the researcher, historical experience is in a way a kind of transformation. Thanks to the documents, he slowly learns to rid himself of his prejudices, his mental habits, his too-particular type of humanity—and he learns to forget himself in order to become open to other kinds of lived experience, to make himself capable of understanding and encountering those of the past.

If, going from ethics to logic, we seek clarification of how this is possible, the answer must necessarily be that this difficult ideal (which will never be more than partially attained) imposes two methodological rules on the historian. First, he must learn to think rigorously and to give a specific meaning to the words he uses (defined contents for each of his concepts), contrary to the habits of daily language usage.

Thus in the relatively simple field of military history, for instance, what is to be called "victory"? Killing more of the enemy than one loses? Occupying new territory? (For the Greeks of Thucydides' time, victory meant retaining control of the battlefield, to be able to bury the dead and erect a trophy). Modern men believe they have improved this idea by defining it as "Making the enemy bow to the victor's will." But in what way, and to what extent?

When it becomes obvious that some modern concept is not applicable as such to a context of the past, the historian must (consciously and rigorously) construct a more general concept which, by abstraction or transposition, is applicable to an enlarged domain. We must be careful not to jump to conclusions about the universality of such concepts in a true and rigorous sense. We must be aware of the traps that the ruses of the imagination plant in the path of reason. The philosophy of the natural sciences here carries warnings for the historical theoretician which are well worth meditating.

When scientific experience reaches into a new field, the concepts used up until then are found to have been dependent on the experimental conditions under which they were formulated. This is striking in physics, but no less true in mathematics. Euclid, for example, thought he was using a truly universal concept of "space." Since Lobachevski and Reimann we have learned the special characteristics of Euclidian space (homogeneity, three-dimensionality, non-curvature, infinity) and its obvious dependence on empirical evidence.

The same is true of history. The proposition "Nero was a parricidal maniac" makes use of an apparently universal concept; but the definition "a parricidal maniac is a killer of one of his parents" implies the idea of a responsible actor, and gives the concept weight. It would be inapplicable, for example, in a "primitive" society which practiced ritual sacrifice of the aged.

Often, experience alone (present experience as well as the ever-renewed and enriched past experience) will teach a feeling for these limits, but there is no call for scepticism. There is difficulty only for narrow and rigid rationalism—an authentic theory of knowledge has no difficulty recognizing the inevitable interference, and the necessary cooperation, of experience and reflection.

From these observations we must conclude that the universality or the generality, the validity, of concepts used by the historian are not so much relative as dependent—not exactly on the historian's personality, mentality and period, but rather on the validity of the philosophy, implicit or (preferably) explicit, which made it possible for him to elaborate them. All our ideas about man are the instruments whereby we strive to recapture the human past, and are related to a philosophy of man. On the truth of these concepts, implying the limits of their validity, depends the truth of historical knowledge. It is not up to the historian (except accidentally) but to the philosopher as such (and to the anthropologist) to establish, to specify and verify this validity. History is not, as the Positivists dreamed, sufficient unto itself; it is part of a whole,

11

of a cultural organism in which the philosophy of man is like the axis, the framework, the nervous system. With it, history stands or falls. We must dare to recognize the strongly structured nature of knowledge and the unity between the various products of the human mind.

b) Care must be taken to distinguish between true concepts as formed by generalization, and the analogical or metaphorical use of them which the historian may find expedient for some special image.

In opposition to "Nero was a parricidal maniac," let us take the proposition "Nero was a tyrant." If we are to be rigorously precise, we must state it as: "Nero's behavior with regard to the senatorial aristocracy, considered from their point of view as a function of their acceptable norms, showed the same characteristics of cruelty and illegality as the Greek democratic tradition of the fifth and sixth centuries emphasized in its recollection of the τύραννοι of the sixth."

I will leave Croce[5] at this point. His preoccupation was to furnish a rigorous analysis of the historian's task, and he was satisfied to describe it in terms of formal logic: historical knowledge becomes a composite of judgments of the type S is P and I is U, stating a universal predicate from an individual subject. These predicates could be "functional concepts" which would be rigorously defined, elaborated by reason and philosophy ("philosophy is a methodology of historical thought"), and would make it possible to confer a rational character on the strange, or rather (this is a Heglian speaking now) to extract the immanent rationality of a strange reality. Croce insists on the non-empirical, extra-temporal origin of these universals. (This is quite a different thing from our

5. This is one of the strongest points of Croce's "protean" thought; he constantly returns to it in *Logica*, pp. 103 f., 108 f.; *Téoria e storia della storiografia*, p. 49; *La storia comme pensiero e come azione*, English translation pp. 134 f., 265 f., etc.

previous concepts—"bald," "parricidal maniac," and the rest—which are borrowed from the various sciences which study man. I imagine that Croce would have excluded them as not being specifically historical.)

Let us borrow from Croce his favorite example: the notion of the "baroque." For him, this is a concept that the historian receives from the philosopher (more exactly, here, from the aesthetician), and whose context can perhaps be expressed by a definition, as for a geometric term. The baroque, that type of ugliness, he said is "the vice of artistic expression which substitutes for beauty an effect due to surprise or to the unexpected."[6] A precise definition, but one in which I do not recognize the idea of baroque as modern art history and culture use it. It is an idea which, to be truthful, is much more comprehensive, more nuanced, more subtle and (though possibly less precise) much more fruitful.

If I analyze the use of the baroque (as I have sometimes done[7]) it seems that I see in it not a species of "ugliness" but a movement in the evolution of a style. Following the classical period where, after some blind groping in archaism and primitivism, art reached a perfect mastery in its means of expression, two things can occur (other than a revolution) that can stop the homogeneous development of this style. Either the tradition is congealed in a strict and timid imitation which soon becomes sclerotic and thus academic; or, on the contrary, it flourishes with exuberance, pushing each principle to the limit in an orgy of experiment and innovation. This is what we could call baroque.

This second definition does not exclude the first, nor does it pretend, in turn, to exhaust the contents of the idea. Others will come, or have come, who will try to explain it otherwise.

6. *La storia . . .* , English translation, p. 136.
7. As a disciple of Focillon and through him of Wölfflin, in *Saint Augustin . . .* , *Retractatio,* p. 670.

For example, E. d'Ors presents the baroque as a fundamental aesthetic category completely opposed to the classic. Instead of defining it, he tries to suggest it through a series of examples: the baroque is round and not square; an ellipse rather than a circle.[8]

In fact, we find two very different uses of the term. When we say that the Church of Santa-Teresa-a-Chiaia is baroque, or more boldly, "the discovery of the circulation of the blood by Harvey is a baroque invention," we are not using a universal idea, but a definite and special idea tending to express the common traits of many artistic creations in Italy during the seventeenth century. In the same way, other forms of thought and expression characterize the same period. We say baroque art and baroque age as we would say gothic or Renaissance. We shall later examine this type of special concept. We will now concern ourselves only with its "universal" use. When we qualify the grand Temple of Baalbec or the rhetoric of St. Augustine as baroque, we are not speaking of the same concept, but merely of an image, metaphor or an analogy (difficult to decide at times) based on an implied comparison. Between the sober and balanced art of Augustus or Trajan and that of Baalbec, I see a relation similar to the one that I said exists between the classicism of Michaelangelo and Bernini's baroque, on the one hand, or between the style of Cicero or Isocrates and that of St. Augustine, on the other. If this is an honest comparison, I can very well explain the reasons and find exuberance, studied effect, expressive deformation, and dissymmetry at Baalbec as well as in St. Augustine or Bernini. But this analysis will not necessarily exhaust the importance of the implied comparison.

For such a use would not come from the geometric spirit,

8. See the collection of essays translated into French under the title *Du baroque* (1935). E. Castelli suggests an entirely different conception: *III. Congresso intern. di studi umanistici* (Venice, 1954).

from that strict use of the concept by which Croce hoped to reach the very essence of the historic object and to exhaust it rationally, but rather from the spirit of subtlety. It must be defended as such, for historical knowledge, which seeks to seize the lives of men of the past in all their delicacy, their infinite nuances, their subtle truth, could not be satisfied with the strict but narrow and limited resources of mathematical logic. An implicit comparison of the type examined above might well permit us to understand those aspects of reality which would escape us if we sought to enclose them in explicit definitions.

Undoubtedly the truth of such a metaphorical utilization is in proportion to the partial point of view under which the historian chooses to consider both his object and the term of comparison. Nor should we forget that all confrontation is lopsided, and that there is never, in the strange realm of history, either a perfect parallel or an absolute renewal. The use of such analogical and metaphorical procedures, therefore, demands precautions, integrity and sophistication: qualities which are, furthermore, indispensable in forming that delicate instrument of knowledge which the mind of the historian must be.

When we proceed from the development of knowledge in the historian's mind to its expression for public consumption, the figurative use of special images will present greater difficulties. How can we be certain that the reader will understand all that the author has put into this rapprochement, and within what limits he has enclosed it? I have had the occasion to compare the idea that the Fathers formed of the obscurity of the Bible with poetic obscurity as understood by Mallarmé in contrast with Rimbaud. A critic has objected[9] that such ultra-modern comparisons "tend to obscure the argument

9. Cf. G. S(arton), in *Isis*, vol. XLI (1950), p. 332, criticizing my *Retractatio*, p. 649.

rather than to clarify it." Evidently he had not read Mondor! In spite of these difficulties, the suggestive richness of such a figurative use is such that the historian would hesitate to renounce it.

c) In contrast to these truly universal concepts that we examined in a), the historian uses technical ideas whose validity is limited in time and space or, shall we say, in relation to the given milieu of a civilization. This is the case for all the special terms designating institutions, instruments or tools, manner of acting, thinking or feeling, in short, all the facts of civilization. Thus, for the history of the Roman Republic: patrician, consul, toga, atrium, *molae trusatiles* (the handmill), adoption, *deuotio, mos maiorum* . . . are all concepts obviously relating to that one determined sector of the past, except in metaphorical utilization.

Here the limits of validity are those of our comprehension. The problem is to discover exactly what a Roman of the Republic meant by the words "patrician" or "consul." Roman public law existed before Mommsen; we need only reconstitute it and the truth will progress with our knowledge. Let us compare the extremely rich, precise, accurate image that we can form of the idea of "pharaoh," thanks to a century of efforts since Champollion, to the very summary one—probably also true though very limited—that an educated Carolingian could have had, who knew nothing of the Pharaoh except what he learned from the story of Joseph in Genesis and from the account in Exodus.

A rather more complex case is that of the concepts that we find elaborated in our sources by the historians, or more usually by intermediary witnesses who link us with the past. Such is the notion of "Roman virtue" that Plutarch offers us, and of "Athenian democracy" expressed by the Pericles of Thucydides. Truth and validity are suspended here upon two mental operations; the historian must understand what Thucydides or Plutarch meant, and then weigh the legitimacy of their construction or their evidence. Finally, such concepts are sometimes built up by today's historians, even if they indicate them by a term borrowed from the language of their heroes, as the geographers like to do, giving technical meaning to ordinary expressions.

The danger in that case is not, as above, to put less than the entire truth of the past into the idea, but rather more, or something different. It is this that constantly threatens the historian of philosophy, of thought, of mentality, who will be tempted to attribute to the man of another age the clear and distinct idea which he has himself formed, extrapolating the often slim and imprecise facts of his documentation.

Let us take the famous and indeed valuable book by the great Lutheran theologian A. Nygren, *Eros and Agape, the Christian Notion of Love and its Transformations.* It is clear that the extremely systematic picture he proposes of two concepts of "Eros" (love—desire, increasing, aspiring to possession of its object), and of "Agape" (love—self-bestowal, decreasing, widely distributed) is infinitely more precise, with more internal structure and severity, than the sense these words are given in the writings of Greeks, pagans or Christians. It is a more formal recognition than the ancients could have reached with their own real feeling.

Here we move toward quite another category : only a vague borderline separates the special concepts, elaborated by the historian, and those we are about to study :

d) To indicate this other class, we shall retain the term *Idealtypus,* borrowed from Max Weber,[10] who has defined this type of notion with special care and who made systematic use

10. The reader will find a first initiation to the theory in R. Aron, *La philosophie critique de l'histoire,* pp. 232–235; M. Weinreich, *Max Weber, l'homme et le savant* (Paris thesis, 1938), pp. 96–113.

of it in his work as a historian. Not, indeed, that he invented
the expression, properly speaking, nor was he the only one
to use it:

I shall take as an example of Idealtypus the notion of *The
Ancient City*, as elaborated by Fustel de Coulanges (1863).
We continue to use his notion (even when we criticize or
deny it): that is, the city-state is conceived as a confederation
of the great patriarchal families (γένη, *gentes*). It is assembled
first in phratries, then in tribes. The unity of each of these
social groups, ranging from the family to the city, is expressed
and consolidated by the existence of a specific worship directed toward the ancestor or hero, and practiced around a
common center.

As this example shows, it is a question of a plan of relatively
general value built up by the historian from rudiments observed in the study of special cases, an organic scheme of
mutually dependent parts. This organization is not arbitrary.
It is based on structural relations brought out from analysis
of peculiar instances—in fact expressed with precision and
severity by the historian in a definition which exhausts the
contents. The "ideal" attribute stresses the share of its
original construction comprised by the notion. It is not a
mere generic figure, reduced to the common characteristics
only, as are the concepts of the systematic in biology, which
merely retain characteristics presented in identical form by
all the individuals of the species or genus. The characteristics
retained by the *Idealtypus* are not necessarily those supplied
by the most numerous examples, but rather those supplied by
the most "favorable" examples—namely, those which suggest
to the historian the most coherent, the most significant and
the most intelligible idea.

If, unlike Croce's "universal predicate," the genesis of the
Idealtypus assumes a phase similar to that of the elaboration
of the Aristotelian Abstract, the share of the original con-

struction, which then follows, remains essential. Doubtless, Fustel de Coulanges did not entirely invent his ideal-type of the ancient city. For this, he used the comparative study of special instances represented by the various constitutions, πολιτεíαι, of cities known to classical Greece or to archaic Rome. Nevertheless, his ancient city is something different and something more than any of his empirically observed cities.

Once in possession of this pure idea, the historian returns to the concrete and uses it to obtain a better grasp of particular instances, the only "realities" presented by our documents, and this in two ways. First, insofar as individual examples, when superimposed on the theoretical picture of the Ideal-Type, reveal a greater or lesser correspondence to it, reality has henceforth acquired some intelligibility, doubtless partial but authentic. Second, to the extent that comparison results in a negative opinion (where the instance of the reality does not prove identical to the *Idealtypus*), this opinion allows a precise knowledge of the singular as such, which till now could not be seen clearly in its autonomy and in its absolute heterogeneity.

H. Jeanmaire, attempting to specify the originality of the Lacedemonian city, declares that Fustel's hypothesis is "doubtless the one which appears the least suitable as a starting point for the explanation of Sparta."[11] A mere dismissal? No, what follows shows that the comparison between hypothesis and documentary data aids Jeanmaire in grasping and dating the extremely late development of the aristocratic family in Sparta.

Weber's restatement of the idea of *Idealtypus* has sometimes been acclaimed as a decided progress in the theory and practice of history, finally provided with a precise instrument. However, it may be necessary to curb this enthusiasm. First,

11. *Couroi et Courètes,* Works and Memoirs of the University of Lille, 21 (Lille, 1939), p. 468.

as shown by the foregoing, the Ideal-Type is not the only way in which the historian can obtain knowledge, nor indeed is it the most frequently used. Then again, its formulation proves extremely difficult to achieve if optimum efficiency is to be assured to this type of concept. As a matter of fact, to the extent that the *Idealtypus* differs from a simple general concept engendered by abstraction, it tends to become arbitrary (on the same grounds as the "universal predicate," which Croce showed us as springing from *a priori* ingenuity of philosophical thought). However, one is free to define words, and it is within my power to define any Ideal-Type as I please. But in order to help the historian, this concept would have to possess an inner logic full of significance conferred on it by its own intelligibility and lucidity. At the same time it must be one where the characteristics are very easily found, at least in a participated sense, in the individual cases shown to exist by our documents. From all this many practical difficulties arise.

Still apropos of the ancient city, a controversy arose in 1937 between V. Ehrenberg and H. Berve[12] about the date of its appearance. Ehrenberg claims that it dates from the eighth century; Berve tended to make it a good deal later —600 or 500, if not still later. Each defines his Idealtypus of the *Polis* in a different manner. Berve speaks of the democratic city, and to recognize this he awaits the elimination of all "dynastic" principles; whereas for Ehrenberg the city's form of government is established, in its main points, as soon as the community attempts to impose sovereign law on the autonomy of its citizens.

12. V. Ehrenberg, "When Did the Polis Rise?" in the *Journal of Hellenic Studies,* vol. LVII (1937), pp. 147–159, criticizing H. Berve, "Fürstliche Herren der Perserkriege," in *Die Antike,* vol. XII (1936), pp. 1–28; *Miltiades, Studien zur Geschichte des Mannes und seiner Zeit* (Berlin, 1937).

Both conceptions are legitimate and the debate could continue forever were it not for practical requirements. Of the two concepts, which is the most useful to the historian? In my opinion, it is obviously that of Ehrenberg, which embraces a greater generality; Berve's city does not really attain its complete development until 450 and its decline begins with the internal tension caused by the Peloponnesian War (431). Reduced to such a short period, the notion loses some of its usefulness.

Finally and above all (as Max Weber emphasizes with some insistence), it is only legitimate to use the *Idealtypus* as long as the historian remains fully conscious of its strictly nominalistic character. Very rightly, Max Weber loses no opportunity to emphasize the constructed, unreal and fictitious character of these concepts. A useful reminder, since the natural inclination of the human mind is to over-estimate the value of its own ideas. The idealistic temptation lies ever in wait for the historian. If he is not careful, he will spontaneously be inclined to bring his "ideal-types" into being and reify them, using them as though they were really Platonic Ideas, Essences, tending in their ideal purity to be more real than the authentic historic reality. It is this elusive reality that always escapes to some extent, and is finally unamenable to all our efforts at that rationalization which is a condition of all knowledge.

I do not believe I am pointing out an imaginary danger. Over-attracted by "clarity," the rational limpidity of the ideal-type, the historian risks confusing the means with the end, of exchanging the substance for the shadow, and of substituting a set of constructed abstractions for the authentic knowledge of the concrete which should be his aim.

Take Athens in the time of Pericles. We could analyze it and, for instance, find $x\%$ of the true "ancient city" (man defined by his participation in the superimposed communities, with which he is identified), $y\%$ of the survival of archaic personification (the moral philosophy of the Homeric-type hero); and $z\%$ of individualism already announcing Hellenistic man; $x+y+z$ forming a total which more or less tends toward 100.

We find the same inconveniences that we found with Croce's universal concepts, who invited us to analyze the art of a given period in $x\%$ baroque, $100-x\%$ of non-baroque, Dante's work in a similar combination of poetry and non-poetry.

I have purposely chosen safe examples. I allow the reader to engage in an argument with Marxist historians, in whose work it would be easy to find a real intoxication of idealism. Under the pretext of reaching profound reality, we find them quite ingenuously substituting a set of reified abstractions for the authentic reality: social classes, productive forces, feudalism, capitalism, proletarianism and all the rest.

We can never be too insistent. No, it is not through "ideal" concepts that we reach the essentials. They are mere outlines, diagrams, constructions of the mind. They attempt only to seize something of a "reality," whose confusing complexity escapes on all sides from the moulds that would encompass it. Over-rating the ontological value of these instruments of thought results in a really imaginary history. The past appears less "real" than these intelligible entities, for it never appears capable of fully incarnating them; the historian would spend his time in searching the past for something that is not there, or at least not there in sufficient quantity.

Handled without care, the *Idealtypus* tends to be no more than a stereotype or prejudice. The ready-made idea, intervening between mind and reality, ever threatens to blunt the historian's curiosity (which should be untiring, in quest of an ever closer and more direct contact with the concrete).

Thus for true historians, the practical use of ideas first

defined as Ideal-Types involves an instinctive reaction against this idealistic deformation and salutary amendment or correction. When, for example, a historian of antiquity makes use of the term "civilization of the ancient city," he actually uses it to recall, in a complex understanding, the ensemble formed by the facts in conformity with the definition of the "type" and by the exceptions noted in the work of verification through a comparison between the abstract idea and special cases. For him the word evokes the systematized whole which was directly or indirectly tied to the community ideal of the πόλις in the life of the ancient Greeks and Romans. At the same time, he also sees the elements of this same civilization which escaped from the scope of this ideal (survival of the Homeric knightly spirit, foreshadowing Hellenistic individualism), and finally the thousand and one characteristics which the same historian may learn from special cases called Athens, Thebes, Sparta, Rome. In accordance with its formulation, historical knowledge reveals its radical nominalism, much more radical than Max Weber ever imagined it, in spite of his profession of faith. Used in this manner, these technical terms are no longer, properly speaking, *Idealtypen* but mere verbal tags. They in no way prejudice the complex and at times even incongruous contents of the card index, of which they allow a convenient description. With these directions for use, we have actually reached a fifth and last species of concept (if one can retain the name) of historical notions:

e) We have only too many examples to choose from: thus Classical Antiquity, Athens, the Pentecosioétiade ("Between Two Wars"—between the Persian and the Peloponnesian Wars), the Second Sophistic, the Spätantike, Byzantium, the Renaissance, the Baroque (this is where the term, used in its proper sense, finds its true place), and perhaps again, the French Revolution.

In the nineteenth century, the historians of the Liberal Era (see Michelet) thought out the French Revolution by means of a veritable *Idealtypus*. For them, it was a coherent system of thought and action ("The Revolution forms a unit," said Clemenceau). Today the term recalls the tumultuous aggregate of what we are able to learn of all that occurred in France, and under French influence, between May 5, 1789 and the 18th *brumaire an VIII*.

This time, it is a matter of particular terms that are incapable of exhaustive definition. They denote an ensemble, for example a more or less vast period of the history of a certain human milieu, or of the history of art or of thought: the totality of all that we are able to know of the object thus defined. The use of such ideas is perfectly legitimate if we are always careful to retain their strictly nominal character. The word is only a verbal symbol for a reality that has a more or less organic, more or less anarchical, structure which it does not prejudice. After many years of study, the historian may close his eyes and recall all he knows of his subject by means of a single word—as a lover whispers the name of his beloved.

The danger remains—here we must also know how to guard against it—of hypostasizing these ideas and conferring upon them, in turn, the value of an idea, of an essence, of a superior reality, of a principle of cohesion and intelligibility.

The process of error is this: for some reason the historian decides to designate a period by what appears to him to be its dominant feature. For example, seventeenth century Italy will be called the Baroque Age. Then through an unconscious inversion, he (or his readers on his behalf) tends to make a principle of this name and to "explain" the phenomenon observed by "Baroque"—forgetting that the notion has no individual existence.

Thus history becomes somewhat populated with phantoms,

which is another way of making a set of abstractions, those vain shadows. Lord Acton was angered at the sight of diplomatic history continually calling on these stereotyped actors: Great Britain, France, where one should say the ruling class, the government, the Foreign Office, the Quai d'Orsay, or rather such and such a minister, in truth such and such a young attaché, on duty on that particular day in such and such an office. Not indeed that these abridgements are necessarily to be proscribed. Thus our sports reporters—another form of history—willingly say: England has won or lost a match, while they really mean a team of professional players. (However, when one witnesses the outburst of collective passion provoked in any country by the news of one of these national "victories" or "defeats," one is obliged to recognize some truth in this metonymy.) The conscientious historian, however, must always make clear the meaning he attributes to any such substantial use.

Once these necessary precautions have been taken, history should not, cannot, refuse to use these designations, which really belong within the limits of its development. The ultimate stage of knowledge cannot be represented by general concepts or abstractions (such as that of the *Idealtypen*), since the reality of the past is always richer, more nuanced, and more complex than any of the ideas that we may elaborate to embrace it. It is this concrete particularity that ever defeats and disconcerts us, surprises us by something unexpected, something new, something radically different. A narrow rationalism would be saddened, as if by a defeat, but the true historian, on the contrary, is gladdened; for it is in this aspect of human reality that the originality and fertility of history resides. The experience of the past is of such a nature as to burst out of the over-symmetrical settings, ever too simple, in which human reason would spontaneously enclose reality. Parodying the famous words which Hamlet addresses to his friend Horatio: "There are more things in heaven and earth . . . ," we could say that the nature of history is to remind us constantly, and to allow us to discover, that there are more things in man and in life that can be dreamed of in the small concepts of a philosophy.

The foregoing allows us to answer in one word a too-long disputed question[13]: the division of history into periods, the *Periodisierung* as the scholars call it (the constant prestige of the German word). It will only be a matter of labels, ever temporary, relative to the point of view adopted at the time. Their role, of a practical and pedagogical nature, should not be over-estimated. It will never be a determination of essences! Does the civilization of the Africa of the Vandals belong to that of antiquity, or does it already belong to the Middle Ages? It depends entirely on the perspective chosen for its study!

13. I will simply refer the reader to J. H. J. van der Pot, *De perio-disering der geschiedenis, een overzing der theorieën* (The Hague, 1951).

CHAPTER VII

Explanation and Its Limitations

At the outset of this study (Chapter 2), we had stipulated that historical knowledge should not content itself with reflecting the tumultuous reality of the past, with its at first sight disconcerting wealth. We concluded that it should strive to project upon it, or better still to disengage from it, intelligibility. At this stage, the reader may wonder whether the complete nominalism we have just professed will not lead to unintelligibility pure and simple. It is therefore necessary to lose no time in showing that when history seeks to apprehend its object in the most precise and complete manner possible, it does not at the same time let up in its concern to "make it understandable"— to furnish, in a certain sense and within certain limitations, an "explanation."

To begin with, let us consider the relatively simple case of the historical scene: Athens in the time of Pericles, French social life on the eve of the Revolution—in short, the effort which the historian makes to grasp the spectacle presented him, seen at an instant t of its evolution. It is this past of mankind, or better, the always limited sector of it, which is the object of the authentically historical enquiry. It is not true, as it might seem, that the datum upon which this effort of comprehension is exercised (the whole of what the documents reveal to us), presents itself as a confused swarm of facts, a fine powder of little elementary acts. Analysis discovers in it, with certainty, the phenomena of coordination and structures.

Of course, the object of history always belongs in the

category of the particular. And it is also true that the actors of that history are always men, human individualities (the individual, the person, is the historical unit, the "atom" in the Greek sense of the word). But as Rickert has so well emphasized,[1] there are historical realities that, without ceasing to be particular, possess a certain general character in the sense that they encompass an ensemble of elementary phenomena, less comprehensive in character, that appear with respect to it as parts relative to a whole.

Take the example proposed, Periclean Athens. Athens was not only the empirical union of a specified multitude of representatives of the human species. Among all its inhabitants, there were several thousands who, bearing the title of citizens, found themselves broken down into demes and tribes, sat in the ecclesia, furnished the courts with jurors, and so forth, in short, constituted the organized skeleton which transformed an amorphous mass of human individualities into that precise political organism which was the democratic city of Athens.

Similarly, a whole series of rituals, of customs, of beliefs was organized around a central hope concerning life after death. This constituted the cult of the Two Goddesses which for simplification we designate by the term the Eleusinian Mysteries, and so on.

In such complexes of particulars, the component parts do not simply appear linked by a global intuition, but find themselves unified, among themselves and with the whole, by relationships of interdependence which lend them a complete intelligibility, and constitute their "explanation."

Actually, this observation is not really at variance with the remarks made in the previous chapter concerning nominal

1. See for example, "Les quatre modes de 'L'Universel' dans l'histoire," in the *Revue de synthèse historique*, II (1901, pp. 121–140, and especially pp. 131–134.

determinatives such as "Athens" and "French Revolution."
We stated that the use of such labels is not indicative of the
more or less organic structures of the entities to which they
are applied, but we did not mean to deny the existence of
these structures themselves. We intended merely to encourage the historian to check the reality of each structure
and then to define its limitations. For each time he ascertains
that such structures are real, he discovers that they—or rather
the "ideal-types" which we invent in the hope of understanding them—never cover more than a certain portion of the unit
of history which he wishes to catalogue and which they at
first appear to systematize. In the final analysis, historical
reality is always richer and more complex than any unified
structure could possibly be. Let us consider two characteristic examples of the partial success and inevitable shortcomings of all organicist hypotheses.

My first example is that of the ideal-type of the Ancient
City. In the hands of such an expert historian as Fustel and
of those of his successors who perfected it, this working
hypothesis proved fertile, revealing the existence in the civilization of classical antiquity of a whole network of relationships. *To a great extent,* ancient man was indeed, as Aristotle
defined him, ζῷον πολιτικόν. That is, he was an animate
being who (instead of living in herds, flocks, hordes, hives,
or swarms) was characterized by the fact that he lived
κατὰ πόλεις, in the definite social organism constituted by
the πόλις. We actually ascertain that *a large number* of the
main characteristics of ancient life—economic, artistic, religious, and moral ones, to mention a few—apparently find, *at
least to a certain extent,* their explanation (their *raison d'être,*
their meaning) in their direct or indirect relationship to the
social organization of the city.

But analysis soon reveals that this "political" structure did
not embrace the whole of ancient man. Although the unity

of classical Greek civilization was astonishing, particularly if we compare it with the pluralism or the anarchy which reigned in nineteenth-century western Europe, it is impossible to relate all the aspects of Greek life to the ideal of the City. Except perhaps in Sparta, intellectual education, for example, was not profoundly influenced by this ideal. As W. Jaeger[2] has shown, future citizens of the "city of hoplites" were brought up on Homer's poems, and from them they absorbed a system of ethics—the ethics of the hero seeking personal glory through some outstanding feat—which was at wide variance with the ideal of complete subordination of the individual to the community. Furthermore, it is not true, as Fustel tended to believe, that the various social forms of religion—the cult of the home, of the clan, and of the City—were sufficient to satisfy ancient man's religious instinct. Nilsson has very appropriately pointed out that, after the early period of the sixth and seventh centuries B.C., the mystical and ecstatic currents of personal religion always definitely and forcefully clashed with the formalized aspects of civic worship.[3]

Let us now consider the example of medieval Christianity. It is undeniably true that many of the characteristics of Western civilization in the Middle Ages can be explained in terms of their strict subordination to the Christian ideal of religion. Thus arts, science, technology, society, the state, and patterns of life and of sensibility appear as means, or symbols, ultimately subservient to the Faith which held together the members of this Christian civilization.

But on the other hand, it is also obvious that certain factors of medieval life remained quite unaffected by this synthesis. These factors, foreign in origin, were only superficially Christianized—an external varnish, which merely disguised their

2. *Paideia, die Formung des griechischen Menschen,* I³ (1954), Chap. III; cf. my *Histoire de l'Éducation dans l'Antiquité*³ (1955), pp. 33–39.

3. *Grekist religiositet,* English translation (Oxford, 1948), pp. 20–65.

true nature without really integrating them into the framework of Christendom. Let us cite a few random examples: the survival, particularly after the twelfth-century renaissance, of the ancient ideal of empire and of the autonomy of public law; survivals of paganism that can easily be discovered in the popular religion or in the occult practices of witchcraft; dualistic heresies (the Catharists were certainly not Catholics and probably not even Christians); the profane ideal of the passion of love (whether courtly love came from the Moors by way of Spain or from the Celts through the *roman breton*, it is still out of keeping with the principles of Christianity). We might also mention innumerable aspects of the economic and social organization of feudalism. The existence of these aberrant sectors does not destroy that of the hierarchical domain, but it reveals the fact that the concept of Christianity does not completely cover the nature of the Western medieval world.

In other words, one must prove and not merely postulate the existence of a unified structure, of a coherent whole, of a *Zusammenhang*. Unity is a problem, not a primary principle to be used as a point of departure. That is why the true historian (and by that I mean the historian who possesses a keen sense of the irreducible quality of historical reality, not the mere dry narrator of history) is inevitably repulsed by most of the theories of civilization which so increased during the period between the two World Wars, to the extent that these theories accept the postulate of coherence and structural unity.

The true historian must reject not only the mad lucubrations of Spengler, who, once he has applied the metaphor of the "organism" to the great civilizations, proceeds to exploit it in a systematic and paradoxical manner. He must also refuse to accept the synthesis which was so conscientiously and so reasonably worked out by the great and noble intelligence of Arnold J. Toynbee. Although Toynbee's empirical sense of the positive and his historical sense of the concrete make him wary of the temptations of the idealist system (incidentally, he criticizes Spengler's extreme organicism), he nonetheless falls victim to this system himself when, for instance, he defines the twenty-one (or twenty-nine) "civilizations," which he has somewhat arbitrarily cut out of the fabric of history, as being "entities forming a whole *all* of whose parts are in reciprocal cohesion and mutually affect each other."[4]

Our theorists on civilization, the "culturologists,"[5] are not the only ones who have abused this hypothesis of unity. Ethnographers have also made the same error often—those for instance who have defended the notion of "cultural cycles" and of "primitive" civilizations defined by the association of various techniques (this association supposedly proved empirically, though in a sense it is inevitable as well). Thus the "boomerang cycle" (Australia, Upper Nile Valley) would associate together the use of the bull-roarer for musical purposes, the ritual extraction of certain teeth, monotheism, lunar mythology, exogamy, and the equality of the sexes.[6]

This myth, for it is a myth, of the structural unity of civilizations is one of the forms of the great idealistic temptaion that the historian must avoid. He is in constant danger of inferring from certain obvious juxtapositions that a hypothetical unity, the "spirit" of civilizations, the "genius" of peoples, and the *Zeitgeist,* do actually exist.

For instance, it is well known that the civilization of Southern France in the twelfth century included the following factors: the survival of Roman law, Romanesque art, the Catharist heresy and troubadour poetry. This suffices for

4. *A Study of History,* vol. III, p. 380.

5. Term launched by Prof. L. A. White of the University of Michigan to designate these theoreticians of civilization.

6. See for example G. Montandon's article, "Culturali (Cicli)," in the *Enciclopedia Italiana,* vol. XII, pp. 104 A–113 B.

certain people to affirm that the troubadours were Catharists![7]

The real structure of the various civilizations cannot be postulated. It becomes evident only after a complex and precise examination. Of all those who have attacked the problem in the past thirty years, it seems to me that the one who has best grasped the reality of the phenomenon "civilization" in all its complexity, and more generally the nature itself of the historical object, is the Russian-American sociologist P. A. Sorokin.

Reduced to its principal results (for his doctrine passed through considerable evolution in the course of a quite considerable amount of work[8]) and freed of its paradoxes, it stands out as a correct interpretation between two opposing errors. On the one hand, there is the "atomistic" theory of superficial historians who think they are describing a civilization by making a haphazard inventory of its diverse aspects; on the other hand, there is the "integralism" of the organicist theoreticians of the Spengler-Toynbee type. Once Sorokin has set forth the exact characteristics of the facts of civilization (which form what he terms the "socio-cultural": (meanings, values, norms), he analyzes their manner of existence in a very concrete way.

According to Sorokin, the elements of historical reality which constitute the facts of civilization may present themselves in an isolated state; others can be met in a purely empiric juxtaposition of "congeries"[9]; others, and here appears the really organic structure, constitute systems (that is the case especially of various technologies: classical Greek

7. As Denis de Rougemont, *Love in the Western World* (1939).

8. See notably *Social and Cultural Dynamics* (New York, 1937–1941, 4 vols.); *Society, Culture and Personality, their structure and dynamics, a system of general sociology* (New York, 1947); a helpful initiation will be found in F. R. Cowell, *History, Civilization and Culture, an introduction to the historical and social philosophy of Pitirim A. Sorokin* (London, 1952).

temple architecture constitutes a "system"). Systems in their turn may combine themselves into large syntheses (in the manner of the great religions such as Mahayana Buddhism, Sunnite Islam, Roman Catholic Christianity, that combine in a truly organized way feelings, beliefs, moral principles, liturgy, and social structure). Ultimately, the possibility of an "ideological supersystem" may be conceived that would have the ambition to rule a whole civilization (again we find the examples studied previously: the city of antiquity, Western medieval Christendom). But this is an eventuality that could have existed only under the form of an ideal in human consciousness that was never completely embodied in any civilization. As we have shown with the cases cited above, a real civilization shows itself an analysis to be much richer and less unified than the idealistically intended supersystem.

Finally, and especially, whether it is a question of isolated elements, congeries or systems, or more or less large syntheses, experience reveals that in a specific sphere of civilization three cases are possible that verify themselves by turns: integration, antagonism, neutrality.

Because it is easy to use, let us again take the case of the Western Middle Ages, and more precisely that of the twelfth century. Roman architectural technique is neutral in relation to the ideal of Christendom. (What does it matter to Christendom whether or not a cathedral is covered with a multi-figured framework or groined vaults?) Courtly love surely is antagonistic; grammatical culture, tightly subordinated to the study of sacred books, is satisfactorily integrated. The strain, plainly seen for example between Abelard and St. Bernard, proves the fate of philosophical culture (dialectics)

9. I borrow the word from our Alpine dialects (where it is a meaningful word in the sense of "a pile of snow accumulated by the wind"); Sorokin uses the Latin *congeries*.

to be a difficult one: we know that, at first antagonistic, it will finally be integrated by Scholasticism.

The historian must endeavor to understand the totality of reality. His knowledge will have to record intellectual structures as well as anomalies. He must state precisely, as far as possible, the relations existing between the various elements, congeries, or systems that he will have been able to discriminate. And even in the case in which his analysis legitimates a synthetic view, he must remember in time—as we underlined in the beginning of this chapter—that the specific sphere that "really existed" is neither the fact of a civilization nor the system or supersystem, but the human being whose individuality is the only organism genuinely supplied by experience. Even here idealistic temptation awaits the historian; for by reading certain contemporary works, one has the impression that historical actors are no longer men but entities: ancient cities, feudalism, capitalistic middle class, revolutionary proletariat. There is an excess here.

Even if it appears by examining all documentary data that a given historical phenomenon is accounted for by one of those socio-cultural abstractions, the historian must continually remind himself, and remind others, that what is in question here is only a mental construct. This is undoubtedly unavoidable (being the only way to understand the complexity of reality), and legitimate within the limits of its use. It is nevertheless an abstraction, a derived product, and not the reality itself—and it is especially not a super-reality, as one ends by believing.

But now let us give up the observation of the historical scenes at instant t. Let us now reinsert the historical phenomena in the flow of duration and follow out its development, its evolution through time (and that is normally the essential task of the historian). We find the same rational claims again: the mind cannot satisfy itself with a simple enumeration in which all kinds of events and facts succeed one another, arranged simply according to chronological order.

J. Delorme has compiled for us a useful *Chronologie des civilisations* in which we find well classified in analytical tables all the great dates of universal history, from 3064 B.C. (foundation of the Egyptian monarchy) to December, 1945. It is a memory aid, an everyday work tool, but one in which nobody would expect to find the sum nor the summum of our historical knowledge.

History attains intelligibility only to the extent that it shows itself able to establish and to disclose the relations that join each new stage of human progress to the past and to its consequences. Just as a historical situation, taken at an instant *t*, reveals itself always more or less structured, so the development of instants is not simply a discontinuous line of atoms of reality, isolated like the beads of a rosary arbitrarily told by God's unfathomable will (as Islamic theology likes to imagine). The experience of history that the conscientious worker acquires through contact with historical documents enables us to discover that intelligible relations exist between the successive moments of history. Of course, everything is not linked. There are hiatuses in temporal development as there are limits to static structures; but the historian's task is to discover those sequences, wherever they exist. This is what is commonly expressed by saying that history must not only "establish facts" but also search for "causes" and their consequences. I insist upon that again, for it matters as much to a comprehensive appraisal of a historical element to establish what it may have caused as to know out of which cause it has issued.

This notion of "cause," as we receive it from common thought and daily language, turns out on testing to be very difficult to use for historical knowledge. It is meaningful only in elementary cases in which historical investigation is very

close to that of judicial inquiry: Who is the responsible
author of a voluntary action? Or, taking again the example
imagined by Collingwood: Who killed John Doe? But these
situations rarely occur in genuine historical research.

For most often what is most important is less the identity of
the murderer than the reconstruction of the system of values
which has made that man its agent. Motives or causes—conscious or unconscious—superficial or profound . . . the historical "cause" of Caesar's death does not properly speaking
lie in the actual group of conspirators assembled around
Brutus and Cassius, but rather in the opposition of the
senatorial aristocracy to Caesar's monarchical politics, combined with the special resentments or reasons for vengeance
that each plotter privately nourished against the dictator.

The search for "causes" was meaningful only when considered within the framework of a strictly circumstantial view
of history similar to old-school political or military history.
This concerned itself with what it called categorical events
(royal accessions or demise, diplomatic negotiations or trea-
ties, sieges or battles), fragments of historical reality set apart
by the mind that one could arrange at will into a linked series
of cause and effect. Today, we have come to be wary of the
artificial character resulting from historical events so conceived. Far from finding in it the most profound meaning
of the past, we have learned to recognize in it a system of
mutilation and selection (legitimate only if consciously done
and logically justifiable), which plucks an isolated event the
historian deems worthy of examination out of the composite
whole that constitutes the past.[10] It is from this very moment
that the danger arises of treating as distinguishable phenom-

10. See especially H. Lévy-Bruhl, "Qu'est-ce qu'un fait historique,"
in the *Revue de Synthèse historique*, vol. XIII (1926), pp. 53–59; "Une
notion confuse, le fait historique," in *Recherches philosophiques*, vol. V
(1935–1936), pp. 264–274.

ena (as cause from effect), what may in reality have no autonomous existence. Of course, the problem ceases to exist when one studies the most involved aspects of the past, such as social institutions, ideologies, techniques or the arts. These do not flash like meteors into the historical heavens, but are the results of long periods of incubation. They are comprehensible only in terms of their own evolution, during the course of which they are constantly subject to imperceptible and profound transformation.

But we must stress the central difficulty that confronts us here, which arises from the impossibility of isolating one component or one aspect of the historical entity, except in thought. The ordinary idea of "cause" may be strictly applied only in cases where it is possible by experimentation to construct a closed system in which a determined cause can be isolated in order to establish undeniably its effects in all their variety.

In physics, for example, let us take Galileo's classic experiment of the inclined plane. Once friction has been reduced to a minimum, the moving body with mass m which slides on the plane is only proportional to the weight of $mg.\ sin\ a$. Therefore, by modifying angle a, which is the angle of the plane with the horizontal, we can vary the intensity mg. and measure the various consequences.

But this is only a very elementary example. Even among the natural sciences, when phenomena becomes more complex the application of such formulae rapidly becomes more difficult and experimental techniques much less manageable.

We shall attach particular significance to the difficulties of methodology, often quite analogous to those of history, encountered in such disciplines as geology and physical geography. Here the study of the past is also involved and purely scientific experiments are similarly impossible, since whatever experiment is attempted upon a reduced scale can be only of comparative value.

We can in no way manipulate the past; on the other hand, bound by our knowledge of individual things we cannot hope to find in mere repetition an equivalent to the variety of experiment achieved in the laboratory. Therefore, it is again by reason of the purely "speculative" character of historical evaluations, as opposed to those of a compelling nature, that we can at best offer in this quest for "causes" likely hypotheses based on the calculated probability of hindsight. I have taken this expression from R. Aron[11] who in this instance seems to have judged the conduct of the historian perfectly.

He is notably correct in contrast to the Hegelians[12] who in the name of the rationality of the real and of the necessity which emerges from it reject as illogical and anti-historical all speculations as to "what might otherwise have been." It is doubtless laboriously futile to imagine like Renouvier in his *Uchronie,* "the development of European civilization such as it never was, such as it could have been," but it is established, on the other hand, that "every historian in order to explain what once was must ask himself what might have been."[13]

Confronted with a historical situation, we recall its multifarious antecedents or its consequences. Then by reflection we mould one or the other in turn, trying in each instance to find a synthesis which might be derived from them. In such a fashion we form for ourselves an idea of the relative effectiveness of the various "causes" involved: intellectual experiment replaces the impossible scientific experiment—but

11. *Introduction à la philosophie de l'histoire,* pp. 159–187.

12. See Croce, "*La storia come pensiero e come azione,*" English translation, pp. 27–31: "*The historical signification of necessity.*"

13. R. Aron, *Introduction,* p. 164 (underlined by the author).

its conjectural nature grievously affects the significance of its conclusions!

What is even more serious is the fact that the historian can resort to the idea of causation only at the price of creating an arbitrary system, a crude oversimplification of reality. One example will illustrate this.

A. Brun,[14] a worthy scholar, accurately traced the progressive stages by which the French language asserted itself in the regions of the "Langue d'Oc." Having treated simultaneously and in a parallel manner the royal policy of political unification during the same period (about 1450-1550, the significant years being 1500-1550), he emphatically concluded that the one is the cause of the other. Thus concerning the well-known edict of Villers-Cotterets (1538) on the exclusive use of French in public proceedings, he writes: "It is henceforth to be admitted that its significance was almost overwhelming."[15]

Yet it never entered his mind that his conclusion was based on reasoning derived from an arbitrarily chosen hypothesis by which he *selected* the "royal policy" aspect and placed it alongside the aspect of linguistic evolution.

This has been shown clearly by L. Febvre.[16] He shifted (or more exactly, enlarged) the scope of the argument, disclosing the contrived nature of the relation of cause to effect which was established between the two phenomena. They are both nothing more than individual manifestations of the same historical unity seen as a whole: the expansion of French civilization during the period in question, which followed the successive crises of the Hundred Years' War, shows itself

14. *Recherches historiques sur l'introduction du français dans les provinces du Midi* (Paris thesis, 1923).

15. *Ibid.*, p. 421.

16. *Combats sur l'histoire*, pp. 169–181 (reprinted in the *Revue de Synthèse historique*, vol. 38, 1924).

in all spheres—economic, artistic, religious, as well as political or linguistic—with the same burst of powerful vitality (that is, the French Renaissance and Reformation). At a stroke the "cause" mistakenly interpreted vanishes and the interdependence established between the two processes, originally selected out of their historical context, becomes illusory.

Who could remain insensible to the importance of such a conclusion? The problem, instead of being resolved, is engulfed in one even more complex, which remains an unsolved question. However, it cannot be denied that the "explanation" of the original problem (the "frenchification" of the land of Oc) has been furthered by this new operation. Undoubtedly there is greater clarity. By thus creating a closer network of inter-communications between the concomitant phenomena, the historian succeeds in grasping better and more authentically that particular aspect of sixteenth-century French life—but it is increasingly evident that this "explanation" is no longer of the cause-to-effect type.

It would be about time, therefore, that the theory of history proceed in its turn (as the theory of natural sciences has done since A. Comte) with a revision of the idea of cause. Physicists and naturalists have practically replaced it with the idea of "required conditions." This is both more general and at the same time better defined (given the phenomena A, B, C, we will observe the phenomenon X). Similarly, history must abandon the search for causes, it seems to me, for that of coordinated developments. This idea is only an extension of the static idea of structure to the new dimension of time (some historic phenomenon is found linked to another by a clear-cut relationship: one understands the Spartan morality when one has understood that it is tied to the totalitarian idea of the City).

We would compare historical reality to a muscle. We study its structure by means of a cross-section of a given level (this is the "historical scene" whose case we examined at the beginning). Just as the muscle shows itself to be divided into bundles subdivided into fibers and fibrils, the past reveals a more or less perfectly stratified structure of the facts of civilization, conglomerations or systems, and ideologic supersystems (to retain Sorokin's terminology). But a deeper study will require that the anatomist follow, from plane to plane, the continuity of each fiber or fascicle, that he analyze their nature and the relationship of their gradual changes. Similarly, the historian will discover that each element of the historical reality, from the isolated or elementary fact of civilization to the vaster synthesis, is surrounded by continual development. And during the course of this development it never stops changing, as relationships established with neighboring elements (of neutrality, antagonism or integration) never stop changing.

This brings us to the essential point: explanation in history is the discovery, the comprehension, the analysis of a thousand ties which, in a possibly inextricable fashion, unite the many faces of human reality one to the other. These ties bind each phenomenon to neighboring phenomena, each state to previous ones, immediate or remote (and in a like manner, to their results). One may rightfully ask oneself if real history is not just that: the concrete experience of the complexity of truth, a grasp of its structure and evolution, in which both are ramified in this way. This is a knowledge undoubtedly elaborated as deeply as it is broadly understood, but it is something which assuredly remains closer to actual experience than to scientific explanation.[17]

It is easy to foresee that many of my readers will react with surprise or indignation to such a conclusion. What! Could this be the explanation we are seeking, the awaited enlightenment? Who will simply accept it and be satisfied with it?

17. Cf. R. Aron, *Introduction*, p. 106.

Undoubtedly, as can easily be seen, the kind of knowledge we have just acquired is very different from the raw data as it appeared in disorder on first contact with the documents. Analysis has been able to extract some elements of order and classification, some principles of understanding, some links. We no longer need to speak of causes and effects, but of developments. Between these developments relationships of interdependence and often hierarchy are established (as within the great "system" or "ideological super-systems" in which is glimpsed the unity, at least ideal, of an entire civilization).

Paradoxical as it may seem, on going deeper into the question this work of coordination among the various aspects of reality results as much in complicating as it does in systematizing our knowledge of the past. This has already been shown to be the case at the concept stage. In the same way, it is no less true at the higher stages of variously graded synthesis. Each explanation leaves its aftermath. In the plain facts of history there are always "more things than have been dreamt of"— than have been envisioned by an ideal-type, a system or principle of elucidation. Better, or rather, worse: the deeper our investigation probes, the closer our effort to understand follows on its heels and the more do the illimitable facts of history betray themselves possessed, in their innermost being, of structural affinities, interdependent links and co-ordination between different stages of development. This is true to such an extent that this same network of relations, on which we hang our hopes of tapping ultimate truth, soon shows itself to be as complicated, as tangled up and as confused, as that first factual shapelessness it was our business to unravel and make clear.

Let us take up once more that instance previously advanced (p. 69) of the history of monachism in ancient Egypt. Though obscured by the dust of individual scraps of information—

13

such as that some monks in certain hermitages or communities, at some epoch or other, gave vent to certain apophthegms, or behaved in a particular manner—there can remain but little doubt that the historian's effort succeeds in substituting an intelligible sequence of development. The phases have been enumerated as follows: economic function, social phenomena, spiritual technique, Christian sanctity. And yet it is the same monk, Arsenios or Poimen, who is found to be at once a business man, a secret resistance leader, an ascetic and a disciple of the Gospel. It is at this level that complexity comes out accoutred in fresh trappings. How is one to coordinate such different, such seemingly self-contradictory lines of explanation?

Without flattering himself that he has done full justice to each shade of long-dead contemporary feeling (this would be an illusion), nevertheless, the conscientious historian should do his utmost to give each category and principle its proper place and function. But if instead he merely jots them down side by side, in so doing he falls into inextricable confusion, much the same as that inherent in empirical description pure and simple. To reconstruct a truly intelligible image of the past, we must be able rigorously to confine these various principles of explanation to their separate channels. We must systematize all this complex network of relationships. We must emphasize their dominant characteristics and introduce some sort of unity and order. But is this possible? Indeed, is it even a legitimate operation, with due respect to that ideal of truth and accuracy to which all knowledge should aspire?

Here we find ourselves confronted—and this from a well-nigh irresponsible direction—with a fundamental demand of the human spirit, obsessed essentially, as it is, with a passion for order, simplicity and unity.

I remember that I once heard a young woman, a philosopher, maintain one day that "in the eyes of many, the aim of philosophy is to explain everything by a single principle, a single concept, a single name." For her part, however, she was delighted to remain a dualist. She prided herself on her pluck, since "among philosophers this epithet passes for an insult, or at least a term of reproach."[18] Yet the true historian will not be so easily satisfied. The two-stop flute still seems to him too primitive an instrument to modulate, in its infinite variety, that baffling and elusive melody that he has grown conscious of from his contact with the past.

It is inevitable that the historian in turn should experience that temptation, peculiar to philosophy, to reduce all things to one. And he will frequently fall into its snares. He will scornfully reject that scrupulous (and, as it seems to him, cowardly) analysis which attempts to weigh the shades of meaning and to tabulate presumed relationships. In place of this he will deem it his duty to substitute the powerful construction, the glamorous hypothesis. He feels by this that he will restore unity to the multiplicity of historical data and make it possible to envisage, from a satisfactory viewpoint at last, the events, life, period and civilization under scrutiny. This operation, in a sense, may well be inevitable. It is even possible, at a pinch, to invest it with a measure of utility on the pedagogic plane. Yet it would be the merest illusion to hope to extract from it (I will not say a complete work, or a sublimation of history, but even) so much as one solid step forward in the accumulation of knowledge.

Moreover, there can be no doubt that during our entire analysis we have continually discovered, at each progressive stage of elaboration, a massive intervention of the historian's personality. His thoughts, his classifications and his inner requirements occur at every turn to shade historical consciousness, to mould its form and color its aspect. It must be

18. S. Pétrement, *Essai sur le dualisme chez Platon, les Gnostiques et les Manichéens* (1947), p. 1.

admitted, of course, that this personal construction finds nourishment and justification in the material data, shapeless but factual, provided for it by the documents. But, on the contrary, it is right here that we reach the limit. The human mind, obedient only to its subjective arbitrary requirements, shows up like some wild pulley that has run off the lines. This tendency to visualize the structure of the past as something simpler and more homogeneous than it really is, represents one of those hidebound prejudices, those mental totems, pregnant with error, so hotly denounced in the past by Bacon. It falls directly under the first of the categories in which he classified them—most appropriately named *idola tribus*.

My task is quite easy here. First and foremost, it consists in showing the practical consequences following on a truth which has been well established by my predecessors. To illustrate fully the implications of the evidence, it will be sufficient for me to quote briefly two classic aphorisms of Raymond Aron:

Theory precedes history.[19] Theory—that is, the position (conscious or unconscious) adopted by the historian as he confronts the past: the choice and limitation of subject, questions posed, concepts put to work, and especially the types of relation, systems of interpretation, and the relative value attached to each. This is no less than the personal philosophy of the historian which dictates the selection of systematic thought-technique in function of which he is about to reconstruct and—so he believes—cast his searchlight upon the past.

The richness and complexity of the fabric of human facts (and consequently of historical bed-rock reality, as we have already demonstrated) opens up a practically inexhaustible mine for the efforts of rediscovery and comprehension. Yet, to quote again: *inexhaustible as it is, historical reality is at*

19. R. Aron, *Introduction*, p. 93.

the same time highly equivocal.[20] Subdividing and super-
imposing themselves on the same point in the past, there are
so very many different points of view, so many and various
forces in action. The historian's mind can never fail to find
the specific element that, along the lines of his particular
theory, must strike him as preponderant. It is this that will
command his immediate recognition as the key to the historical riddle—as *the* one true explanation. The compiler
of history is free to pick and choose at his own sweet will.
The data lend themselves complacently to his proofs and
accommodate themselves impartially to every system. He
always finds what he is looking for—whether solar myths (or
Indo-European myths), religious requirements, social up-
heavals or economic structures. But let his triumph be
modestly unpretentious. He will have risked nothing, since
it is a well-attested fact that human life possesses simultaneously economic, social, religious, and other components. And
—be it remembered—from the start our good man is in possession of a doctrine that informs him in no uncertain terms
which of these multifarious aspects is determinative, fundamental—in short, is real.

Suppose we take the most elementary case: factual history
applied to what is termed inquiry into "causes." Faced with
the multiplicity of possible causes that a fairly serious investigation will always reveal, he must take sides. He must
distinguish between accidental causes and profound causes,
between simple favorable circumstances and the impetus, the
initiative or the vital decision. Who does not perceive the
role that arbitrary conclusion plays in any attempt at explaining in that manner? The historian can always praise or
deride his hero, attribute his conduct to the highest motives
or the basest impulses.

More generally speaking, he will constantly find himself

20. *Ibid.*, p. 102.

torn between the two types of explanation that his experience has opened to him. Following his personal balance he will choose one or the other—or one of the thousand combinations possible between the two. Or he may be sharply aware of the feeling for historic inevitability. Do we not often have the sensation that everything that happens to us occurs through an invincible force and that our whole life is ordained by forces which, *volentes nolentes*, conduct or push us on? The Christian will feel that he is in the hands of God, while the pagan will talk of Destiny . . .

Was it not Fate, that, on this July midnight . . .

Very naturally, then, the historian is led to look for what he calls the underlying causes and to describe the past as a majestic development where the particular nature of the details, perhaps contingent in themselves, are automatically set aside for the benefit of an integrated movement, delineated with the exactness of a graph. History becomes evolution again, and the development of humanity participates in the dignity of Nature.

But lived experience suggests to us also the opposite assumption of a fundamental contingency: the mythical conscience of humanity has called on the idea of blind and inconstant Fortune or luck as much as on that of immutable Destiny. Here the experience of the man of action joins that of daily life. It is because I flipped a coin about spending a day of leisure that I had this unforeseen encounter that oriented the development of my entire life. Thus the historian thinks that . . . "if Cleopatra's nose had been shorter . . ." and he underlines, contrary to what has just been said, the unforeseen circumstances, the pecularities of sequence which made history what it is—and which it very well could not have been.

Accident or fate? Underlying causes or chance? Considering, once again, the imaginative quality of the mental processes by which, weighing the pros and cons, we make a selection among the various interpretations, how can we not perceive the incertitude, the basic gratuitousness, of any chosen solution?

This is still only a rough example. One will find again the same consoling, but uncertain, diagramming in the great hypotheses by which historians have sometimes tried to gather up the essence of their knowledge in a supreme synthesis (or at least in which the public, always in a hurry, willingly condensed the frequently much richer and varied contribution of their work).

Such were the proposed answers given in turn to the question asked by Edward Gibbon (what was the "cause" of the decline and fall of the Roman Empire?): triumph of religion (Christian) and of barbarism (Gibbon himself); elimination of the elite, *Ausrottung der Besten* (Seeck); physical degeneration (Kaphahn), or racial (T. Franck); climatic crises, drought (Huntington); impoverishment of the soil (Liebig, Vassiliev); decline of slavery and a return to a natural economy (M. Weber); class struggle, the Red Army of the peasant soldiers against the urban "bourgeoisie" (Rostovtseff); disaster from without—"the Roman civilization did not die a natural death; it was murdered"— by the barbarian invasions (Piganiol); the conjunction of an outside peril and the disaffection of the masses (Toynbee) . . . I do not claim to give a complete list.[21]

By shifting the problem, one can locate the line of rupture at a much later date. According to H. Pirenne, antiquity is prolonged through the "barbarian" period, and it is only the Arab conquest of the southern shores of the Mediterranean which destroyed, together with the Mediterranean unity, the

21. The analysis of these principal themes will be found in M. Rostovtseff, *Social and Economic History of the Roman Empire* (1957), pp. 610–619; A. Piganiol, *L'Empire chrétien* (1947), pp. 411–422; S. Mazzarino, *Aspetti sociali del quarto secolo* (1951), pp. 8–29.

economic unity of the ancient world. Here the synthesis attains
its perfect form: the complete theory can be summed up in
two words, *Mohammed* and *Charlemagne*.[22]

Such suppositions must be subjected to the same criticism
we applied to other over-ambitious concepts: *There are more
things* . . . In historical facts there are always more things
than can be embraced by the most ingenious hypothesis. The
hypothesis is only an expedient for a presentation that, in
order to aid memory, underlines in red pencil certain lines
lost in a diagram whose thousand curves cross one another
in every direction. It is only one way of looking at the reality,
and it cannot pretend to bring together all the truth of our
knowledge of the subject in the brief formulas above in which
I summed up their opinions. This is attested by the very great
care they take in calling attention, one after the other, to the
main hypothesis of their predecessors, in specifying for each
(each a totalitarian ambition in itself and exclusive of all
others) that part of truth it can disclose—or cause to be discovered through criticism. The real picture that their varied
and thorough exposés leaves in the mind of an attentive reader
is made up of the superimposition of these different touches
and brush marks. As we emphasized above, it is less an explanation, bringing the detail back to the whole, than a
thought-out description evoking little by little the complexity
of these multiple coordinations which make up the structure
of reality.

In fact, nothing is more revealing than to observe the valid
use the true historians make of these hypotheses. Let us read
over the final chapter which Michael Rostovtseff or André
Piganiol devotes, each in his own way, to the study of the
problem, "End of the Ancient World." It is quite clear that
neither one claims to reduce the observed multiplicity in in-

22. Title of the posthumous book (Brussels, 1937) in which one finds
the last stage of the theory.

formation to a few principles that, coming closer and closer, would explain the reality truly and entirely.

Therefore, in theories of this kind, we cannot perceive the higher form, the culmination of historical knowledge—the equivalent of the "great hypotheses" of physics (kinetic theory of gases, electromagnetic theory of light, relativity)—to which they were carelessly compared. But undoubtedly they have their advantages and can, in some measure, help discovery.

No one better than L. Febvre knew how to describe the use of "these general hypotheses that group thousands of small and scattered facts and clarify them by gathering them, giving rise to a fruitful task of checking, of demolishing, and of rebuilding."[23]

They can, however, easily become "some of those big anti-comprehension machines."[24] Through their comforting simplicity, their dazzling clarity, they finally blunt the historian's capacity to see reality in its authentic and irritating multiplicity.

That is what happens to the lazy minds which confidingly accept ready-made theories—or even to the master himself when he has grown old and has lost the rapidity of his reflexes. Then he allows his schemas to become static at the point at which he was justified in fixing them as a result of his investigation. The fossilized hypothesis becomes a theory which one substitutes for reality and which one insists upon verifying at any cost. This may happen to the greatest of scholars, as it did to H. Pirenne. The line of my research once crossed his apropos of the "conditions of lay education in the Merovingian epoch."[25] The "Mohammed and Charlemagne"

23. *Combats pour l'histoire,* p. 96; cf. p. 358.

24. I take the formula from the same L. Febvre, *ibid.,* p. 308, n. 1, who thus corrects himself.

25. Title of the memoire published by H. Pirenne in the *Revue Bénédictine,* vol. 46 (1934), pp. 165–177; for the contrary position, see my *Histoire de l'Éducation dans l'Antiquité*[3] (1954), pp. 444 and 569–570, n. 9.

theory required that ancient education continued after the barbarian invasions, therefore one *must* find "lay" schools of the Roman type under the Franks. Pirenne was convinced that he had found them, but all the texts he invokes to this end he has understood in a mistaken sense, for they really concern "clerical" schools of the medieval type.

Accordingly, these generalizations are most often valuable only as aids to teaching. They represent a method of presenting events concisely and provisionally, the equivalent of a handy summary, a first sketch to be finished later. Complicated and outdated, they are far from being the pure essence of history or a fine distillate retaining the flavor of knowledge!

G. Wiet published an article on "The Neo-Byzantine Empire of the Ommiads and the Neo-Sassinid Empire of the Abbassids,"[26] a magnificent sketch brushed by the hand of a master, a stimulating, intellectual success. But in it one finds no more than an introduction to the Islamic history of these two centuries. Wiet, a real scholar, of course makes no pretense of explaining them completely within the framework of these two concepts.

In order to remain faithful to our nominalist principle it is more than ever essential to attack any attempt to establish an ideal pattern. The historian must guard against overestimating the logical value of his hypotheses and of his concepts as well, as we have insisted that he do. Unless he exercises the utmost care, he will almost invariably find himself extrapolating them.

The mechanism is the following: a theory is always formulated (limited by the intellectual resources and theoretical knowledge of the author) to solve a specific and limited problem. It is, therefore, based on a selection (this is the "mark of the red pencil" of which we spoke earlier), a choice

26. *Cahiers d'Histoire mondiale*, vol. I (1953), pp. 63–70.

among the innumerable facets of this particular historical reality. The historian retains only those elements which, in his opinion, help him explain the event or events under consideration. This is a legitimate exercise provided one never forgets that it represents an abstraction.

But the peril is great. The historian risks forgetting that those things exist which he has chosen to ignore. Thus theory is like a searchlight. Its thin beam pierces reality and illuminates violently those objects that present themselves in a favorable aspect, leaving the rest in total obscurity.

This image is not satisfactory (no comparisons are) since it suggests that, to obtain a more complete truth, all that is necessary is to increase the number of these partial illuminations and add the amount of light. Thus, one clarifies the Ancient City from a religious point of view with the searchlight "Fustel de Coulanges," economic and social conditions in the light of "Marxism," and so on. The result is generally an illusion.

It is, in fact, almost inevitable that every explanatory hypothesis tends to escape the limits for which it was conceived (and within which, if correctly formulated, it retains its value). It begins to exhibit an increased intellectual tyranny through which it attempts to explain everything. The historian thus finds himself re-evaluating and reconstructing that portion of history under study (and sometimes the entire history of man) to conform to a system based on selected facts. Since the threads of historical reality are closely interwoven (though there are numberless combinations among the different facets of this reality), no matter from which angle one approaches it, sooner or later the historian is imprisoned by the illusion that everything, or almost everything, is explained by his theory. He is then astounded at his achievements. He sees them as experimental verifications of the truth of his system when, in fact, this re-examination of history simply embodies

in itself (but is incapable of proving) the validity of the theory
in whose service it was formulated.[27] The prime example of
this, crudely caricatured, is Marxism as used by certain
communist historians, particularly in Russia.[28] Marxism appears to the historian as a theory formulated by its author
(mostly by the device of "ideal-types": capitalism, middle
class, proletariat, social classes, productive forces) within his
own personal philosophic framework (that of a disciple of
Hegel and Feuerbach) in order to explain a collection of social
phenomena related to the Industrial Revolution in the nineteenth century. As such, it is a theory which has shown itself
to be remarkably fertile, operating with a large measure of
success on the problems for which it was originally formulated.

But, once an attempt is made to apply it to sectors of
reality no longer close to the specific area— the socio-economic
—for which it was developed, its bearing on the facts, its
significance, and its importance rapidly diminish. This is
equally true in the domain of aesthetics and of religion.

Soviet criticism[29] asks us to compare the work of Mussorgsky
with the revolutionary "democracy" of the 1860's as well as
with the lower middle class and the anarchism of the "Popu-

27. Cf. R. Aron, *Introduction*, p. 95: "Is not a [re-examination] of
history doubly bound by the theory and point of view of the historian?
It embodies in itself, and cannot prove, the truth of the philosophy of
which it is an integral part."

28. These few observations make no effort to discuss the problems
posed by Marxism itself, but only to explain one use to which it has,
in fact, been put. The elementary aspects of this use are a result of the
conditions of Soviet culture following the Revolution: the Russian in-
telligentsia were decimated, practically wiped out by "liquidations" and
emigrations. Thus the culture of Russia was forced to start from scratch,
in a climate almost Carolingian: it was, in fact, a return to the Middle
Ages.

29. See the curious preface published in "The Musical Edition of the
State" for the critical edition of the *Khovanchtchina*, by P. Lamm (1932),
pp. 5–6.

lists." The inherent contradictions of a social class are revealed in this study: the unseated nobleman who, having broken all economic ties with the landholding class, is still incapable of the effort necessary to absorb serious revolutionary concepts. Does this interpretation in itself constitute a genuine historical explanation of a work such as *Khovanchtchina*? Does it assist us in understanding—which is the real purpose of history—the aesthetic values of this music, the surprising technical originality of its style and, finally, the human significance which makes this "popular" drama one of the masterpieces of religious art?

The relationships invoked are real, but they appear decisive only to those who choose to examine the work through the Marxist lens, an apparatus incapable of performing tasks for which it was not designed and which analyze all reality in socio-economic terms, disqualifying all the rest as superstructure. But such a Marxist history of music is incapable of containing anything except that which is, in fact, nonmusic!

The contrast between reality and theoretical pretension is the more glaring as one moves further away from the "capitalist" period, as when we find two Soviet historians of the Stalinist era grappling with ancient Rome.[30] What a painful contrast between their profession of Marxist faith, their reiterated conviction that a new and authentic scientific concept of history comes from this, and the academic tableau which they present. (No historical cliché is avoided: not the seven kings of Rome, not even the choice of the deposition of Romulus Augustulus as the closing date!) Why? Because the "Marxian searchlight" offers[31] only a feeble illumination

30. N. A. Machkine, *Istorija drevnego Rima* (Moscow or Leningrad, 1948), and S. I. Kovaliev, *Istorija Rima* (Leningrad, 1948).

31. With two *obiter dicta* of the "genius," Comrade Stalin, French translation in *Questions du Léninisme*[2] (Moscow, 1947), pp. 432 ("the revolution of slaves"?), 453 (Rome as racist!)

and a single principle: slavery (between the "primitive" community and "feudalism"). Who can explain the immense variety of Roman history by reference to this single concept?

The exaggerated dogmatism which certain partisans of historical materialism exhibit compels one to insist on the illusory nature of the logical exercises in which they see a proof of the theory's truth and effectiveness. Once again, the theory precedes historical reconstruction. They see nothing except what theory permits them to see and call "history," an image selected to support the doctrine—a deformed and partial image. Thus one such historian believes he is "explaining" Racine by correlating his work with the religious, social and political events of the time.[32] He is astounded at the unexpected results, at the narrow correlation such comparisons show:

1675

1675–1677	
Racine wrote *Phèdre*. Returned to tragedy. Again took up *Mithridate* but in a tragic context. History does not exist, conflicts are insoluble, no compromise is possible.	After a calm lasting from 1669–70, popular insurrections started again in Brittany, Le Mans and Bordeaux. Tensions increased, etc. . . .
	. . . .
	1676
	May 30, anti-Jansenist warrant against Henri Arnauld, posing again the problem of the signature of the formulary.

But we must oppose the same objections to his reasoning as those which L. Febvre made to A. Brun (p. 190): it is only because the author chose to set up his material in two columns that the connection appears so convincing. It would be sufficient to add a third, concerning for example Racine's

32. L. Goldmann, *Sciences humaines et philosophie* (1952), pp. 137–145; but in practice the author showed himself quite different from what was announced by this theoretical manifesto; see *Le dieu caché* (1955).

sentimental and sexual life, in order to obtain yet another explanation (the stormy liaison with Champmeslé . . .). Finally, if a psychoanalyst examined the case, the privileged position of the socio-political comparisons would disappear!

Another paralogism in reasoning of this type is that Marxism, having succeeded in explaining the development of capitalism ("the materialist concept of history is no longer a hypothesis but a scientifically proven doctrine"[33]), therefore asumes that it can be legitimately employed in the study of other societies. But this is not so. The value of scientific theory is closely related to the body of experience for the explanation of which it was originally formulated. "Every theory finally loses its usefulness, even its meaning, as one moves further and further from the experimental conditions under which it was conceived."[34] If Marxism had in the past,[35] and still has, a general fertility for history, this usefulness does not reside in employing it literally, but in transposing its analogies. Thus the role of Marxism has been to suggest that the economic aspects of history could possess a fundamental importance and to encourage research in this area. The true importance of Marxism in the study of the history of Rome is not in these pitiful Soviet manuals but in the fertile works of M. Rostevtseff in his studies in the *Stuchen zur Geschichte des römischen Kolonats* (1910), and the *Storia economica e sociale dell' Impero Romano* (3rd edition in Italian, 1933).

This discussion exhibits the essential reasons why, for a century and a half if not more, professional historians have opposed and refused to admit the validity of philosophical

33. Cf. V. Lenin, "Ce que sont les amis du peuple . . . ," in *Oeuvres choisies* (Moscow, 1948), vol. I, p. 94.

34. I quote here the physicist and rationalist, J. Perrin, *Les éléments de la Physique* (1929), p. 21 (underlined by the author).

35. It is necessary to emphasize, in view of the naïve pride of the Soviets and Western communists, the importance of the "Social-Democratic" period of Marxist influence.

speculations on history. The speculative philosophers, it seems to us, have surrendered without resistance to the impure prestige of the *idola tribus*. Insofar as they confront the intellect with an explanation, total and unified (which flatters and satisfies its secret demands), they substitute an invalid system for that authentic history which forces itself "patiently to clarify the tangled threads of history" by meeting head-on their "extreme complication."[36] Such speculations destroy the original importance and the rich diversity which is so rightly a part of historical research (and which we can summarize in the verse of *Hamlet*: "There are more things . . ."). What is the purpose of history if philosophy tells us in advance, at least in essentials, what will happen! History, then, becomes a simple mechanism for registering events to confirm their occurrence as forecast. It is reduced to a process of verification. As Péguy says so aptly in his *Note conjointe*: "If Jesus had fulfilled the prophesies by automatic deduction, a mechanical deduction, purely and strictly determinist, if the *life* of Jesus had been nothing more than an automatic occurrence, the mechanical realization and methodical culmination of the prophesies, then we would have had no need for the Gospels and neither would Jesus himself."

The example is much more striking today than it appeared to be in Péguy's time, since, in the meantime, "historians" have appeared—such as G. A. van den Bergh van Eysinga—for whom Jesus is precisely nothing more than the methodical realization of the prophesies. These historians have concluded that Jesus no longer possessed a valid reason for existing and, with rigorous logic and utter seriousness, they therefore contest that existence.

One is struck, in going from Marx to Hegel, from Hegel to Fichte and thence to Kant, by the perfect frankness of the philosophy of history which, very early in its development,

36. As H. Berr puts it so well in *La synthèse en histoire*[2], p. 205.

proclaimed the lack of qualifications of empirical history. Thus Kant, for example, develops in nine propositions the genuinely philosophic *Concept of a Universal History*,[37] "leaving it up to nature," he says with naïveté or casualness, "to produce the man capable of writing history according to this principle." This is somewhat as if Leverrier had left to the humble astronomer the useless task of verifying the presence of Neptune at the point indicated by his calculations.

In thus confirming the conclusions suggested previously, this study of the limits of historical analysis has allowed us to isolate the existence of a specific level at which it is possible to establish the validity of history as knowledge of the human past. We have chosen to ignore the problem, but if it were possible, or became possible, to develop a true science of the evolution of humanity and to establish in a rational or experimentally convincing manner the existence of laws or general principles explaining human actions in history, the validity of the direct confrontation of the past, of that unique knowledge which history represents—and which, as we have seen, implies an analysis both structural and temporal—would continue to conserve its innate value, its specific level of usefulness. In the same way the existence of general laws of botany (anatomy and physiology of plants, laws of evolution) does not invalidate another level of knowledge of plants, that of the farmer, the amateur gardener, or of the systematic botanist who describes the characteristics of each species.

In what we have written here so far we have not, in fact, considered anything more than the possible analysis of individual historical phenomena—the proper goal of the historian. I believe that it is indeed useless to attempt to formulate historical "laws" in the strict sense (as opposed to the analytical laws of the philosophy of history whose proponents

37. French translation of St. Piobetta: Kant, *La philosophie de l'histoire, opuscules* (1947), p. 61. For Fichte, cf. H. Berr, *op. cit.,* p. 22.

14

assume that they have evolved a more profound system than that available in a direct confrontation of historical phenomena —a system which reduces these phenomena to a more essential reality such as economic infrastructure or sexuality).

Why? Because the historical reality revealed through experience recorded in documents offers only individual phenomena essentially incapable of being further simplified. If it is possible to make comparisons between some of these phenomena, the inferences which one can draw are valid to a very limited extent as imaginative abstractions produced by the intellect, but they are not reality itself. We discover, in connection with research into causality, the consequences which result from the impossibility of isolating, through experiments with closed systems, this or that element of reality. The observations of supposed general characteristics which are often proposed as "laws of history" are nothing more than partial similarities. They are of value only within the momentary point of view that the historian has chosen in his attempt to define this or that aspect of history.

Some of these "laws," of a psychological or sociological nature, derive, in fact, not from either of these sciences but from the art of the moralist (in the style of La Rochefoucauld or Vauvenargues). They are simply "maxims" of limited importance and based on a restricted experience, which gain weight through their sentencious or piquant presentation as general laws. Thus, the favorite aphorism of Lord Acton (and of Alain): "Power corrupts . . ."

On the contrary, it is my belief that the great statesmen— the true "leaders of the people," whether they are called Pericles or Churchill—prove that a great soul develops in greatness and integrity with the exercise of power. If others (such as Caligula, Nero and certain cabinet ministers) were corrupted, it was because they were weak and unworthy of their high positions.

I attribute the same totally relative value to the "laws" of the development of civilization which Toynbee, in his clever and patient study, believes he has discovered by comparing the twenty-one civilizations contained in our history: challenge and response, breakdown, Nemesis of creativity, and the rest.

It is useless to return to the arbitrary premise on which the *Study of History* is based—that of the organic unity of civilization, summarily defined as the "intelligible field of history." If there is no doubt, for example, that the Nile played a decisive role in the development of the agricultural civilization which produced Egypt, the historian still hesitates to explain the entire civilization of the pharaohs by a *response* to the *challenge* presented by the drying out of Libya following the last Ice Age.

I am personally well aware of the interest which a study of the graphs of development as defined in Arnold J. Toynbee's system possesses for the historian. However, it is clear that his theory has not succeeded as well as he had hoped in formulating the specific laws of the phenomenon civilization. He analyzes with subtlety and sureness certain aspects of the historical process, and formulates some "laws," if you like, of human behavior. But in these systems of conduct, the elements of the curve are capable of being applied on different scales to historical phenomena of different strength, and thus they cease to be characteristic of the development of civilizations.

Toynbee is too intelligent not to have been the first to realize this. Noting that the rhythm *Ying-Yang, Rest-Dynamism,* which he used to characterize the transition of primitive civilizations to major ones, was recurrent in the *Withdrawal-Return* in the personal life of great men, he says, "This time the rhythm is tuned to a shorter wave-length."[38]

Here again we are not dealing with laws of scientific

38. *A Study of History,* vol. III, p. 376.

nature formulated from the observation of well-defined phenomena. It is merely a question of undoubtedly legitimate approximations that emphasize partial resemblances which are
stressed by the particular point of view that the author wishes
us to share with him. The validity of these development plans
seems to me similar to those similar or metaphorical concepts
of the "baroque" type analyzed before (pp. 163-166). Indeed,
it is surprising to see that Toynbee gladly uses for the formulation of his "laws" such figurative expressions as "Time of
Troubles," "proletariat" (internal or external: two successive
degrees of analogy), *lingua franca,* and so forth.

To say, for instance, that the period from the Peloponnesian
War to the founding of the Roman Empire represents a
"Time of Troubles" for Hellenic civilization is a mental
exercise similar to that which terms the art of Baalbek
"baroque," an exercise which within certain limits might be
perfectly legitimate and fruitful. What this means is that
this period was analogous for the Greek world (to what degree? that is the question!) to the period of dynastic, national
and social perturbations of the Russian people in the period
from 1584 to 1613. That period was correctly termed the
"Time of Troubles," *Smoutnoïé Vrémia.*

As we have seen, such comparisons are suggestive and rich
in expression for one who knows how to keep them within
limits. But it would be a pity to expect too much of them.

CHAPTER VIII

The Existential Element in History

Up to this point we have been considering history in relation to what might be termed its object, that is, the past to-be-known; or, in any event, history in relation to knowledge in process of elaboration. Shifting from the periphery to the center, to the origin, we should now envisage history from the point of view of a knowing subject.

The strict objectivism of the old positivism would have liked to be able to reduce the historian's behavior to a fixed and seemingly indifferent gaze directed toward a dead past. In opposition to this positivist conception, history now seems to us rather as the fruit of an action, of an effort which is in a certain sense creative. It is an effort that brings into play the "kinetic energies" of the spirit, as we understand this spirit by its capacities, its mental quality, its technical endowment and its culture. History is a spiritual adventure wherein the historian's personality is brought into play. History is thus endowed, for the historian, with an existential value, and from this existential value it receives its importance, its meaning and its value.

As previously stated, this conception forms the very heart of our critical philosophy, and the focal point around which all else takes on order and clarity. Indeed, the really useful task before us is less to prove this assertion (which has already become quite evident) so much as to verify it; to make its truth more precise, and to determine its limitations.

The time has come to consolidate positions already won. We must abandon turgid formulas, extravagant pretentious-ness, and the paradoxes we have used (sometimes even abusively). Let us admit frankly that in this regard we have all sinned more or less.

Let us begin with the great Dilthey himself. Despite a good deal of truth, there is also a certain exaggeration in his insistence on biographical and autobiographical considerations, on the knowing by the self in and through its personal past. Dilthey located this personal past at the origin and veritable center of all history. In his view, my inquisitiveness and my inquiries grow out of my personal history, and it is my inquisitiveness and my inquiries that, by spreading from individual to individual, finally engulf the whole of humanity.

Raymond Aron, with his customary flair for pithy observations, has neatly summarized this doctrine in a triple aphorism: "At a given moment in time, an individual reflects upon *his* adventure, a collectivity upon *its* past, humanity upon *its* evolution: thus are born respectively autobiography, individual history, universal history."[1]

This point of view is quite acceptable, but it is necessary to explain how the accessible past of humanity can, in a sense, be adopted by each man as his own. Otherwise the history of, say, the Hittites would have hardly any meaning or existential value except to present-day Turks, the Hittites' successors in Anatolia and, to quite an extent, their descendants.

And what are we to say of such paradoxes as Croce's "All history is contemporary history"?[2] There is, of course, a certain element of truth in this: every genuinely historical problem[3] (which Croce contrasted with the "anecdote," that

1. R. Aron, *Introduction*, p. 82.

2. *Contribuzione a la critica di me stesso*, French translation (1949), p. 110: ". . . the *Théorie et histoire de l'Historiographie*, wherein I undertook to determine the nature of genuine historiography considered as an ever 'contemporary' history—that is to say, as one rising out of the intellectual and moral needs of the moment."

3. *History: Its Theory and Practice*, English translation, pp. 118–126.

comes from curiosity pure and simple) is a drama enacted in the consciousness of a present-day man, even when it concerns the most distant past. Every genuinely historical problem is a question which the historian poses to *himself* in the contextual situation of his own life, his own milieu, his own time.

But by over-insisting on this subjective consideration, by assigning a highly exaggerated role to the "presence," as it were, of a revivified past in the consciousness of the historian, one runs the risk of destroying, of emptying from within, the distinctive character of history. By definition (see p. 34), history is, after all, knowledge of the past, of the what-has-occurred, of human reality considered as a "having-been," *dagewesenes Dasein*.

Considerable light has been shed on this point, as on so many others, by Heidegger.[4] In his works there is much to be learned, provided one can read with discretion. Thus, in the highly personal commentary he has made on the conception (so cherished by Dilthey) that man (*das Individuum*) understands history because he is a historical being,[5] Heidegger writes:

> [The rediscovery of the past] already presupposes the *historical Being*—historical in relation to human-reality as a having-been-Presence; that is, [the rediscovery of the past] presupposes the historicity of the historian's existence. It is this very historicity which establishes history as a science existentially, down to its least apparent structuring—to the minute details of scholarship.[6]

4. *Sein und Zeit*, §73, French translation in *Qu'est-ce que la métaphysique?*, pp. 179–180.

5. *Der Aufbau der geschichtlichen Welt . . .* , *Gesammelte Schriften*, vol. VII, p. 151.

6. *Sein und Zeit*, §76. (I have reproduced the system of ingenious, although rather curious, equivalences conceived by H. Corbin, whose rendering of this "transcription"—one can hardly call it a translation—is much more obscure than the original German text.) In the works of Dilthey himself, the phrase "man is a historical being" emphasizes particularly "the latent presence of the objective spirit in each person" (language, concepts, monuments, techniques inherited from the past): R. Aron, *La philosophie critique*, p. 87.

I would hardly venture to assert that he was always so inspired. There is no question that Heidegger's influence is very largely responsible for that shrill lyricism and precious style affected by our younger philosophers, who take this as a proof of profound thought—mere verbal gymnastics with an etymological foundation, copying *Cratylus*. Barely acceptable in German, they become completely ridiculous when transposed into French, a language in which the meaning of words is defined by consensus and not by etymology.

Indeed, the primary aim of Heidegger's philosophy was not our scientific or historical knowledge, but what I have termed (without any illusions about the value of his principles) the analysis of the ontological condition of man who, "temporal to his very depths, does not and cannot exist other than historically."[7]

It was tempting, and in a sense inevitable, that one who found his fundamental basis in the finality of temporality,[8] in striving to relate the historicity of "human reality" (*Dasein*) to historical knowledge (from *Geschichte* to *Historie*), should present us with this deeply pathetic description abounding in tragic images: destiny, dereliction, care and anxiety, "Man is a Being made for death."

It is a dangerous example to imitate: for it results in the tendency (become so general) to bring an over-emotional attitude to the existential nature of historical research. Our link with the past then becomes a ponderous, anguished communication where the historian, engaged in the struggles of the present, seeks in the heat of action to obtain some illumination from the past that might help him in his effort to shape the future.

As Aron says, "Inasfar as he lives historically, the historian tends toward action and seeks the past to gauge his own

7. *Sein und Zeit*, §72 of the same translation, p. 176.
8. *Ibid.*, §74, p. 191.

future."[9] Or as E. Dardel puts it, "Interest in the past already reveals a historicity that is in the process of evolution." This is readily seen, but why (concerning this) speak of "dizziness" and "anguish"?[10]

Sooner than investigate maliciously what my predecessors have written (possibly a little excessively), I prefer to repeat: we have all sinned. It once happened[11] that I succumbed completely to the prevalent influence and adopted Sartre's theory of "existentialist psychoanalysis," transferring it from the ontological to the level of empirical expression.[12] I maintained that historical research, at least for a historian of real vocation (the man to whom history is not merely a light pastime or a part-time occupation), is a symbolic manifestation of this primitive and fundamental "projection," in which and by which the individual himself seeks to become incarnate, to "find his inner reality," and where, in some sense at least, he expresses himself entirely.[13]

I simply wanted to say that if he is really a man and genuinely engrossed by history, the historian will not waste his time quibbling over questions which "disturb no one's sleep" (according to Jean Prévost's brutal expression which was taken as a challenge by all the scholars of my generation); that is to say, unless he is merely a learned man, busy weeding out material for future history. On the contrary, in his personal confrontation with the past he will busy himself with the development of *the* question which disturbs *his* sleep—of the problem which is primary for *him*, whose solution completely

9. *Introduction*, p. 337.
10. *L'histoire, science du concret*, p. 121.
11. *Revue de Métaphysique et de Morale*, vol. LIV (1949), pp. 259–260.
12. A transposition legitimate in itself, as much so as that which Sartre himself imposed on the original idea of "pro-ject" (*Entwurf*). In Heidegger this signified something quite different ("the man flung to being, flung in pasturage to being") from what Sartre suggests!
13. Cf. J.-P. Sartre, *L'être et le néant*, pp. 643–663.

engages his life and person—sought though it may often be by devious and mysterious paths.

Need I still convince my readers? As we have seen (Chapter II), history does not exist until a historian appears to summon the phantom of the past, and, harrying it with questions, bend it to his will. It is from the very depths of the historian's own being that these questions arise, questions that direct and pre-determine the entire inquiry in advance. At least this is so in its general outline, for as we have seen, as the dialogue is prolonged the question gives way before the resistance of the object and changes its shape in order to conform to it.

A close analysis will always emphasize this essential link, this umbilical cord linking history to its historian. Let us begin with the choice of subject: a researcher's reasons for undertaking a particular task may often appear quite extrinsic, but upon closer examination the existential nature of his choice will soon emerge.

I published the *Histoire de l'Éducation dans l'antiquité* in 1948 because I had been asked to do so in 1943 by the *Éditions du Seuil*. But the publisher is a friend of mine, and if he urged me to undertake this project it was because he knew how dear to my heart it was. And if it was he who first spoke of it, it was because he knew that I had it in mind. Moreover, if I welcomed his proposal when I had refused so many others without even considering them, was it not because I instantly recognized his idea as my very own?

But the choice of the subject is nothing in itself: what really matters is the manner in which it is outlined, directed and understood—and most particularly the way in which it is realized. The more the mind becomes involved in it, the more historical research sets in motion the mind's entire resources; thus it is not surprising that the mind should leave an indelible imprint there. What his research becomes depends very strictly upon what the historian is, and it does not really exist at all except insofar as he *concerns* himself with it passionately, engaging his total being in the act.

From this point of view we could recapitulate all the previous analyses, but it is so self-evident that time thus spent would be wasted. Now, here is the point on which I must insist: we must give to the assertion of the existential value of history all its shades of meaning in order to mark its exact scope. Too much emphasis upon it risks distortion: we must not place history upon too high a pedestal, nor expect or demand too much from it. It is due to just such exaggerations that critical philosophy has sometimes discredited itself in the eyes of professional historians who can no longer recognize their humble and conscientious work in the highly colorful and stirring version of it given by the theoreticians. It is all very well to talk about "existential anguish" to a historian of economics who is concerned with fluctuations in the production and the price of silver in nineteenth-century America—fluctuations that are recorded and "understood" with almost the same objectivity as those of, say, rainfall. In both cases, the specifically human element is outside the phenomenon, which can and must be observed first of all by and for itself.

It is therefore necessary to state clearly that if all historical knowledge is in fact endowed with an existential value, nevertheless it is not always *in actu* with the same intensity, with the same immediately useful import. All the elements of the science of history are not on the same level: a great deal of indispensable knowledge function as means subordinated to an end—that higher understanding which alone is true history, but which could not exist at all without these means. Such is the case with all of the elements accumulated with infinite patience by our auxiliary sciences. The compilation of a *Corpus* of the trademarks of Roman potters is in itself a mental operation weighted with no more existential values than that of the *Collector* imagined by Jean Capart who collected,

classified and identified the trouser buttons he picked up in
the streets of Brussels. But then such a *Corpus* is not an end in
itself, and its justification is the use that may be made of it by
a historian of the Roman Empire.

On the other hand, one must not have too narrow, too
readily utilizable an idea of the existential scope of some
particular segment of knowledge. The politician or diplomat,
bent under the weight of his responsibilities, will first look for
a historical culture that will enable him to understand his
own times: he will consider it more important to know what
happened at the Yalta or Potsdam conferences than what took
place in ancient Rome or Byzantium. But that is a limited
viewpoint, unworthy of a truly cultivated man, for in order
to understand the international situation today it is indeed
necessary to know the distant past of which today preserves
the heritage: Byzantium does help us to understand Moscow,
"the Third Rome."

Thus, in order to enrich it, the notion of the existential
stake must be made more flexible. Here we should comment
on Dilthey's doctrine of universal history as an extrapolation
of autobiography—granting all the truth it contains. It is
certainly true that history touches us more clearly, more
directly (I do not say more profoundly) if it seems in some
way to be *our* history. But we should not limit this to a simple
retracing of our direct biological descent. Again, to take the
case of the Hittites: if they seem more remote to us than to
the Turks, it is nevertheless a fact that their discovery aroused
considerable interest in our Occidental milieux from the
moment it was certain that they were Indo-Europeans (or at
least that their ruling class used a language related to our
Indo-European dialects). They at once became ours—much
more interesting than the Elamites, for example (although the
civilization of Elam was more original and more fecund).
Knowledge of the Hittites clarified another aspect of our

origins, for if they were not our fathers, they were at least our uncles, or our cousins.

I remember the great joy that greeted the publication of a Hittite treatise on the training of horses[14]: for wasn't this a kind of verification of the thesis, notably defended by Max Weber, of the Indo-Europeans as nations of horsemen?

It would hardly be an easy task to determine exactly how much to include within the meaning of the term "fraternal." Everything depends on the limit given to the "I," that subject of values. The national traditions of our old Western countries have taught us to identify ourselves with the national community, and with its past. French children from Dunkirk to Perpignan have learned to feel in tune with Vercingétorix, Clovis, the Capetians, and the rest, as do all French citizens. But there are many of us already who consider ourselves Europeans, even members of an Atlantic community (some of us—others, of a Soviet community). There are men of good faith in the UN and UNESCO who are working courageously to engender a planetary consciousness: and the logical corollary to this is that they have undertaken to promote the writing of a history of the scientific and cultural development of humanity.

This last-named extension is still in an imperfect state, for the cultural unification of the world is not yet an accomplished fact. Here another factor intervenes: that of the personal vocation.

To me, a Westerner, the history of China remains foreign, in spite of all, since I cannot immediately assimilate that rich and singular past which constitutes the heritage of the Chinese people; but if I decide to learn her language, her literature, her art, I am no longer excluded. When Louis Massignon

14. B. Hrozny, "L'entraînement des chevaux chez les anciens Indo-Européens d'après un texte mitannien-hittite provenant du XIVᵉ siècle avant J.-C.," in *Archiv Orientalni*, vol. III (1931), pp. 431-461.

speaks of Al Hallaj and Ibn Dawud we sense that the Arabian past is not unfamiliar to *him*; if I knew Arabic as well as Massignon, the history of Arabia would also become a part of *my* past. Thus, there is no necessarily imposed limit upon the extension of curiosity and the comprehension of cultural history. Nothing human is *a priori* prohibited to me. One could transpose the verses of Vigny speaking of his ancestors:

> It is in vain that I am descended of their blood:
> If I write their history they descend from me.

On the contrary, if we consider men as foreign as possible with respect to the biological heredity manifest in my chromosomes, I ask: what is the importance of not being related by blood, *for if I write their history I too am descended from them henceforth*—if I have shown that I am capable of understanding their past, it is because I feel the family relationship.

Let us acknowledge that this is a question of fact. We must now pose a deontological question in order to continue our treatise on virtue: is it necessary to abandon oneself without control to the pressure of the existential—to this passion, conscious or secret, which is found to animate the activities of the historian—in order to awaken and orient his curiosity and sustain his effort? Especially with respect to this practical aspect, it seems to me necessary to react against current notions of the existential and of "engagement." I summon to my aid all humanist tradition and classic wisdom with its counsel on the dangers of passion (a source of blindness to reason), its defense of the virtues, temperance and prudence (so ancient and so Christian at the same time), moderation in everything (perfect equilibrium and the art of composing a mixture well dosed with all the necessary elements). *Ne quid nimis* . . . One should not have too much of it, for in pressing too hard on the existentialist pedal one runs the double risk of endangering both the reality and the truth of history.

Its reality we have defined as an encounter with the other, a departure from the self and an enrichment of one's being. But if man is too self-conscious about his encounter of the self and of life, he becomes closed up and haunted by the gravity and urgency of the problems which are imposed upon him. He is radically incapable of putting his preoccupations "between parentheses" temporarily, of this *epokhè* which alone makes possible and fecund the departure from the self, the engagement and understanding of the other. Nothing is more instructive than to follow the development of contemporary existentialism. Here is a philosophy that begins with Heidegger by forcefully affirming the characteristic historical aspect of man's situation and ends with "the ahistoric thought of Sartre" which "imprisons man in the straitjacket of his liberty" and "bars the road," "excluded by his very method" from what we call history, rendering it "absolutely impossible to integrate."[15]

The danger that I point out here is not simply theoretical nor does it menace only the philosopher, for historical literature is witness to the fact that much work of limited or debatable value is a result of this defect. A study dominated by the existentialist imperative (that is, over concerned with immediate anxieties about the problem posed, *hic et nunc*, to the historian and to his contemporaries, and seemingly obsessed by the anticipated response) rapidly loses its fecundity, its authenticity—its reality.

It would be easy to multiply the examples, some of them harsh. I have chosen a mild one. Much work was done on St. Augustine in the seventeenth century: Jesuits against Jansenists, Augustinians (Noris, etc.) against Jesuits, Catholics (Harlay . . .) against Protestants. But very often these works are too deeply and narrowly oriented towards the theological

15. J.-L. Ferrier, "La pensée anhistorique de Sartre," in *L'homme et l'histoire* (*Açtes* of the Strasbourg Congress, 1952), pp. 171–175.

controversies of the epoch to ever be really useful. Too preoccupied in seeking out immediately useable arguments in the
works of St. Augustine, no effort was made to discover, to
experience, to know St. Augustine himself, for himself.

It is at this point that we can resume again our previous
discussion of the criticism of documents (Chapter IV): history
as friendship. Anyone who thinks too much, too soon or solely
of using his friends can neither really love them nor know
them; friendship and business relations are not to be confused. History furthermore assumes a centrifugal[16] rather than
an egocentric inner attitude, and an opening out towards
others which demands that we mute our existentialist preoccupations.

Certainly, this can never be completely eliminated and
always *epokhè* (the "putting in parentheses") is not only
provisional but relative. I am not at all forgetting that our
analysis has revealed the essential interdependence of history
and the historian, but the approaches must not be confused:
there is the ontological analysis and the empirical method. It
is a question of degree, of proportion, of finesse, of nuance,
and above all of good sense. In opposition to an unruly ex-
altation of existentialist values, our ethics will rediscover with
profit the wise rules formulated by Cicero or by Tacitus:
"avoid the least suspicion of favoritism or of hate,"[17] "speak
of no one with love or resentment."[18] I count on the reader's
intelligence not to confuse this necessary impartiality made
calmly and based on a need for understanding, with the illusory attitude of detachment advocated by the positivist
theoreticians, "to consider human acts from the outside, as
things."

16. M. Nédoncelle, in his communication to the same Congress, *ibid.*,
p. 145.

17. *De oratore*, II, 15(62).

18. *Histoires*, I, 1, 5.

But there is a real danger, more vague perhaps, but none-theless menacing: the obsession with the existential can go so far as to compromise the very truth of history. One can begin by denouncing, and validly in a sense, the "myth of objectivity." One can also emphasize the fact that every historical work—not only by virtue of being a choice of one among the infinite possible aspects of the past—assumes and reflects a choice, an orientation that the mind of the historian imposes on it. One might say that there are only three pos-sible cases: the position of those who know themselves to be partisan but call themselves objective—gross hypocrisy; those who believe themselves objective, but who reflect their prej-udices without conscious knowledge—unpardonable naïveté. One cannot help but prefer the last solution—a history truly engaged, the story of a struggle, proud of being just that.[19]

One might say, for example, that there is no impartial history (especially contemporary). No matter what you may do you are part of the scene. You merely have the choice between a history which is "middle class," "capitalist," "imperialist"—and a communist or at any rate "progressivist" history. It will either be a gesture in defense of the class in power, menaced in its privileges by the economic and social evolution, or it will be a conscientious evaluation of that evolution and a revolutionary gesture.

Yet from the moment stress is thus laid on action and its efficacy, what is to become of our patient and persistent re-search into the past for all accessible truth—whatever it may be?

The historian will soon be solicited by the demands of the battle in which he is engaged. First, he will be notified that

19. P. Vilar, "Défense de la paix et objectivité historique," in *Trygée,* November 15, 1953, pp. 25–26, an intelligent and sincere argument, but all the more distressing because Vilar is an old companion of mine and I must be frank with him.

15

certain truths should not be told, whereas the essence of historical research lies in facing the unforeseen and the inopportune at every moment.

I continue to take my examples—a borderline case—from Soviet or Western communism of the Stalinist period. It was a counter-revolutionary gesture to recognize the part played by Trotsky as People's Commissar for the Army and Navy during the critical period of the civil war at a time when Stalin was busy eliminating Trotsky from power and consolidating his own position. To conceal this blinding truth became a duty.

Next, he is persuaded that he is no longer one of the "former species of armchair scholars" but, for instance, "a combatant for Communism" at the service of the people[20] or its leaders. Our historian is reduced to the level of a propagandist, requested at a given time to produce from his files (or put back into them) the bundle of papers which provide a useful precedent or convenient illustration; he must make a moving commentary on the leading temporary trend; he must construct a tangent to the chart and the thousand unforeseeable changes of direction of the "general line" drawn up by the chiefs of the moment. It is an undignified and worthless role.

Nothing is more distressing than the lot of the historians of the non-Russian peoples in the U.S.S.R. If the liberal outlook of the "policy of nationalities" increases, they are asked to consider the past of their little country and extol former heroes. If Moscow worries about the inevitable recrudescence of "bourgeois nationalism," then these heroes become mere reactionaries. The historian on duty will henceforth apply himself to the task of describing what a joy it was for the Cossacks or Tchetchenes to have been united to the great Russian family by the Imperialist conquest at the time of the Tsars.

20. I. Kon, "K voprosu o specifike i zadatchah istoritcheskoj nauke," in *Voprossy Istorii*, no. 6 (June 1951), p. 63.

One step more and how will the historian be able to withstand a Machiavelli who appears one day and insinuates that a certain cleverly contrived lie will be more effective in the fight that is being fought (or will serve the cause better) than those small, minutely established factual truths? What does it matter if things did not happen in that way? Why not relate them as they should have happened, for that history will be "politically" *true*?

They were not content with passing over Trotsky's exploits in silence, nor were they content with unscrupulously falsifying such documents as photographs. But they even sought to exaggerate the part actually played by Stalin side by side with Lenin in managing State affairs during the early years of the Revolution.

Such criticism may seem simplistic and unjust. I have not forgotten that this romantic philosophy, Marxism, endows its followers with a theory (which they hold as truth, considering it to be based on reason and experience). And I know that it provides them with the truth of the purpose of history and its process of materialization, prior to any properly historical research bearing on factual questions. In their case again we find the conflict between history and historical philosophy to be one in which the latter reduces the former to a simple process of verification.

Of course the Marxists, these neo-Hegelians, are men who deny transcendency; historical truth for them is only to be found in, and in relation to, contingency and the present moment in human evolution. However, I am writing this treatise for people who "believe frantically in truth," like the "conscientious little Breton who fled terror-stricken from Saint-Sulpice because he believed he had discovered that part of what his masters had taught him was not true."[21]

21. E. Renan, *Préface* (1890) to "L'Avenir de la Science" in *Oeuvres complètes*, vol. III, p. 718.

This is why I reiterate, still quoting Cicero, " that the first duty of history is to say nothing false, the second being to dare to say all that is true," *ne quid falsi dicere audeat, deinde ne quid ueri non audeat.*[22] I shall put my disciple on his guard against such naïvely monstrous applications of our theory of historical knowledge by urging him to realize more and more acutely the essential personalism of historical knowledge— and this as a natural consequence of the dignity of his part and of the responsibility he assumes. As a man of science, the historian finds himself delegated, so to speak, by men, his brethren, to conquer truth.

Isolated by the very technicality of his research, he sits there alone confronting his conscience as he struggles in the shadows where his convictions are worked out. It is useless to deceive oneself about a corroborating check. As far as the essential components of his contribution are concerned—those precise details of truth he alone has been able to perceive and grasp— it is hardly likely that a colleague following the same trail would retrace his exact path again, and be in a position to check his conclusions before a long time has elapsed. Truth in history is made of subtle judgments, the weighing and arranging of a thousand various data; it is the fruit of an experiment of the mind which cannot easily be repeated in another's test tube. Finally, scientific truth depends on the mental integrity of the research worker, on his personal quali- fications, attention to detail and, in short, his conscientiousness: therein lies the truth of the science.

This is why we are scandalized when we find it betrayed— for instance when R. Draguet states that the great Dom Butler himself once committed the sin of superficiality by neither comparing nor actually using for his critical edition of

22. In the same passage of *De oratore,* II, 15(62).

Palladios a certain fundamental manuscript (of which he knew, however), merely glancing through it carelessly.[23]

Aware of this responsibility, the historian will do his utmost to make himself capable of grasping the maximum of truth. To that effect he will subdue his passions, and in the first place calm those which his existential commitment kindles and keeps burning. Of course, we too shall advise him to be aware of that central passion, of the presuppositions and the inevitable prejudices that are involved in it—like forms of structure, and the limitations of his own mind—and we do this so that he will learn how to watch over himself and, if possible, never be self-deceived. We shall advise him to place himself under the best possible conditions for seeing, hearing and understanding.

The historian will impose upon himself that effort of self-mastery, of strictness, indeed of asceticism, all the more rigorously to the extent that he thinks less in the beginning of the external use—of its influence and usefulness to others —that will be made of his knowledge once it has been consolidated and made public. The historian does not work for a public as a primary motive nor essentially, but in fact he works for himself. Thus the truth of his findings will be sought all the more passionately, and will be all the more clearly disengaged and surely attained, if the problem has been conscientiously studied. As we have stated, it must always be *his* problem, one upon which his very personal being and the sense of his life depends.

Again I will contradict the formula dear to my positivist predecessors. To their illusory ideal of "knowledge of value to all," I will oppose that of the truth of value *to me,* for I see therein a guarantee of serious thought, of exigence and of strictness. In history, it is always easy to convince others.

23. Consult on this subject the note published in *The Journal of Theological Studies,* 1955.

There is no need of even a little urging, but simply a slight dexterity in the presentation, a bit of the lawyer's artfulness. On the other hand, it is far more difficult to convince oneself when working in a new field, in contact with the fundamental ambiguity of the sources, the difficulties of the information and of understanding. It is there above all that one measures the importance of the existential risk.

I would like my disciple to meditate often upon that admirable reply that Plato attributes to Socrates. The Sophist Hippias was sunk as usual in an inextricable problem and, as a man for whom truth had little importance, offered as solution, "Perhaps our adversary will not be aware of the difficulties?" Socrates replied, "By the dog, Hippias, they will not escape the attention of the man before whom more than any other I would blush if I reasoned badly and spoke empty words." "Who may that be?" "Why, myself, Socrates, son of Sophroniscus, who would no more allow myself to advance an unverified affirmation lightly than to appear to know that of which I am ignorant!"[24]

24. *The Greater Hippias,* 298 bc.

CHAPTER IX

The Truth of History

We have now arrived at the threshold of the ultimate question that we have never lost sight of, for which all of our investigation has prepared an answer: what is the truth of history? At the outset, we proposed that history should be defined insofar as it could shed new light on truth. Has it shown itself capable of this? On the point of answering, and of answering "Yes," I beg my reader to recall again what domain it is that we have been exploring. It is concerned with the understanding of Man—of man in his rich entirety, his baffling complexity, his immensity; and so it is a domain of the refined mind, of a feeling for subtleties. The truth in question is not amenable to the harsh reasoning of the geometric mind, or at least of those narrow categories freely designated by this term, for true mathematics demands more flexibility.

We must take care to avoid both forced assimilations and summary dichotomies. The theory of historical truth was led astray by the simplistic attitude of the positivists. Even after so much reaction, much remains distorted or posed in misleading terms. To formulate history on the bases of the natural sciences was to go astray, as it was to make objectivity the supreme criterion and even a unique path to truth. Whatever he may do, as we have insisted throughout our analysis, the unfortunate historian will always introduce some personal element into his thinking and knowledge—that dangerous and deplorable "subjectivity." To require that he end by isolating at the bottom of his test tube, once his operations are over, a residue that is 100% objective is to impose an impossible task upon him. With such an end in view, either one mutilates history, reducing it to a few meager factual observations, or one opens the door to scepticism—a path that many have rashly taken.

But conversely (and here, too, the reader has been warned by our preceding remarks), it is a very dangerous solution to do nothing more than oppose the two groups as irreducible facts: the natural sciences, the sciences of the mind—as if historical truth were of another order entirely. The irrational factor here lies in wait for us. I understand perfectly and can even share the concerns of our predecessors who were confronted by these theories of knowledge which tends toward a metaphysics of intuition. Human reason is one single thing, however diverse its adaptations, however flexible its behavior. A logician discovers no impenetrable barrier between the mental operations of the physicist, of the naturalist, and of the historian.

It is only too easy to oppose the magnificent "objectivity" of experimental science to the contradictions of history. But one cannot simply affirm, for example, that the laws of physics "impose themselves upon all those who desire truth."[1] Knowledge valid for all? Certainly not for everyone: it is not assimilated by the primitive, the child, the simpleton nor the ignorant—but only by the competent physicist. It can be said of physics as Aron once said of history: "It is true for all those who desire its truth—that is, for those who construe facts in the same fashion and who use the same concepts."[2] For strictly speaking, it exists only for those minds which have accepted the tradition of Western science and have agreed to bow to a certain discipline: that of our laboratories. This has taught them to tabulate experimental facts by means of operational procedures selected with a view to obtaining results

1. R. Aron, *Introduction*, p. 88.
2. As he reminded me in a letter of June 5, 1954.

of a determined order. An exacting philosophy of the sciences would not fail to insist upon the active contribution of the scientist in this "stylizing of the real." It implies a positive intervention, a "theoretical construction," a veritable "creative toil."[3] Selection and strict defining of the phenomena, procedures of analysis and measurement (all of which shape physics, for example) confer upon it its form and its structure, just as we have seen that history is shaped by the hand of the historian—even if with physics it does not occur in the same measure or to the same degree.

The analogies or parallels could be multiplied: here, for instance, in its glass case, is the pendulum of an old grandfather's clock.[4] In order to study it scientifically I must first eliminate from my knowledge of it all personal sentimental implications (this clock is a family heirloom whose monotonous movement recalls a thousand childhood memories). It is through this effort of abstraction that the knowledge I am about to use *becomes* objective.

Yet even on the plane of scientific knowledge itself this same object is susceptible of a great many conceptualizations. I am able to see it, in turn, as a pendulum integrated with the mechanism of a grandfather's clock; or again, my eye being caught by the play of light which appears on its surface, as a convex mirror; or it may be as an alloy of copper and tin. In a less complex domain of reality than that of human history, is this not the equivalent of the "equivocal and inexhaustible" character that we have attributed to history?

And there is another common zone: the role of authority. The further the phenomena studied are located from the the experience of daily life, the more rare and difficult it

3. I borrow these formulas from M. Vanhoutte, *Theses* (Louvain, 1953) (D. Thomae Aquinatis Schola, no. XXV), 25, 27.

4. Cf. the same example in F. von Hayek, *Scientism and the Study of Society* (1952).

becomes to possess a first-hand knowledge of them. We do not repeat an experiment as complicated to work out as that of Michelson and Morley every week; we cannot repeat certain clinical observations at will. In all these cases the physicist or biologist accepts the veracity of these results or these facts that are based on the testimony of an authoritative colleague, in exactly the same way as the historian trusts his witnesses. Each believes that were the experiment repeated or the observations renewed, the same results would be obtained, just as the historian believes that if he had been the observer in place of his witness he would have noted the same event.

I hope that the reader will not misjudge the scope of these analogies. I am not attempting to assimilate historical knowledge to that of the natural sciences. Thus with respect to the case just mentioned, the historian cannot verify the testimony in which he has placed his confidence, whereas on the contrary the physicist, at the price of an often considerable effort, can repeat the experiment. The clinical worker can reasonably hope to encounter analogous cases at one time or another; and the repetition, even though often merely virtual, undoubtedly makes a great difference. I have wanted simply to stress the analogy between the historian's and the scientist's psychological and gnoseological behavior.

One cannot, therefore, speak about the objectivity of the natural sciences without qualification. It must at least be explained that one does not thereby mean the type of knowledge which I defined as "100%," derived from the object without any involvement of the knowing subject. The knowledge is objective in the sense that by means of the techniques and procedures introduced by the scholar, it attains something which authentically belongs to the object. But then in what, *mutatis mutandis* and taking into consideration the necessary adaptation to an infinitely more complex object, in what way would the position of the historian be substantially different?

The possible number of questions that could be raised over an identical portion of past experience is so great that for practical purposes it could pass as infinite, particularly when compared to the physicist's or chemist's limited questionnaire. Since these questions are of so subtle a nature, the concepts that would aid in arriving at their solution are at once far more numerous and less simple to define than those which the mathematician, for example, would use. It becomes much more difficult to find, off hand, two historians who (presented with the same object) would undertake to systematize it by means of the same operational procedures, and "interpreting the facts in the same way" would draw the same conclusions. But that does not mean, as the relativists and the sceptics would so readily claim, that history is therefore afflicted with a radical "subjectivity" (in the sense of an arbitrary fact, of a falsehood).

I insist upon this, because such formulae (employed in a polemical context) have sometimes caused us to miscalculate the importance of our critical philosophy. Against the positivists' objectivism, we were for a long time obliged to insist upon the "subjective" factor introduced into history. As we have seen, this is true in all science, by the active, constructive and (in a sense) creative intervention of the knowledgeable subject. That subjectivity is not, however, the sceptic's.

Two historians, posing a problem in the same manner and having at their disposal the same documentary facts and the same technical and cultural equipment for their use, will not find two different solutions, nor construct two different histories.[5] The historian is not imprisoned in his subjectivity; and the existence of historical science can testify to this. The contradictions which divide us have been greatly exaggerated. As a matter of fact, we manage to convince each other, and

5. That simple and sensible verification has already been made by von Hayek, ibid., p. 80.

the debates among specialists (though animated and sometimes impassioned) in no way resemble dialogues between stubbornly opposed points of view. They are quite comparable to those which periodically divide scientists. The history of the sciences—of each of the "positivist" sciences—proves with what difficulty new points of view, original discoveries and daring undertakings are accepted. In this we observe the role, and the destructive power, of the authoritarian mind.

For all the simple historical problems, such as those which concern the establishing of "facts" of an objective nature (reality, determining dates, and the like), competent technicians agree upon the methods of procedure. They must single out the fact, isolate the phenomenon, criticize the testimony, weigh reasons for belief. Despite the hyperlogical criticisms of Pérès and Whately, the existence of Napoleon Bonaparte and the major dates of his life are established in the same manner by all historians with the same degree of satisfactory probability. Yet all these "facts" cannot be defined with the same precision, just as all the physicist's measurements are not obtained with the same degree of exactitude.

As the questions become more complex (more interesting and richer in human value) it clearly becomes more difficult to obtain unanimous agreement from the very beginning. But there, once again, the historian's vision is not marked by an unrelenting subjectivity. At the price of an effort to explain on the one hand, and an effort to understand on the other, we gradually come to share the same conviction, and learn to see what the other has first seen, adopting the same point of view and using the same techniques of investigation (concepts, etc.). This is not always easy. In order to agree, two historians must share in common the same mental categories, the same cultural basis, the same affinities. With the exception of the color-blind, all men realize that they perceive light waves in the same fashion. Agreement is not so easily reached on the facts of historical experience, such as values, meanings, or indeed intellects, characters, personalities. Nevertheless, it is not unobtainable.

I do not pretend to eliminate all subjectivity from historical knowledge by these remarks. At most, it is conceivable that a residue, a portion which retains a personal nature will always remain. We may never find two persons who have seen exactly the same things in the same light, but what I alone will have grasped because I alone was in the mental position which qualified me to grasp it, will not be less true, less authentic or less valuable . . . on the contrary!

As we have seen (p. 137), the positivists' effort to attain a knowledge valid for all, had it been followed through, would have ended in mutilating history by causing it to lose its human substance, its depth, its fecundity. For it would have been necessary to limit its truth to a meager common denominator among all the numerous diversified perceptions. A few basic "facts" would be reduced to their objective components, stripped of their value and their meaning. On the contrary, for us the historian's task is not to limit himself to what he is certain would be seen alike by everyone, but rather to comprehend all that he is himself capable of attaining.

We are coming to see that as a historian I am not seeking primarily to satisfy a public, nor *a fortiori* all men; I am seeking to convince *myself* of the truthfulness of *my* understanding of the past.

This means that we will not imprison our historian in a knowledge which would be valid for him alone. In the conclusion we will show the social role which devolves upon him. Here let us simply reiterate that this knowledge developed by and for the historian will be equally valid for all who prove themselves capable of sharing it, that is, of understanding it and recognizing it as true.

The solution to the problem of historical truth must be formulated in the light of all that our critical analysis has caused us to discover: it is neither pure objectivism nor radical subjectivism. History is both knowledge of the object and at the same time a spiritual adventure of the knowing subject. It is this ratio:

$$h = \frac{P}{p}$$

established between two planes of human reality—that of the Past, of course, but also that of the historian's present, where he acts and thinks with his existential perspective, with his orientation, his probing instruments, his aptitudes—and his limitations, his blind spots. (Because I am I and no other, there are certain aspects of the past that I am neither capable of comprehending nor even of perceiving.) Within this knowledge there is necessarily something of the subjective, something relative to my position in the world, but this does not thereby deny the possibility of its being an authentic grasp of the past. Indeed, once history is true, its truth is double, for it is composed of truth both about the past and about the testimony offered by the historian.

Nothing is more revealing than an examination of the successive images which historians of different periods, intellects and orientations have, each in his turn, developed from the very same past—those images, for example, which are offered us of Roman history by St. Augustine, Lenain de Tillemont, Gibbon, Mommsen, as well as others I could cite, for instance Gaston Boissier or Rostovtseff. From what they consider the sad spectacle of their "variations," relativists or sceptics draw conclusions which I refuse to accept. Assuredly, considered globally these various images cannot be superimposed. But a more thorough critical analysis succeeds in discerning clearly what exists as an authentic grasp of the object and what is a manifestation of each of their personalities (a personal equation which explains at the same time what is true and what is false or lacking in their vision). As heirs, we utilize these old texts of course, sometimes for the study of the very past with which they are identified, sometimes for a study of the past which became the present of these historians of another day.

Take, for example, the evocation of the Roman past contained in the *City of God*. I perceive the subjective nature of this image quite clearly, so that it is simple for me to establish contact with the existential point of view that St. Augustine held. His work is dominated by a double polemical preoccupation, directed against both the pagans of his time and against the Pelagians. This awareness allows me to criticize his testimony, and does not deter me from using it. With the necessary precautions, I shall make use of the *City of God* for ancient Roman history (to the extent that my evaluation validates the fact that St. Augustine, in a certain way and within certain limitations, knew it authentically). And at the same time I shall also make use of it for the history of St. Augustine himself or of his time.

We might make the same kind of analysis for each historian I mentioned. It is because he was a liberal under the Second Empire that G. Boissier wrote *L'opposition sous les Césars;* because he was a White Russian that M. Rostovtsev stressed the "class revolution" character of the army's interferences in imperial affairs in the third century. But it would be childish to suppose that their eye was distraught because it was attracted in a particular direction.

I do not want to recall here the image of the projector aimed at a predetermined azimuth. I have already pointed out the inadequacy of such a comparison, which opens the way to the consoling but largely illusory theory of "perspec-

tivism." In order to have a more complete or total picture of
the past, it is not enough to increase the number of pro-
jectors and viewpoints (p. 203)! No, the image that each
historian gives of the past is so profoundly and so organically
modified by his personality that in the last analysis their
various viewpoints are not so much complementary as mutually
exclusive. In order to exemplify our theory of historical knowledge, the best illustration is one which I will borrow from the
art of the portrait artist.[6] If we stand before a painting by
Holbein, Titian, Rembrandt, La Tour, or Goya, we find
ourselves confronting a work (just as in history—the self-
portrait corresponds to the autobiography) in which the object has been authentically grasped. (Even though we have
not known the model, we are sure that the resemblance is
really there.) On the other hand, like the historian, the artist
is also completely incarnated in his work. The portrait itself
is true with a double truth: in Raphael's "Balthazar Castigli-
one," in the Louvre, I find not only the author of the
Cortigiano in his entirety, but all of Raphael as well.

An experiment wellknown to psychologists will supply an
answer to the illusions of historical perspectivism. By super-
imposing various profiles that we have of Cleopatra we can
declare that we have thus, by mechanical means, obtained *the
true visage of the queen*—which is an absurdity. Cleopatra is
too poorly represented (plastically and historically) for such
an experiment to be convincing when carried out upon her.
Or let us take Louis XIV. To superimpose the views which
have been worked out and offered us by Rigaud, Mignard, Le
Brun, and many others, would be meaningless!

The understanding of man by man, history is a knowledge of
the past through and in, a human, living, absorbed thought. It
is a complex—an indissoluble mixture of subject and object.

6. Following the example of W. H. Walsh, *An Introduction to Philosophy of History,* p. 113.

To those who are upset or annoyed by such a servitude, I can only repeat: such is the human condition, and its character. Unquestionably, for this reason a relative element is introduced into historical knowledge; but all human knowledge is similarly marked by man's situation in his being and in the world. We need only reflect upon what we have learned from the physicists concerning relativity. We now know that our perception of space, and our conception of Euclidian space, is a function of the speed of light! The fact that something of the historian himself is embodied in the make-up of history, and that this is absolutely unavoidable, does not prevent its being at the same time and in the same act an authentic comprehension of the past.

Let us go back and complete the formula at which we had arrived (p. 143). I will now say: history is true to the extent that the historian has *valid reasons* for placing credence in what he has understood of the documents he has examined. Once more, the historical case cannot be examined apart from the more generalized problem of knowledge, of the experience of the other. The fact that it bears upon the past does not cause a fundamental difference, as we have seen. We enter into possession of the human past on those psychological and metaphysical terms that in daily life permit us to increase our knowledge of the other. No philosophy can disguise the fact that this knowledge is relative, imperfect, "human, all too human." (I do not know my friend—he does not know me—as we are, both of us, known by God.) Any logician will stress the hypothetical character of such a knowledge, its unrestraining, completely practical nature. Yet no one, again, except the even more hypothetical solipsist, would contest its reality or even its truth (within bounds which are often difficult to define).

I have shown that history comes before the bar of human reason with the same claims to credibility as all experience of

16

the other. The meeting of the past and the meeting of man in lived experience impresses us with the same value of the *real*. At the start (Chapter I) I confronted authentic history with all these imaginary types of representation of the past. That was not merely a formal distinction, but definitely the expression of a deep experience. It is the character of reality that permeates its entire being which differentiates history from its falsifications or its imitations.

We might speak of the "suffocating atmosphere of Utopias,"[7] and the historical novel lends itself to the same observations. The patient work by which the historian, or successive historians of the same period of the past, attempt to draw closer and closer to the authentic otherness of their object marks their knowledge (insofar as it thus shares in the category of the real) with a value that cannot be confounded with any other. Even when a great writer, novelist, dramatist or poet has fixed upon a historical figure and marked it with the imprint of his own creative genius—even when that creation is admirable, moving, grandiose, and true with a certain ideal humanity—the historical truth, be it ever so humble, remains precious in itself and always desirable, because it has the ring of genuine humanity.

Thus even after *La dernière à l'échafaud* and the *Dialogue des Carmélites*, it is still true that *La véritable passion de seize Carmélites de Compiègne*[8] deserves to be known for itself. The astonishing character that Bernanos has created for Mother de Croissy—a tragic incarnation of anguish in the face of death—cannot obliterate the real person who can be discerned through the documents: the real Henriette de Croissy, that

7. R. Ruyer, *L'Utopie et les utopies* (1950), pp. 109–113.

8. Such as it has just been reconstituted from archives and other documents by P. Bruno de J.-M., *Le sang du Carmel ou la véritable passion* (sub-title quoted), 1954.

noble figure who "defied the blade of the guillotine"[9] to the very steps of the scaffold.

But we cannot stop at these general considerations. Our theory (and it is in this that its real fecundity lies) puts us in possession of precise standards that allow us to judge history's pretensions to possess some truth, wherever it has been empirically determined. The time will come when we must undertake a critical revision of the historical literature which at the start we accepted as fact. My reader will not be surprised when I declare that everything does not have the same value, indeed that not everything has value, in the historical production that has accumulated in our libraries since Herodotus.

There is no need to emphasize the inevitable role of that imperfection which is inherent in all human enterprises: the errors, the gaps due to blunders, to negligence, and similar causes. Even our good Homer sometimes dozed off. The greatest among our masters, those most strict with themselves, all have on their conscience some false reference, some unfortunate meaningless remark. It is also useless to insist upon the inadequacies of certain ancient works whose authors could not apply our research methods with the scrupulous precision that has been developed in our day. How many published texts or documents need to be revised, through lack of strict criticism; how many archeological sites have been devastated by the brutal methods of the seekers of yesterday! It is normal that historical research (like every intellectual discipline which develops continuously) should have progressed in the course of time, going from recognized failures to fruitful initiatives.

But this is not very important. It is rather that in historical writing we find a great deal of false history, of pseudo-history, and of material which is not history at all. Because historians

9. *Ibid.*, Bruno de J.-M., p. 5, quoting one of his sources.

were not guided by a critical philosophy, because they did not have a rational and precise theory of historical knowledge (of its conditions and especially its limitations), they became involved in pointless enterprises. At this stage of our inquiry is it really necessary to convince the reader of this fact? If so, we would have to ask him to join us in a re-examination of the entire preceding analysis, chapter by chapter. At every turn we would place the rigorous demands of historical reason side by side with the hesitant and uncertain practice of historians—a hazardous practice that was, and too often remains, theirs. Yet however rigorous this critical balance sheet might be, it would be made out in a spirit wholly different from that destructive game in which scepticism has so often and so readily indulged ever since there has been talk of a crisis in history. (Yet did we not indicate that the denial of history forms just as much as part of the continuing tradition of Western scepticism as does the parallel game of seeking contradictions in the writings of the philosophers?) We would do more than merely show that errors of sometimes enormous proportions can be found in the works of historians, that they contain what are at times crude failures of understanding, immense areas of uncertainty, pretentious judgments and syntheses which are as ambitious as they are illusory. We would underline in every case the logical root of these fallacies, for we are now in a position to do so.

We would discover almost every time that historical writing commits the sin of *hubris*, that it is guilty of a lack of moderation which made it forget the meaning of its limitations, the extent of its dependence, the humbleness of the human condition. Oh, pretentious, excessively ambitious Icarian Clio! How often you crashed to the ground because you were too sure of your wings, because you wanted to fly higher than your powers permitted.

But rather than meting out blame and praise to past his-

torians in this fashion, I prefer to turn toward the history yet
to come. Still intent on completing this treatise on the virtues,
I shall continue to indoctrinate my student: you know now
what reason is capable of in the study of history, under what
conditions it operates and what its confines are. Γνῶθι
σεαυτόν, learn to know yourself as you really are. Do not
let the discovery of your limitations overwhelm you: for
surely you are only human, you are not God. You can
know something of the past, but you cannot know everything.
Be humble, do not succumb to illusions, learn to gauge the
strength of your arm and the length of your days. Graciously
accept the logical and technical limitations which restrict the
scope of your effort, which circumscribe and determine the
area of its application, for they will force themselves upon you
in any event.

There is, for example, a limitation with respect to documents: it is pointless to raise problems that will never be
solved because the available documentation is inadequate,
simply for the sake of raising them. And most important, there
are demands of a logical nature: learn to think, to assure the
coherence and rigor of your reasoning. History has had to
pay very dearly for the historians' indifference to the philosophical problems posed in the course of its elaboration. We
need only think of the large number of naïve fallacies contained in their analyses (such as the excessive, unwarranted
use of the argument *e silentio*). Even when they took such
great pride in having become "scientists," they remained too
purely literary—that is, they remained rhetoricians, and their
expository skill (which is simply the talent of a ropewalker)
served to conceal the inadequacies of rational demonstration.

But there are not merely the demands of logic—philosophy
as a whole has its requirements. The positivist scholar relied
upon his critical method, that instrument which unfailingly
produced certainty. This is why he was so terrified by "meta-

physics," as he put it, a fear which soon extended to any careful thought about man and the world.

I remember that old scholar whom a witty woman complimented in my presence, and not without some irony, on a lengthy and foolish book he had just published. "Ah, Madame, isn't that so! But here, at least, there is no danger of getting lost in ideas!"

Such an illusion is too convenient! We have already seen (p. 161) that there is no true history independent of a philosophy of man and of life. It is from this that it derives its fundamental concepts, its explanatory framework and—first and foremost—the very questions it will ask of the past in the name of its conception of man. The truth of history is a function of the truth of the philosophy used by the historian. Since this is so, how can any one fail to do everything possible to become conscious of these presuppositions, and to elaborate them rationally?

Finally, there is the limitation (or rather the creative dependence) not only on his own doctrinal framework, but on his culture, his orientation, his existential position—on the historian's very being. Particularly among our elders, there are still many historians who feel too reticent about this "Copernican revolution"[10] effected by critical philosophy which now causes the whole system of history to gravitate around the historian's mind as its center and source of energy. It seems to these men that this would question again the value of all the effort expended since the time of Niebuhr and Ranke (and perhaps even since the time of Lenain de Tillemont) by which history was freed from "literature" and

10. The expression, which appears to originate with Lord Acton, has become the *schibboleth* of the new historical spirit: all (Meinecke, Croce, Collingwood) adopt it, without always giving it the same meaning: contrast for example M. Nédoncelle and P. Thévenaz, *L'homme et l'histoire* (*Actes* of the Strasbourg Congress, 1950), pp. 145 and 220.

given a rigorous structure. To reassure them, we need merely persuade them that our new historical spirit does not attempt to reject the ideal of our predecessors, but rather to accept and transcend it. We shall recur once more to an image already familiar to the reader: what we are dealing with is not linear progress (which would be naïvely optimistic) nor the path of a pendulum (which would justify the anxiety of the pessimist), but rather a helicoidal movement: that of a conical spiral which becomes at the same time larger and deeper as it turns.

We only seem to be contesting the axioms of the positivist method—actually, our theory integrates them, if only at that rather superficial level at which they are valid. The problems raised by the new theory of knowledge lie on an altogether different plane: we have moved to another point along the spiral. Positivist ethics as used by the historian were as elementary as his logic: the historian was to be exact, precise, prudent, critical and impartial, and we readily agree to this. But the moment we have seen in what very realistic and profound sense one has to understand the axiom "as you value the worker so you value the work," it will be necessary to become more demanding. The value, by which I mean the truth, of historical studies will be proportionate to the historian's own human resources. The more intelligent and cultivated he is, the more he has himself experienced, and the more open he is to all human values, then the more able will he be to discover things in the past—the richer and truer his knowledge can become. Because everything has at least a potential relevance to any subject of study, the ideal case would be that he know everything—that he have seen and read and remembered all that exists.

The strict conscience of the scholar, satisfied with having checked personally all the items of a bibliography intended to be exhaustive, is a thing of the past. I once knew a great historian who did not hesitate to cross Europe in order to check a reference to some otherwise unavailable pamphlet. One cannot be too thorough. But today we know that the truth of our studies often depends less on some detail of erudition than on an idea left at the back of our mind by something we read in our youth or a reflection resulting from some experience or other.

Let us not abandon the real conditions of research. Because the historian will always be only a man, his competence will be defined by what we have called his personal equation, that is, the structure of his mind, his intellectual capacity, his education—and these have not only their positive aspects, but also and necessarily their limitations. He will know the past to the extent that he shows himself capable of understanding it. Our earlier reflections (Chapter IV) on the necessary role of sympathy in the understanding of documents have a general applicability: the best historian of a period, of a human problem or of a great personality is one who is able to respond with a harmonic resonance to the object he is studying by the very structure of his intelligence, and can echo it through recognizing the full range of vibrations which define it.

If it is the personal qualifications which thus guarantee the richness and the truth of historical knowledge, nothing is more vain or more hypocritical than the attitude imposed on the historian for so long a time—that detached and quasi-impersonal, *unimpassioned* view of his subject: the "objective" manner. This is still fashionable. Sometimes a scholar, who is fond of logical rigor, dares set down his postulates and bring himself into the picture by saying, "Thus I was led to ask myself if . . . I thought that . . ." And criticism immediately becomes indignant and protests against this intrusion of the detestable self.

Here again, of course, there is an elementary level. Historical writing must eschew the style of the pamphlet as it must the style of the panegyric. A certain moderate tone corresponds to the composure, the mastery over existential passion that we have demanded as a guarantee of level-headed judgment. But at a deeper level—and since it has been established that historical truth is a function of the historian's self—it is completely illogical and can become dangerous to think that this variable has been completely eliminated.

Personally, I would go very far along this line of reaction. It has always been understood that an honest scholar had to furnish his readers some means to check the validity of his affirmations: this is the reason for footnotes, for precise references to sources. And it is one of the incontestable merits of positivism to have taught us to become very demanding in matters of detail in such indications. But it is no longer enough for us to guarantee simply that the document utilized has been placed in its proper context. The reader must, it is true, be placed in the position of determining the fact that it has been understood. But he must also be able to see how it has been understood (for every understanding is necessarily subjective, and therefore partial).

It seems to me that honesty in scientific matters demands that the historian make an effort to become aware of the orientation of his thought and then define it. He should give a clear account of his postulates (insofar as that is possible); he should reveal himself in action and allow us to witness the genesis of his work; he should tell us why and how he chose and limited his subject, what he was looking for, and what he discovered. Let him describe his interior itinerary, for every genuinely productive piece of historical research implies a progress in the very soul of the writer: the "encounter with the other" goes from wonder to discovery, for it transforms and thus enriches him. In short, he should furnish us with all the materials that a careful introspection can bring to what, using an expression borrowed from Sartre, I have suggested calling his "existential psychoanalysis."

I am describing here an ideal without concealing from myself that its practical realization will always run into partly insuperable impediments. Most often this examination will be made from too close up. It will not be sufficient to bring out the internal structure of a historical work, for the fundamental postulates, the central option are too deeply rooted in the author's personality to allow for a total self-judgment. Nor, above all, for an immediate one. Experience shows that a few years later the development of his personal evolution will lend him (with the necessary proper perspective) an almost objective detachment that will remain associated with a direct comprehension. But even if it will not suffice for a complete and exact explanation, as long as it is frank and brave this retrospection can supply extremely valuable elements of appreciation.

I have been greatly taken to task for adding to my *St. Augustine* (in re-publishing it after thirteen years) a 90-page *Retractatio*. Yet this was not self-complacency, nor (aside from the choice of the title) a desire to compare myself with my subject. I had intended to follow the example of Dom C. Butler, for I had noted how much the *Afterthoughts* (added to the second edition [1927] as a foreword) contributed to the comprehension and the exact appreciation of his *Western Mysticism*.

When an author cannot himself bring a point to a successful issue, his reader will have to pursue it as far as he can, in order to use the work critically. Undoubtedly, this will not be easy for him! We are cut off from the experimental verification that psychoanalysis in the literal sense finds (or thinks that it finds) in its effective cures. Our "existential psychoanalysis" will often lead to the formulation of hazardous hypotheses. Is it not a question of unearthing secret intentions, all the more determining and decisive the deeper they have been hidden in the unconscious of the researcher? Such hypotheses would take the form of ungracious indiscretions, thoroughly insufferable to any historian subjected to such investigations. This is so true that I do not advise anybody to indulge in such attempts on a living author, for such an "existential" criticism would run the risk of coming within the provisions of the libel law!

At the risk of appearing unrelenting against the memory of Charles Babut, I will mention his case briefly once more. This conscientious historian would certainly have been grievously offended if one had diagnosed in his writings a "Camisard* complex"; yet to say that he expressed through his principal subjects the resentment built up within himself against Catholicism because of the persecutions imposed in the past on his Protestant ancestry remains the most likely assumption—and in the end the least disagreeable one—to explain the patent incomprehension he displays with respect to the orthodox popes and bishops of the fourth and fifth centuries.

But there is no doubt about the legitimacy of such a "psychoanalysis," and for the necessity of it, whatever the practical difficulties of its application. And this is true even though the first attempts that have so far been made may be thought of as caricatures.

The most characteristic one that I can mention is by Daniel Guérin at the end of his two volumes on *La lutte des classes sous la première République: Bourgeois et Bras Nus*, 1793-1797 (1946). Here he reviews the principal historians who preceded him in the study of the revolutionary period,

*Translator's note: Camisards—Protestant insurgents of the Cévennes mountain region in central France who, from 1702 to 1713, rebelled against Louis XIV as a result of the religious persecutions that followed the revocation of the Edict of Nantes (1685). Their name is derived from their peasant smocks, called "camiso" in local dialect.

and strives to pass critical judgment on each, sifting out (as we have suggested here) the theoretical presuppositions of his research.

This very commendable undertaking has been carried out, unfortunately, with the elementary dogmatism and relish for base insult that Western communists—whether Stalinists or (like D. Guérin) Trotzkyites—have so irritatingly borrowed from Soviet rhetoric. It is distressing to hear him say that our respected master A. Mathiez, that fine man, had been (in his capacity as a civil servant) in the pay of the capitalist Republic—was he not rather one of its victims? It is naïve to pretend that all the "bourgeois" historians have something to hide—in strict logic, it should be said that their position necessarily hides something from them—and that the Marxist historian, for his part, has nothing to hide (from his point of view, of course, which is also just as partial itself).

Thus our history can unfold itself freely without having to choose between a blind dogmatism or a disheartened scepticism. History is quite properly open to a truth that may be authentic even though it is dependent on the instruments of thought that have brought about its elaboration. If the reader has kept in mind the stages of our analysis, he will remember that each of the successive elements of our theory of knowledge impressed on history a new boundary while at the same time it set up a possibility. The truth of history in its authenticity is limited on every side by the demands inherent in man's condition. History is true, but this truth is only a partial truth. We are able to know things out of mankind's past, but we are not able to know this past in its entirety. Nor can we know all about any given aspect of the past, whatever that aspect may be. Nothing is more ineffectual than these endeavors to fathom the mystery of the person—than these historians who judge their heroes, mistaking themselves for the Eternal.)

It follows from all this, in particular, that a universal history is theoretically impossible (the elementary level of the textbook excepted, of course). I am referring to an authentic history that would make the pretension to know Amenophis IV as directly and as thoroughly as it would understand Queen Victoria—and to know all that it is possible to understand about everybody. There is no one man capable of gathering in the microcosm of his knowledge the macrocosm of this "equivocal and inexhaustible" matter, nor would a collective synthesis in its turn overcome the difficulty.

We must first put to one side the fact that history is confined to the zone enlightened by intelligible documents, and reaches back only over the last few millenia. It will always be ignorant of the long childhood of pre-history during which humanity took decisive options on its future. Even ignoring this, it follows from what we were saying that a philosophy of history drawn from experience is an impossibility. We discover that we can never have a history built on a scientific foundation, if the term is preferred—by which I mean a doctrine, in the classical sense, pretending to bring out the meaning or the general laws of humanity's advance through time.

CHAPTER X

The Usefulness of History

As the limited, incomplete nature of historical truth (and therefore of history itself) becomes more apparent, the question so often discussed by our predecessors—without a satisfactory resolution—imposes itself with ever greater urgency. In what sense is history useful? What role should it assume in our culture?

Our reply will be qualified, as well as complex, for history in fact serves several ends, and at several levels of being. Invoking once more the now familiar image of the conical spiral, I will say first that the process of exploring the past does not always develop in the same depth nor to the same extent. We must return to the two distinctions sketched in Chapter VIII relating to existential value. The two questions are linked together, or we might better say that basically they are one: that is useful which is shown to be given weight in some way by the existential factor—but history may be so weighted in many different ways and to different degrees.

True, we have agreed with Heidegger and all existentialism that "there is no history except in and through the historicity of the historian." That is, the past can only be known if it is brought in some way into a relationship with our existence. But we must immediately add this further (and to us, fundamental) qualification: if the past matters to us, this contact may sometimes be made from a great distance and in a very indirect fashion—at the cost, as Plato was fond of saying, of a "long detour," μακρὰ ἡ περίοδος.

Is it not true that the historian may be obsessed by his involvement in change, and seek to understand his present situation only to direct his very next action? I am distressed by the excesses to which an egocentric notion such as Dilthey's may lead, organizing, as he does, the entire concept of history from the starting point and focus of the knowledge of the ego. On the contrary, we have found that historical knowledge is based on a dialectic between the Self and the Other, necessarily implying an essential element of otherness.

In the very narrowest perspective, history may aim at nothing but the comprehension of my historical situation by reconstructing the line, in a genealogical sense, of my antecedents. Obviously, in this case, I come to know these previous stages, these ancestors—even these immediate predecessors through an autobiography of my self of yesterday. Yet I also know them as different (since past), and as irreducibly other than that present self of mine which is straining toward the future.

Thus historical knowledge always implies a detour, a circuitous route. It supposes an initial centrifugal movement,[1] an *epokhè*, a suspension of my most urgent existential preoccupations, a movement outside myself, an exile, a discovery and an encounter with the other.

It is here that it is important to distinguish levels and scope. In its most superficial form, history will appear to the moralist as the result of simple curiosity. It is, first of all, the discovery of sheer otherness. In those days, in that country, men lived who were this or that. They spoke such a language, had a certain type of social organization, practiced such and such techniques of production; such was their clothing, their cooking.

First there is what might be called the elementary level,

1. No one has better emphasized this point than M. Nédoncelle, in the previously cited article in *L'homme et l'histoire*, p. 145.

that of the child learning for the first time in primary school: "In the past, our country was called Gaul." Then, on a secondary level, there is the person discovering the Pharaonic civilization. And the same thing also exists on a higher plane: the other day I was listening to Mr. Charles Virolleaud lecture at the Academie des Inscriptions on the results of Russian excavations at Kamir-Blour in Armenia. We discover the existence of the kingdom of Urartu with the same curiosity that our children discover the Gauls.

This is the equivalent of the botanist's effort to observe and classify the different species which comprise the flora of a newly explored region: he must first know that they exist and what they are before being able to see the really interesting problems they create.

As long as it remains on this first level, history will always be open to the moralist's severe charge of idle curiosity, whether he be St. Augustine, Descartes or (the heir to them both) Bossuet:

". . . This insatiable greed to know history! If it aims to derive some useful example for human life, well and good. One can bear with it and even praise it, provided that some sobriety is brought to this research. But if, as is the case with most curious people, the end is merely to feast the imagination on vain objects, what is more useless than to linger over what no longer exists, than to seek out all the follies that have passed through a mortal's head, than to recall with so much care the images that God destroyed in his holy city—the shadows that he dispersed, vanity's entire apparatus, that plunges back into the nothingness from which it came?"[2]

When it is a question of practical morality, we must always distinguish each specific case. As is evident from the idle

2. "Traité de la Concupiscence," Chap. VIII, cited by P. Mesnard, *L'esprit cartésien, est-il compatible avec le sens de l'histoire?*, same collection, p. 275.

17

questions that readers address to popular magazines specializing in this sort of question, there certainly exists a peripheral zone where historical knowledge sinks into mere vanity. But Augustinianism too, in the name of the seriousness of existence and our stake in it, can sink into a narrow and crass utilitarianism. Human success lies in a balance between opposing demands that is difficult to achieve and always unstable. In culture, health and wealth, commitment and breadth of views are not always compatible.

We have all met those timorous educators who stingily measure out the mind's nourishment. They worry about everything that might trouble it or lead it into temptation, but they are not sufficiently concerned that a plant raised in a closed vase may wilt.

If we consult the psychologist, he will declare that curiosity (no matter how gratuitous it may appear) implies an existential value at its core. This, of course (the moral problem remains untouched), may perfectly well be morbid—escapism, daydreaming, the need to have fantasies that we are someone else, or the need to defy another person.

Consequently, even if history were only the "aesthetic contemplation of singularities"[3] as it has sometimes been defined, it would not be useless or without a cultural function. I should like to stress this specifically aesthetic character. We need think about it for only a moment to see the analogy that exists between the matter of history and the subjects—themes, characters, situations—at work in epic, tragic, dramatic, romantic, or comic literature. Viewed from this angle, history is a grab bag of good stories to tell, a magnificent collection of inexhaustible richness.

Is there a Racinean tragedy that compares, in the intensity and nobility of its passion, to the true story of Heloise's

3. The phrase is Raymond Aron's, *La philosophie critique*, p. 32, summarizing Dilthey's critique of this concept.

loves? For romantic adventure, what could be better than that of King Giannino, the Sienese merchant who was persuaded by Cola di Rienzi that he was King John I of France, the posthumous son of Louis X the Headstrong, deprived of his heritage by his uncle, Philip V? What detective story is equal in suspense to a real espionage story such as the "Cicero Affair" in Ankara during the last war?

There is more than an analogy here. It is always surprising to realize the role historical knowledge has played in world literature as ferment to the creative imagination, from Homer to our own time.

Roger Martin du Gard would never have conceived of the dénouement of *Summer, 1914* if he had not heard of the historical suicide of Lauro de Bosis, the young Italian who flew over Rome in 1932 or 1933 distributing anti-Fascist tracts, and died in the venture.[4]

And what about Balzac? Without Vidocq we would not have Vautrin, nor *A Shadowy Affair* without the kidnaping of Senator Clément de Ris (which occurred in October, 1800), and Esther Gobseck's liaison with Lucien de Rubempré borrows one of its most human episodes from Juliette Drouet's affair with Hugo. This characteristic is not peculiar to realistic novelists; Stendhal's imagination would never have conceived *The Charterhouse of Parma* if it had not been sparked by an old Roman chronicle.

These comparisons will help us become aware of another, and more profound, function of historical knowledge. It is one that theoreticians have too often neglected or dismissed summarily. We have by no means said everything once the term "aesthetic value" has been pronounced. True, we often study history as we read Balzac. But what mind is superficial enough to dare claim that the reading of Balzac is not

4. R. Rolland, *Introduction to* (the private edition of) *Lauro de Bosis' Icare,* in *Europe,* vol. XXXII (1933), pp. 5-15.

weighted with existential seriousness? In both cases, we derive a lesson in humanity from our experience. In reply to the moralist whose narrow intransigence is founded on ignorance, the lover of literature will join the historian in defending the legitimacy and, above all, the fruitfulness of this human experience. Whether it is real or fictitious, and even if vicarious, it represents a true broadening of my personal experience, my experience with man. Much more surely than through literature (whose humanity is always somewhat uncertain), knowledge of history extends—in practically unlimited measure—my knowledge of man in all his many-sided reality, in his infinite capacities, well beyond the necessarily narrow confines of my own personal experience.

And let it be clearly understood that when we say "man" we mean everything that reflects human nature in its personal aspects as well as in its collective manifestations. History studies and knows Roman civilization and the culture of antiquity as well as Cicero's personality.

We study history as we read literature seriously, and as we seek above all to meet and know men in life —"in order to learn what we did not know and what would be practically impossible to find out by ourselves without being precisely the man who is teaching it to us. When we have known and understood him, we have become that man, and we know what he knows. Even if he has lived long ago and far away, we henceforth possess his experience with man and with life."[5]

Similarly, I will assign to history, as one of its essential functions, the enrichment of my internal universe by re-capturing cultural values salvaged from the past.

By the deliberately vague term "cultural value" we will signify, in the most general possible fashion, all that we may know and understand of the true, the beautiful, and the real

5. This paraphrases a fine page of literary criticism by my late friend Gouverneur Paulding, *The Reporter*, December 11, 1951, p. 39.

in the domain of human life. We will let it extend from the most elementary products of civilization (any artifact whatever, a tool or instrument, a work of art, a concept, a feeling) to the vastest syntheses, those "ideological superstructures" bequeathed to us by great civilizations organizing themselves about a collective ideal.

We discover these values first under the category of the Other, meeting them as already existing among men of the past, in the bosom of lost societies or civilizations. But to the extent that we are capable of grasping and understanding them, they again come to life in us. In a sense, they acquire a new reality and a second historical existence, in the womb of the historian's thought and in the contemporary culture to which he reintroduces them. The historian seems to me comparable to a man who, without fear of wasting time (this is *epokhè*), leisurely pokes the ashes of the past. This is literally true in looking for papyrus, when we poke around the heaps of *sebakh* (household refuse) heaped up at the gates of the large towns of Greek and Roman Egypt and find there drachmas left by oversight or golden staters struck in the king's likeness, as fresh and shining as if they were newly minted.

It is not necessary to waste time in demonstrating how real this recovery is—so obvious, for example, in the domain of the history of philosophy or the history of art. Each may judge for himself, in considering his own artistic experience, the contribution of history to the enrichment of our aesthetic consciousness and to the deepening of our taste.

Let us take music (to say nothing of the plastic arts, where Malraux is quite sufficient). Compare the narrowness of the repertory to which a connoisseur like Stendhal was restricted (generally, from Mozart to Rossini) to our present broad range of choice. During my childhood, Bach still appeared to be at the dividing line between "ancient" and "modern" music;

today, he is at the center of a repertory which has increased immeasurably. We have recovered all the polyphonic music of the Renaissance, and its medieval origins, the melodies of the troubadors and the Minnesingers, to say nothing of all the composers who have emerged from little-known periods. (For example, in French music of the classical period we used to pass from Lully to Rameau, but now we have discovered Charpentier, and Lalande, among others.)

The improvement has not been in quantity alone. Thus, the magnificent progress achieved in Greek archeology has permitted us to make a much more refined aesthetic judgment of classical sculpture. Compare our situation to Winckelmann's. He had at his disposal only a vague and synthetic image of "Antiquity"—in which the Greek and the Roman, the highest forms of art and the handicrafts of the provincial Pompeian decorators, were jumbled together—an incongruous and ambiguous general ensemble of highly dubious value.

Having formulated them once myself,[6] I am certainly not unaware of the reproaches one might make, as Nietzsche did, of abuses in the history of art, and of the resulting despondency of the artist and art lover. In extreme cases, burdened down with erudition, they become incapable of feeling and substitute historical judgments for a truly aesthetic experience. A fine work of art is no longer liked or appreciated for its excellence. An arch is located in the development of Burgundian Gothic; the role of Italian or Flemish influence is determined for this one, particular eighteenth-century French painting. For the sake of understanding all, we finally accept everything. Beauty and ugliness, greatness and decadance no longer exist. We pass from Praxiteles to Samaritan or Gothic jewelery, embellished with some spirals and colored stones set in a milled edge. We say there is classic art and there is

6. In a youthful book, *Fondements d'une culture chrétienne* (1934), pp. 50–51.

baroque art. We say that Louis XIV, even he, had taste because he had a taste for a particular kind of thing, even though he exiled the Swiss to the other side of their ornamental lake after having Giradon touch up the unreal and grandiloquent statue sculptured for him by Bernini.

Let us limit the extent of these criticisms: the work of art does not solely concern the history of art. In an attempt at total comprehension, history seizes on all the values to which it is a witness, and some of these values are not of an aesthetic order.

So it is for the symbolic values of iconography. If we study the last of Emile Mâle's great syntheses, *Religious Art After the Council of Trent,* we will learn to take an interest in works which are artistically very mediocre, such as scenes of martyrdom painted by Pomarancio in San Stefano Rotundo, because these dreadful daubings are shown to be very significant evidence of the missionary preoccupations of the Church of the Counter-Reformation. We will deposit these frescoes in the file for religious history. In other cases it will be technological, economic, or social history—even the history of civilization—that will benefit. This desecration may scandalize the artist, but the historian must take advantage of his opportunities where he finds them.

I will not deny that history may have been or may still be put to bad use in this domain, as in many others. For my part, I willingly repeat here the harsh but pertinent remarks of Nietzsche,[7] for whom history could be tolerated only by strong personalities; it disintegrated the weak ones, by throwing their sensibility and aesthetic judgment into confusion. It is they who (for want of self-assurance) go to the history of art for advice: How should I feel, understand, judge, admire? I think I have sufficiently taught my disciples a sense of the limitations of our discipline, and the humility they necessitate.

7. *Considérations inactuelles,* II, §5, French translation, pp. 176–178.

I do not have to prove to them how naïve and disheartening
it is to ask the historian in this way to resolve the artistic
problem—the religious problem, or any other of the great
human problems. It is not for him to replace the aesthetician,
the art critic, the connoisseur or the artist. It is incumbent
on them to make the original judgment which can not be
reduced to any other form of knowledge. It is this that recognizes the work of art's properly aesthetic value, and bestows
its reality on it.

But granting this, the historian sees that he is still needed
to draft some of the decrees of this judgment. I am quite
impressed to see that this subordinate but often indispensable
role is recognized by those very people who are the most
resistant to history's possible encroachments, the most preoccupied with safeguarding the autonomy of the artistic experience, the most hostile to the pettiness of erudite research.
Such a man is our old master, Bernard Berenson. No doubt
the true connoisseur, the artist, is the person who loves a
painting for itself, as one loves a friend, or a child—a person.[8]
But the moment he wishes to deepen this love, he must really
seek to know its object as it is—as it really is—to avoid the
risk of loving a vain phantom in its name. (The reader will
again recognize here our ideal of affection founded on knowledge and the rejection of any illusion.) But from that point
on, how could he avoid, for example, questions of date and
attribution that are decisive for his judgment? However
vexing it may be to have his judgment depend on extrinsic
facts, at this point the artist must call the historian and the
scholar back, after so disdainfully dismissing them.

We see the work of Georges de la Tour, formerly dispersed
among the schools of Le Nain, Zurbaran, Caravaggio and
Rembrandt, in such a new light now that it has at last been

8. Bernard Berenson, *Aesthetics, Ethics, and History* (1948), French
translation, pp. 130, 132; cf. 120, 226.

reassembled and restored to its rightful creator! It is enough to page through the notes of F. G. Pariset's monumental monograph[9] on this restitution to establish the role played by archival holdings, civic documents, account books, and similar items.

Lanzo del Vasto laughed haughtily at those good scholars (like P. Coirault) who were striving so patiently to rediscover the artistic sources (operatic arias, Pont Neuf songs) of our popular songs—"wasted work!"[10] But when we see the aged Herder take the academician Moncrif's mediocre pastiches in the troubador style (1750) for authentically popular art, sprung from the depths of the collective unconscious, or when Lesseur (Berlioz' master) sees in the aria of *Que ne suis-je la fougère?* (a romance from the close of the seventeenth century) a classical air of the early Eastern Church, borrowed by the first Christians from the Hebrews—how can we help laughing? "And that is the reason," to cite Berenson again, "why it is important that attributions be very sure."[11]

In the light of what has gone before, we can clarify a bit the much more complex case of the history of philosophy. In fact we can speak more generally of the history of thought, because "positive theology"[12] poses problems that are largely analogous. Here again no doubt we must denounce the possible misuse of history; but perhaps in an even more urgent fashion, we should disclaim the distortions and caricatures proffered in history's name.

As practiced by philosophers generally, the history of philosophy is a cause of perpetual irritation to the ordinary historian. He sees the past lose its concrete reality in their

9. *Georges de la Tour* (1948).

10. Lanza del Vasto, Preface to his *Chansonnier populaire* (1947); cf. my *Livre des chansons*, pp. 26, 46, 80.

11. Berenson, *op. cit.*, p. 225.

12. See the profound methodological observations of R. Laurentin, *Marie, l'Église et le sacerdoce*, vol. II (1953), pp. 17–18.

hands, and thought becoming impersonal, even timeless. For many philosophers, history (properly speaking) does not exist. There is only the immense storehouse of *philosophia perennis*. From this arsenal today's thinker may extract an assortment of concepts or arguments, chosen from among all those that are lying about side by side.

Even when they speak of a Platonic idea, or of Saint Anselm's argument, it means no more than saying "Pythagorean theorem" or "Carnot's principle." These are just traditional labels to which vague sentiments of homage are attached. They are not really examples of historical awareness.

For others, history is a pretext, a mask (if not actually a false nose). Like Descartes, at the moment of stepping out into the glare of the world's lighted stage, the philosopher seems to say: *larvatus prodeo*! He does not dare or does not desire to expose his own thoughts in his own name; but expresses them, a little fraudulently, in the name of someone whose authority is unquestioned.

It would be very easy to give examples. In the days when the positivist dictatorship prevailed among us, metaphysics dared not venture into the open, and history—quite bad history—served as a refuge for every infamous dogmatism. Yet this way of proceeding can be inspired by the most complicated motives, as may be seen from the example of Plato, which has already been given (p. 142). And with him there are all the "little Socrates" who chose to express themselves in their *Dialogues* through the mouth of their master.

Finally, in the name of a history of philosophy we are often rather ingenuously offered what is in reality a philosophy of history (considered from the point of view of thought). Solidly entrenched behind his doctrinal positions, the philosopher throws a glance down the gallery of his great predecessors and draws up a genealogical table in which is to be found the genesis of his own philosophy. It is rather like the paleontologist who discovers the antecedents of living beings by means of a series of fossils.) He shows the gradual development from the forerunner of long ago to his direct sources of inspiration. He underlines all the obstacles which stood for a long time in the way of the triumph of truth, and analyzes the errors which momentarily delayed or compromised it. Such a reconstitution is an obligation for all thought which wishes to be honest, no doubt. It must consider how it stands in relation to all previous attempts; it must classify the cultural heritage in which it finds itself by relating this to itself; and most especially it must prove its own criterion of truth through giving an account of the errors by which previous philosophers were drawn away from this truth. But we cannot be under any illusions as to the demonstrative value of such a retrospective view: philosophy triumphs without any effort, because it judges the comportment of the other in function of its own principles. Our theory of knowledge has demonstrated this mechanism: here more than ever it may be said that "theory comes before history"—any given philosophy may be classified, in comparison to my own, as either a predecessor or an opponent. But this is not really history. History begins only where the historian forgets himself enough to come out of himself and go forward, open-minded, toward the discovery and the encounter with the other.

Philosophy offers us a major case of the dangers of the existential obsession. We have already denounced this in Chapter VIII. More than any one else, the philosopher is the victim of his own problem, and finds it difficult to drag himself away from it and open his mind to the thought of the Other. And yet the seriousness and the reality of history—and its fertility—are only to be obtained at this price.

I would like to give a personal example, as usual. Moved by a purely historical curiosity, I once studied the Augustinian treatise *de Musica,* which is a disconcerting work the first time it is read and is often neglected. Its study has its place in a survey of the ancient origins of the medieval cycle of the Seven Liberal Arts. While reading it, I was most struck by the fact that Saint Augustine used the word *musica* to denominate not the art which we call "music," but the science of its mathematical acoustical and rhythmic bases. The commentary I gave[13] insisted that this was a misconception which should be avoided, and did not admit that the treatise in question might contain anything of use to the present-day musician.

A few years later I happened to draw up for myself a theory of musical art.[14] I realized after a while, without grasping it entirely in the beginning, that the doctrine which I formulated as the truth (and for which I assumed responsibility as an aesthetician) was nothing more than the doctrine of Saint Augustine himself. It had demonstrated its own validity in this field, needing only some slight transpositions and a few adaptations (which I had made unconsciously).

I am convinced (and the unfortunate experience of certain of my predecessors[15] proves it) that I would never have had this unlooked-for advantage if I had read Saint Augustine with a less open mind, or if I had been too eager to question it about present-day musical problems.

Thus in order to have a genuine history of philosophy we must convert the philosopher to the idea of the historical adventure. We must persuade him that he has both a right

13. In *Saint Augustin et la fin de la culture antique* (1938), notably pp. 199–204.

14. *Traité de la musique selon l'esprit de Saint Augustin* (1942).

15. J. Huré, *Saint Augustin musicien* (1924) who, for example, reading in the *Confessions* the word "psaltery" (it is a question of the psalter), translates it by *psaltérion:* such misinterpretations, based on "wishful thinking" are real "ineffectual acts" in the Freudian sense of the term!

and a duty to take a few days off, "a legitimate holiday."[16] During this time he should allow himself the curiosity necessary to discover other philosophies. It has sometimes been tried by adopting a moral point of view: in the name of the virtue of *docilitas*—which is none other than the fundamental virtue of humility applied to things of the mind. The philosopher in search of truth should begin by asking himself whether others have not by chance discovered something of it ahead of him. But here again we shut ourselves into a prejudiced perspective. I prefer to emphasize another argument: truth is not the only predicate which can define a doctrine. There are thoughts which though true are narrow, poor, strict, barbarous. Historical culture is not an instrument of truth, properly speaking, but a factor of culture.

I can be understood more easily if I make a comparison. Paleography, epigraphy, numismatics and other studies of this type are not sufficient unto themselves (the paleographer who is only that and no more has a very small mind), but offer themselves humbly as sciences auxiliary to history. And it is in the same way, I will say, that history appears as an auxiliary science of thought for the philosopher. In itself it is not all-sufficient, but it is careless not to make use of its services. History teaches the philosopher that he must enlarge his horizons, become more aware of the complexity of problems and of their implications; it proposes to him solutions—or objections—that he might not have imagined or foreseen. It rescues him from the inevitable narrowness that isolation implies, and integrates him into the vast society of minds by means of a constantly enriching dialogue.

That is what Seneca expressed in a fine page, dear to the humanist: "No century is forbidden to us: [through history] the force of our mind may go beyond the boundaries of the weakness of the solitary man: *egredi humanae imbecillitatis*

16. G. J. Renier, *History: Its Purpose and Method*, p. 31.

angustias. We can dispute with Socrates, doubt with Carneades, enjoy the tranquility of Epicurus, with the Stoics conquer human nature, and bypass it with the Cynics. Since the structure of being (*rerum natura*) permits us to enter into communion with all the past, why not tear ourselves away from the narrow limits of our primary temporality and share with the finest minds these magnificent and eternal truths" *quae immensa, quae aeterna sunt?*[17]

Against this last idea certain of my readers will protest. Is this not an anti-historical way of using history? Will we not find here again that false *philosophia perennis* in which, in a sham décor of the Champs-Elysées, Socrates in tunic and barefooted, Descartes in Louis XIII lace, Kant in powdered wig, and Comte in formal black have a discussion in which they each advance against the others disincarnated arguments? But I reply: No. If I am truly a historian, I seize each of these doctrines (and their truth—eternal in itself) in its concrete historicity, within the web of that human reality which is situated in space and in time. I take them in their chronological order and (what is more) in the civilization, in the culture, in the political, economic, and social context which was that of the men Socrates, Descartes, Kant or Auguste Comte. "We have treasure in earthen vessels."[18] Philosophical truth—and all truth (the revealed truth of religious faith is transmitted to me through a Church, a tradition, a Book: *fides ex auditu*)—does not come to us in the form of bits of raw metal in the pure state, but as an alloy or in combination with a human reality.

Our comprehension of a doctrine will be all the more authentic and the more profound to the extent that we grasp it better within the structure of its original reality. We may always have the right to abstract it from this complex, but

17. *De breuitate vitae*, 14, 1–2.
18. 2 Corinthians 4:7.

indeed the surgical operation is so delicate that many of the fine points and the most delicate nuances—those in which the truth resides—risks being damaged or destroyed in the course of the operation.

What progress there is from the *Système d'Aristote* by Hamelin to Werner Jaeger's *Aristotle*. In this work we follow the thought as it is being born; we see it developing and revealing itself through literary forms and on various occasions. For here again the historian puts his preliminary question to the too systematic mind of a Hamelin: about this System, what do you know and how do you know it?

At this point, I imagine, it will be the philosophers who will be upset, should they be listening: "Given (such) a history of philosophies—is there still a question of philosophy?"[19] If we insert the thought too intimately into the life of the men who have conceived it, shall we not dissolve the truth (and hence the reality of the thought) in the temporal flux, and fall into the relativism of *Historismus?* Here we reach that profound reticence (which we have so often observed) of true philosophers in regard to history.

But what shall we say about the theologians! In their eyes you will easily be viewed as a "relativist" if by any chance you are too keenly interested in the past stages of theology— in Origen for instance, or St. Maximus the Confessor, or even St. Thomas, if you go so far as to insist on the fact that he lived in the thirteenth century.

In this sometimes ridiculous, sometimes dramatic[20] misunderstanding, certainly all the faults are not on the side of the historians. If the philosopher dislikes Clio's interference, it is often because she tears him away from his comfortable dogmatism, all ignorance and naïveté. He reproaches her

19. H. Gouhier, *L'histoire et sa philosophie* (1952), p. 138.
20. As much as by H. Gouhier, I am inspired here by P. Ricoeur, in *Offener Horizont (Festchrift für Karl Jaspers,* Munich, 1953), pp. 110–125; French text in *Histoire et Vérité* (1955).

with endlessly complicating problems instead of trying to solve them. But, as we have seen, the mission and the fruitfulness of history consists precisely in constantly recalling: "There are more things in heaven and earth—in the thought of your predecessors—than can at first be imagined by your simple philosophy." She makes us understand that nothing is simple. Confronted by two doctrinal positions which appear to clash head on, the first reaction of the philosopher will be expressed in brutal terms: "If one is true and the other contradicts it, then the second must be false." The historian, an unexpected heir to this situation, will endeavor to seize the original intention of these two thoughts from within, and will often be led to suggest that there is no contradiction, properly speaking, "because it is clear that if these two doctrines are worked out according to two quite different original preoccupations, they will never envisage the same problems from the same viewpoint, and consequently the one will never reply to the precise question posed by the other"; hence, "they can neither exclude nor coincide with each other."[21]

All this is certainly not designed for calming our adversary, the dogmatist. If the effort of disinterested sympathy (in which we have recognized the specific quality of the true historian) causes the mere possibility of a contradiction to disappear, what will become of the notion of absolute Truth? If my effort of comprehension succeeds in recomposing each doctrine according to the perspective in which it appeared as true to its author, it will also appear to me in the same light of truth again—at least as long as I will allow myself to look at it in that perspective. If I succeed in seeing the problem of salvation as Saint Augustine saw it, the mystery of predestination will

21. E. Gilson in the conclusion of his *Philosophy of Saint Bonaventure*, third edition (1953) draws a parallel between Saint Bonaventure and Saint Thomas.

cease to scandalize me, and I will tend to admit even its most extreme consequences. But on the contrary, if I adopt the theory of Pelagius or that of Julien d'Éclane, here I am once more about to become a Pelagian. The peril is not an imaginary one. Let us remember the formulas, so generous but so imprudent, which Péguy used in his *Bar-Cochebas*:

"But the whole assembly of the great metaphysicians of history, who live on in the memory of humanity, must appear again . . . and a gathering of all the great peoples and races of the earth—in a word, an ensemble of all the great cultures; we must call up a people of languages, a concert of voices that often (?) harmonize and sometimes (!) are in dissonance, but which are heard again and again, forever." And earlier, criticizing the philosophy of history which locates successive doctrines according to a linear and continuous progression and shows that they are abolished one after the other, "surpassed" by a progressive movement: "It does not seem that any man—nor any humanity . . . can ever intelligently boast of having surpassed Plato." Or again: "A mind which begins to *surpass* a philosophy is quite simply a soul which is beginning to fall out of harmony with the tone and the rhythm, the language and the resonance of that philosophy. . . ." Then follows the magnificent eulogy of Hypatia, that soul "so perfectly attuned to the Platonic soul . . . and to the Hellenic soul generally . . ., that . . . when everyone, an entire world, was in discord . . . she alone remained attuned even unto death."[22]

It is now the historian who seems to speak the impious word, *Larvatus prodeo*, and who comes forward in a mask. In what we might term the arsenal of thought, he can borrow at his every whim this or that new mask, or some cast-off

22. *Cahiers de la Quinzaine*, of February 2, 1907, text reproduced in the *Morceaux choisis* (posthumous), *Prose*, pp. 173–174, 159, 165–166, 167.

costume ("défroque"),[23] and each time play the role perfectly as a good actor—until he is taken in by his own acting. The temptation is great. Once an interest in historical research has been aroused, the philosopher runs the risk of being carried away (by curiosity, laziness, or a truly humble devotion to some great master of former days)—and so may forget his mission, his personal vocation, *his* problem. He holds back, restricting his ambition little by little, in order to reconstruct another philosopher's teaching, and no longer dares think for himself in his own name. In the end, the perfect historian of philosophy identifies himself with that Other whom he knows so well. He no longer thinks, he rethinks. He plays (the game may be played seriously without ceasing to be a game) at contemplating the world and life "through the other's glass," and with his eyes. He becomes Plato, Plotinus, or Saint Thomas . . . and no longer is himself.

There is a simple remedy once the disease has been diagnosed. He must keep alive in himself an awareness of the existential engagement of the thought, and he must constantly strengthen and renew this awareness. He must not passively allow himself to be invaded by that foreign personality, nor accept this other man's principles or viewpoint as one accepts the rules for bridge or chess. In that dialectic, he must not allow his own self to be suffocated by the other, he must not cease to exist, he must always be someone.

This is where the true danger that history presents lies in wait for the philosopher: in dilettantism—not in relativism. It is not historical experience that is responsible for the ravages of *Historismus,* wherever they may be found, but it is rather an internal disease of philosophic thought that has lost the sense of Truth. Historicist relativism (everything is true only for a time—its time) is the inevitable response to

23. To speak like Marx, excellently commented upon by G. Duveau, in *L'homme et l'histoire* (*Actes* of the Strasbourg Congress), pp. 74–75.

a problem whose wrongly stated terms have been dictated by an already existing, fundamental scepticism. If the philosopher abandons his elaboration of a table of truth-values (for it is also a criterion of past truth), if he adventures lightly into the thickets of the past, how can history lead him to discover— how can it reveal to him—what he was not able to see in his own existential situation?

If he is resolved not to be unfaithful to his vocation, the real philosopher must first of all confront the difficult problem of Truth on the genuinely philosophical level. When he has resolved it (and if he does not resolve it, no one can do it for him), he can then confront the diversity of the past without danger. The differences between the philosophers, his predecessors, will not intimidate him any more than the criticisms of his contemporaries, for the true philosopher is one who knows that he has seized the truth—sure of his position, he is resigned (if necessary) to be right even in the face of or against all others.

Here I will invoke the fable of the troubadour Peire Cardenal, *Una ciutatz fo, no sai cals . . .*: Once there was a city in which all the citizens went mad after an accident, except one of them: "Great is his surprise to see them thus, but even greater is theirs to see him still sane; it is he whom they take for a madman . . . This fable is the image of the world, which is this city full of madmen." If he too is ever alone, the philosopher should know how to resist the *consensus* of the deranged!

If a man does not abandon his personality, he is not unarmed when he confronts history. He reacts to his predecessors as he does to his contemporaries. He weighs their reasons and judges, accepts them or rejects them. But his thought emerges from the dialogue enriched by that confrontation (or reinforced, if it has not been altered), and

strengthened through the trial he has accepted and victo-
riously overcome.

I will invoke once more the testimony of Étienne Gilson,
who is a fine example of a historian who was able to remain
a philosopher. It is no secret that his dogmatism, far from
fading out and being diluted by a wider and wider historical
experience, has rather had a tendency to assert itself with
great clarity and intransigence. In responding to a remark
I made on the peril of becoming a Pelagian, he wrote me[24]:
"I believe it to be a real danger all the more willingly inasmuch
as I remember how dazzled I was when I discovered the
meaning of that doctrine: not a denial of grace, but an
insistence that free will is itself the grace. *Falsa sunt quae
dicitis,* yes; *nova,* again yes; but *pulchra,* yes, as well. The
risk must be run if one wishes his certitude to be the result
of a choice and not ignorance . . ."

The peril envisioned will be overcome if each one per-
forms his own task well (philosopher as well as historian),
and carries it out to the very end. Neither do I wish to hide
the historian's shortcomings.

Reacting to what I have said (p. 265 f.) concerning the perpetual annoyance that the philosopher causes us, Emile
Bréhier stopped me one day in a corridor of the Sorbonne
and said, pleasantly but ironically, "You know, Marrou, the
historian annoys the philosopher just as often as the philosopher annoys the historian"—and it is easy to understand
why.

Through a fear of depersonalizing his hero when studying
a philosopher, a thinker, the historian will insist enthusiasti-
cally on the irreducible difference that distinguishes him from
every other philosopher. As he is anxious to grasp his object
in its concrete reality, he will tend to overemphasize too
easily whatever goes to form his individuality. And it is very

24. In a letter of September 26, 1949.

true that the "continuity of the Platonic tradition"[25] can never be reduced to any kind of permanent abstract Platonism, defined as a pure essence that passed from hand to hand, unaltered. It is incarnated in the series of particular personalities (who are in the final analysis incomparable): Plato, Plotinus, Porphyry and on down through Giordano Bruno and Marsilio Ficino.

For example, in order to grasp the originality that is responsible for the fact that the "lack of faith" of Rabelais is not that of a Lucian, a Voltaire or an Anatole France, the historian will try to "explain" them—that is to say, to understand their mentality, their way of thinking and of feeling—as a function of the cultural and social milieu which formed them.

I have just quoted Lucien Febvre[26]: somewhere he says that Calvin and "the character of a totally gratuitous and unconditional gift which the granting of grace to the chosen assumes (in his writings)" can be compared with the royal conception of justice and of royal "grace" that was in effect in France in the sixteenth century: "Let us recall any account of that time; the guilty man is kneeling, blindfolded, his head on the block . . . the man in red has already brandished his fearsome naked blade . . . And at that precise moment a horseman dashes into the square waving a parchment . . . grace . . . grace! The very word. For the king grants his grace. He does not take any merit into account. Such is the God of Calvin."[27]

Now here is something alive, something "true." The historian smiles with pleasure—but what exactly is the value of

25. R. Klibansky, *The Continuity of the Platonic Tradition During the Middle Age,* I (London, 1950).

26. We recall the title of his book: *Le problème de l'incroyance au XVIème siècle, la religion de Rabelais* (2nd edition, 1947).

27. *Combats pour l'histoire,* pp. 227–228 (republished from the *Annales d'Histoire sociale,* vol. III, 1941).

such approximations? Let us pass over all the fundamental ambiguity in such a comparison. (Is it Calvin who has been subjected to the influence of the justice of his day or rather is it not this very justice that has produced a theological and moral climate to which Calvin is not the only witness?) We must insist at least once more (p. 204) upon the "facile" and the arbitrary element in such a type of explanation.

In imitation of L. Febvre, I might undertake to explain for you the harshness of the theory of predestination as seen by St. Augustine, and his indifference to the inequality of the lot between the Chosen and the Damned by the social climate of ancient slavery. But I could just as well see there a consequence of his physiological constitution—of the distress of the asthmatic that apparently he once was.[28] On the other hand I might embark in the psychoanalyst's vessel, and talk to you of his "Oedipus." Of course that is not all: there is still the racial hypothesis, which would explain the thing to you by the traditions of the Berbers. And how many other possibilities!

But most important, though such hypotheses take into account the *how,* and possibly (let's be optimistic) the *why,* they can never explain the *Quid* of the thought. That cannot be reduced to the empirical conditions which accompanied and, if you like, conditioned its appearance. Whatever may be the reasons that led Calvin to formulate his doctrine, whatever were the ways and means which brought him to that day, Calvinism exists and has an internal coherence, a meaning, a value—a degree of truth which the thinker (here the theologian rather than the philosopher, it matters little) must work out. And what goes to prove all of this is the fact that

28. Cf. P. Alfaric, *L'évolution intellectuelle de saint Augustin,* vol. I, 1918, p. 40. But opposing, Dr. B. Legewie, "Die körperliche Konstitution und die Krankheiten Augustin's" in *Miscellanea Agnostiniana* (Rome, 1931), vol. II, pp. 17, 19.

there have been, there still are and there will continue to exist for a long time Calvinists living in an entirely different milieu from that of sixteenth-century France to whom, despite this difference of environment, his "truth" will be similarly evident. Hence it is insufficient to say that "to restore by an intellectual effort, for each of the epochs which he studies, the mental arsenal of the men of that epoch . . . there is the supreme ideal, the historian's final goal."[29] To explain Cuvier by Montbeliard or the French Revolution[30]—that is to stabilize historical research at a superficial and exoteric level.

Such is not the fine point of our effort. As a matter of fact, if the historian studies a thought of another day by devoting himself with restless and punctilious curiosity to the man who conceived it, to his person and what surrounds him—it is not for the pleasure of collecting anecdotes. It is not that he is moved by the illusory ambition to "reduce" that thought to the conditions of its first appearance—but there is a need to comprehend. And for the same reason he studies the occasions (often futile, always extraordinarily contingent in regard to the doctrinal content) which led the philosopher to formulate it; he studies the works in which it is expressed, their literary type, the vicissitudes of their text—not omitting, as we saw concerning Plato, the least particle of any possible connection.

What is it that we seek, what should we seek to grasp? is, if I may put it so boldly (to talk like the chemists), it is the truth at the very moment of birth, in that "original intuition" of which Bergson has spoken so effectively—that central flash, or *Ursprung*. It is from this core (no matter, once again, what the contingencies may be) that the idea took shape in the thinker's consciousness and demanded his attention. Here I appeal to the experience of all those who, with a docile and

29. L. Febvre, *Combats pour l'histoire*, p. 334 (republished from the *Revue de Synthèse historique*, vol. XLIII, 1927).

30. *Ibid.*, pp. 327, 335.

sincere heart, ever leaned over a page—whether written yesterday or two thousand years ago—that at last understood, revealed to them its authentic, its eternal truth. They will
testify unanimously: no, historical study, carried to its limits,
is not a school of relativism. No, it does not end by dissolving
a thought in its cultural or social (or any other) environment.
It is the occasion and the means of a rediscovery, of a revival,
of an enriching experience.

It was before I studied St. Augustine historically that this
thought seemed to me relative, curiously odd and quite
peculiar. I clashed with him as I might with a foreigner. He
was to me that learned man of the decadence, a representative
of a civilization now long gone and of a superceded stage in
the social, intellectual, and religious evolution of humanity.
It is only now, on the contrary, that I have learned to know
him, to understand him, to think somewhat like him. It is
only now that I can grasp from within how and why it was
that he had been led to assume such a doctrinal position and
to express it in one fashion or another (here hardening it to
the paradoxical in the heat of battle, there expressing it with
a popular and even smiling simplicity, as in the *Sermon*
addressed to his own people of Hippo). It is only now that the
value of his thought is really accessible to me—its value sometimes as Truth, and sometimes as an intimidating objection
that it is necessary to confront and conquer.

It is with this original historicity (which was his reality)
that my own historicity establishes the rapport which constitutes history. It is a complex rapport, and the reader should
not forget (p. 48) that all I can know of the historicity of
intermediate ages intervenes. I do not grasp the Augustinian
doctrine of predestination only in the instant in which it
finishes by taking form under the fire of Julien d'Éclane's
objections, but I think it by assuming at the same time all

that rightly or wrongly it may have become in the thought of Gottschalk, Luther or Jansenius.

In this rapport there is established a fraternal dialogue. His spirit and mine communicate what is most profound in each of our existences because we are, the two of us, souls enamoured of—and capable of—Truth.

I have dwelt on this matter of the history of philosophy at some length because it seems to me typical: *ab illo disce omnes*. We can see that historical knowledge has an analogous function in whatever sphere it may be exercised. We must not demand of a thing more than it can furnish—nor anything different. History will not relieve the philosopher of his responsibility in formulating a judgment concerning the truth. And neither can it pretend to dictate to the man of action for example a decision of a political nature (in virtue of the precedents or analogies which it has revealed to him). History cannot undertake the role of a central vivifying force in human culture or in life. Its true role (infinitely more humble but on its own level very real and very precious) is to furnish the alert mind of feeling and thinking and acting man with an abundance of those materials on which he may exercise his judgment and his will. Its fruitfulness resides in the practically unlimited extent to which it can obtain these from our experience and understanding of man. Therein lies its greatness, its "usefulness."

Let us not hesitate to return once more—in a new and vitalized sense—to the ancient conception of *historia, magistra uitae*. We know what a narrow and ridiculous application the old rhetoricians made of this. In their hands history was reduced to a repertoire of topical anecdotes, of examples designed for the use of the moralist, of precedents for the jurist or statesman, of well-tested stratagems for the tactician or the diplomat.

But this expression is susceptible of a quite profound meaning. It is by investigating men—by meeting men other than myself—that I learn to understand better what man is (and the man that I am, with all his potentialities—now splendid, now frightful). This is clearly evident in the experience of everyday life. Who would dare say it is in vain that we have encountered these men, in vain that we have sought to know them, to understand them—to love them? Since it is itself a Meeting with Others, history reveals to us infinitely more things—on all the aspects of being and of human life—than we could discover in only one lifetime. It is in this way, too, that it renders our creative imagination more fertile, and opens a thousand new paths for our efforts in thinking as it does for our action. (Here I use the word "action" in its widest sense, annexing to it for instance the sentimental life: by listening to the troubadors I can discover, or deepen, the art of love.)

History liberates us from the impediments, the limitations that are imposed on our experience of man when we situate him in a certain place in a certain society at a certain moment of his evolution—and thus it becomes in a certain sense an instrument and a means to our liberty.

But there is more. I have continued to insist on the fact that history is not only the reconstruction of my genealogical tree and of my biological antecedents, but I have not denied that it is. Yet it is very evident that it is also—and in a sense it is first of all—*my* history. It is the reconstruction and through this the realization of the human development that has made me what I am, that has led to this cultural, economic, social, and political situation in which I am enmeshed by all the fibers of my being.

It is here that a difference appears. And it is capital from the point of view of *historiodicy* (the "justification of history"). It is a difference at the very heart of culture and of life— between biological evolution and what we proposed to call, by analogy, the evolution of humanity. If a horse, for example, could become aware of the avatars of his distant tertiary ancestors (the Hyracotherium, the Orohippus, etc.) that would change nothing in his bone structure, nor in his racing technique (and the same is true of man when he reconstitutes his phylogenesis).

But the evolution of humanity as well has transmitted to us a heritage that at first is imposed on us with the same "natural" and tyrannical necessity. Yet from the moment that this evolution becomes history—from the moment when I become conscious of that heredity, when I know what I am, and why and how I have become it—that knowledge liberates me with respect to that heritage, and I can now consider it simply under the aspect of an inventory. I can accept it or reject it (to the extent that it is a question of things within my power). As for whatever is beyond me, I can at least judge it bravely, opposing it with indignant condemnation, for example—and this act in the sphere of thought can in turn inspire and animate a whole line of action with a view to transforming things.

If Stalin had been able to discover where his police technique came from (through a historical study of the notion of personal liberty of the type that Lord Acton had dreamed of bringing about), he might have drawn back in horror when confronted with all that survived in him of Ivan the Terrible and of the Byzantine Basileus. It might have led him to modify the regime of the M.D.V., that heir of the N.K.V.D., of the O.G.P.U., of the Tcheka, of the Okhrana, and so on right down to the *agentes in rebus* of the Later Empire and to the *frumentarii* of Hadrian.

A historical awareness brings about a veritable *catharsis*, a liberation of our sociological subconscious somewhat analogous to that which psychoanalysis seeks to establish on the psychological level. I have been somewhat ironic with regard to their aggressive pretensions when they invade our domain, but it is with the greatest seriousness that I here invoke this parallel.[31] In the one case as in the other, we observe this mechanism (at first view surprising) by which "the knowledge of the past cause modifies the present effect." In each case man frees himself from a past which up until that moment had weighed upon him obscurely. He does this not by forgetfulness but by the effort of finding it again, by assimilating it in a fully conscious way so as to integrate it. It is in this sense, as has so often been repeated from Goethe to Dilthey[32] and to Croce,[33] that historical knowledge frees man from the weight of the past. Here again history appears as a pedagogy, the exercise ground and the instrument of our liberty.

I cannot insist too strongly that history, of its nature, is not capable of claiming that directive and dominating role which the men of the nineteenth century dreamed for it. Nevertheless, its presence within the framework of human culture can confer upon this culture a characteristic and very precious value, which is sufficient to determine the whole atmosphere of thought and life. I will gladly define man the historian: he is the man who delights in history and knows how to nourish himself with that knowledge, who has an authentic grasp of its object (even though it is always a partial one). In contrast to him there is the man of the Philosophy of History—that barbarian—the man who knows (or imagines that he knows) the last word on the mystery of time. A victim of his own illusions, he forgets the arbitrary selections and the deforming mutilations by means of which

31. Following Ch. Baudoin, in his paper to the Strasbourg Congress, 1952, "Assumer le passé," in *L'homme et l'histoire*, pp. 121–130.

32. *Der Aufbau der geschichtlichen Welt in den Geisteswissen-schaften, Gesamm. Schriften*, vol. VII, p. 252; cf. R. Aron, *La philosophie critique*, p. 87.

33. B. Croce, *History: Its Theory and Practice*, I, 8, "Historiography as Liberation of History," p. 44, quoting Goethe.

he has been able to draw up his schematic image of the past and future of humanity. Drunk with a desire for power, he rushes into action with a blind fanaticism. Ah! It is not a good thing to be found crossing his path, nor even (as a reluctant ally) to associate with his drive, if only partially. Suspicious and soon convinced of your opposition to the movement of "History," he will shortly sweep you aside, liquidating you without mercy. At the same time—it is a painfully ironic compensation—this same man is obliged to adhere instant by instant to the very sinuous line which the realization of the Idea traces in the course of time. When he loses the sense of Truth with its absolutes, he loses all his internal framework, autonomy and dignity—he howls with the wolves, adores the powerful, spits upon the conquered.

The real historian, on the contrary, knows that he cannot know everything. He does not try to be more than a man, and he accepts with simplicity the fact that he is not God. He knows things incompletely, in his little mirror—not only in limited fashion but often obscurely. Yet he also knows that he does not know; he estimates and locates the immensity of what escapes him. And in this way he acquires a keen sense of the complexity of being and of the situations of man, in all their tragic ambivalence.

What is our twentieth century in the process of accomplishing? Will it see the emancipation of the laboring class (and of the colored peoples)? Or will we only witness a simple shift of imperialism, sanctioning the decline of Western Europe to the advantage of North America or of the Slavic peoples (while awaiting Asia's moment)? Are the sufferings of the present the foreshadowing of the birth of a humanity that is at last truly fraternal, living on a unified planet in universal peace? Or are we definitely entering upon an era of total war, with all its uncontrollable unleashing of the forces of destruction? Are we to see the dreams cherished by our fathers during the liberal period fulfilled and finally carried out—will there be the triumph of the human person, the recognition of man by man in its fullness and completeness? Or have we instead arrived at the threshold of a new world of terror through the emergence of the totalitarian or police state, and the dictatorship of the technocrats? Will we see a labor civilization develop under that very name, where the servitude of the slave to his task is so sinister and deceptive that he comes to bless and adore the very signs of his servitude? Will we see a base materialism or a spiritual advance? And if a new impetus, will it be a renaissance of the noblest forms of religious life, or rather the triumph of the mongrel and vulgar forms of the collective Sacred? Who knows?

As he struggles with this irreducible ambiguity, the historian acquires the sharpest sense of his responsibility and realizes the meaning of his involvement, the value of his free decision. At the same time, he gains a more profound and much wider knowledge of the immense inherent potentialities that exist for him to choose from. He is man become aware—who walks with open eyes, and who cannot be deceived. He does not go forward like a laboring ox, his neck straining toward the furrow but, head held high, he contemplates the immense horizon open to the four winds of the spirit. He knows that nothing is simple, that the die is not cast, that many possibilities exist which may or may not be fulfilled. He chooses and he judges. He is a man who does not become intoxicated with victory, for he measures its precarious nature, its uncertainty, and its limitations. He is also a man who is not broken by defeat. And when there is nothing more that he can do, he knows how to say: *No.* Unyielding, he knows how to suffer with nobility and how to preserve hope.

The Nature of Historical Work

We first defined history as a form of knowledge and then showed it in turn in the process of being born, of developing, and of coming to fruition—a process taking place entirely within the mind of the cognitive subject, prior to any attempt at expression. But from the earliest stage of this analysis (p. 33) we let it be anticipated that all historical research should normally culminate in a historical work (either in the form of oral teaching, lessons or lectures, or more frequently in a written work such as a thesis, an article or a book). Such a culmination, we said, is a necessity of a practical nature, a social requirement.

I would like to underline this last term, because it provides the finishing touch for our theory which, while it brings out in relief the *personal* link established between history and the historian, should not by the same token be interpreted in any individualistic sense.

It should not be imagined that the historian wanders among the riches of the past in the same way as an idle visitor in a museum strolls past the glass cases and stops here and there when his curiosity or interest is aroused. The historian does not casually encounter a problem here, strike up a friendship with a hero there, or relive an adventure in a given period.

Things do not happen in this way because a historian as a person is not the abstract individual defined in the liberal tradition. He is a man involved in the process of living, rooted by every fiber of his being in the human environment to which he belongs—his social, political, national and cultural background. This has made him what he is and to this everything he does comes back and brings some return.

The historian does not go forward alone to his encounter with the past; he approaches it as a representative of his own group. The question he is going to put (that question which sets the course for the whole development of his research—at least if his research raises a "true" problem with all its weight of existential content) will necessarily express a demand that is common to all the members of his collective group—it will not simply be a matter of concern peculiar to him as an individual. All types of interaction are possible at this point. The link between the adventurous quest of the individual and the needs and deep desires of the community can be more or less close, more or less direct, obvious to a greater or lesser degree. The best history, the work which will be of the greatest real service to society, will not be of the type bordering on propaganda, providing data directly related to what is known as news—of a diplomatic or political character, for example. It is worthwhile recalling the saying of Heraclitus: "Hidden harmony" (expressing a deep underlying interconnection) "is superior to visible harmony" (which is too often a superficial phenomenon).[1]

The work that is felt to be the most personal will often be the one in which the historian (in looking for the solution to *his* own problem) in fact answers *the* primordial question uppermost in the minds of men in his time—without having sought to do so.

Gibbon has told us how the idea for his *Decline and Fall* came to him. It was October 15, 1764 at Rome, on the Capitol, while watching the Franciscans of Aracoeli, "the barefooted friars," chant the office on the very spot where once the splendor of the ancient city had towered. . . . It is a striking contrast, but was it a chance encounter? We can

1. H. Diels, *Die Fragmente der Vorsokratiker*[6], §22 (12), fr. 54.

calculate more fully today the way Gibbon was affected by the irritating and the essential elements in the problem of the "triumph of Religion and Barbarism," the scandal of the Christian middle ages. Yet this was so not only for Gibbon but for all the men of the *Aufklärung*—it was a challenge that they could not fail to face.

Still, Gibbon was a representative of that class which is now practically extinct: the enlightened amateur, the dilettante. Nowadays the historian is almost always a professional: even if he is not salaried on his nation's budget, or by UNESCO, he is fully aware of being a specialized worker, delegated to the search for truth, just like, at his side, his fellow biologist or physicist.

Moreover it is the very conscientiousness of his research, the quality of the results he obtains, that will keep the historian from limiting his ambition to the mere enrichment of his inner experience, to a solitary contemplation of truth. *Bonum diffusivum sui:* insofar as the historian attains truth and a knowledge rich in fertile values, he owes them to his fellowmen.

All this acknowledged, the fact remains that the problem of expression is, in itself, external to history and that it finds its way into history under the impulse of considerations of a different nature. Indeed, our daily experience is there to bear this out: the need (or the duty) to write is felt as a painful bondage. Research is in itself indefinite; historical truth is never final, it is always in the making. To express it is to make it fixed. Then again there are the demands of the writer's art, shall we say: *ars longa, vita brevis*. The historian feels torn between the contradictory demands of these two *artes*—unless he ends by yielding to temptation and sacrificing his social duty to the passion for knowledge. (Here again we meet the moralizing criticism of curiosity, for it can become a devouring and tyrannous passion.)

19

The annals of our profession are marked at intervals with cases such as these. There are men who accumulate knowledge, enrich their experience throughout their lives, and attain unequaled competence. Forgetful of the fact that they are men and not Immortals, they write nothing: "fathomless wells of knowledge, which never give forth any water."[2] But one day they die, useless, leaving nothing but a mass of scribbled notes that are worthless to others. I quote at random from a recent obituary notice (it concerns a musicologist, André Tessier): "He confessed to me that he set no value on anything but discovery, discovery for its own sake; he cared little about publishing it. The knowledge that he had acquired of the seventeenth century, and not only of the music of that period, was greater than has been supposed. It was founded on a large number of minute, obscure facts that had caught no one's attention, but to which he had ascribed significance. I may say that he experienced a proud satisfaction to be the only one able to keep his bearings among so many guideposts. How many times he told me that a study was finished: it was so only in his mind; and the traces recorded on his file-cards marked, merely at intervals, the stages of his thought. I write this to warn others against the misleading, skeletal appearance of Tessier's unprinted notes which are soon to be published."[3] As Thucydides has his Pericles say somewhere: "To have acquired knowledge without the talent of imparting it is just as though one had never thought it!"[4]

It is proper for the historian to submit willingly to these demands of a moral nature that result from the social function he undertakes, and to the technical requirements that proceed from them. Besides he will very often find himself directly recompensed. I would also hasten to add (for it is always

2. L. Febvre, *Combats pour l'histoire,* p. 340.

3. A. Schaeffner, *Revue de Musicologie,* vol. XXXV (1953), p. 152.

4. Thucydides, II, 60, 6.

important to make our doctrine as precise as possible), that the contradiction described is not always, in practice, so absolute. No doubt, as a general rule, research is never finished (one question brings up another which in turn implies others that have to be resolved). But if we consider a definite field of inquiry, we find it necessary to affirm that often it would be profitable for the historian to repeat with Aristotle: ἀνάγχη στῆναι. He is obliged to stop, because he can say (according to the well-known remark ascribed to the Abbé d'Aubigné, (among others): "My siege is finished."* Indeed, there comes a time when his vision of the past—for the very reason that it is systematically adjusted to one point of view, to certain presuppositions, concepts, and method—has attained the measure of truth that it is capable of acquiring. From that time on, research will produce nothing more, documents and observations slip into their proper place among the notations by themselves; less submissive data float on the surface of consciousness like an extraneous body, and can no longer be assimilated. (If the historian is conscientious, and he should be, this unassimilable material will be found somewhere in the notes at the bottom of the page, introduced by a formula such as: "I well know that . . . Cf. However . . . See also . . ." These are points that his successors will not fail to take up.)

At other times research becomes unprofitably exasperating and complicated. It soon reaches its limit, variable according to the circumstances. Beyond this (as our favorite axiom puts it), certitude decreases when precision increases.

There is a final point (and here Paul Valéry's teaching can be retained as valid). Research and expression, however

* *Translator's note:* This saying (more generally ascribed to the Abbé Vertot) has come to mean in French, "I have made up my mind." The Abbé Vertot, who was to do the history of the Order of Malta, had written to ask for information concerning the siege of Malta. He did not receive the information before writing his account; afterwards, when it arrived, he disregarded it, saying, "My siege is finished."

distinct they may be from a logical point of view, actually interfere with each other in practice, and this interference is fruitful. Often it is while seeking its expression that knowledge takes another step forward and makes decided progress. The gaps then show up, proportions are re-established, and truth finally takes shape, emerging at last from that shadowy zone where it struggled between development and non-existence.

Thus once the research is finished or at least well on the way, the historian should take a breathing spell. Reflecting upon this new aspect of his problem, he should ask himself: with what I know and can learn, how can I write the best account, with the richest contents, the truest and at the same time the most convincing, the easiest to assimilate (after all, if I write it is in order to be understood)—how can I write the best book with this material?

We have no intention of completing or of crowning our logical treatise with a rhetorical one for the use of historians. In these few concluding pages we wish simply to bring out the problem and put it in its proper place—to make the reader realize the importance of the work to be done in this field of expression. Once again, the social effectiveness of history is involved and its productiveness with respect to man. History as a science would not have fallen so low in general esteem, and its function would not have been usurped by caricatures (historical romances or anecdotal writings, and servile propaganda) if the serious workers had not looked down on the public to such an extent—if they had not all too often been content simply to dump on to their readers cartloads of data, calling them books, *rudis indigestaque moles*. Too many publications are not history, but only an assemblage of roughly hewn materials from which history can be elaborated. Too many of our colleagues have everything to learn on this point. It is one thing, for example, to accumulate all the available documentation, but it is quite another thing to force one's readers to read it in detail. Justifying conclusions adopted is strictly in the line of duty, but it does not require one to retrace in detail the whole, often winding path taken by thought in order to reach them. To be readable, a narrative must go along at an even *tempo*; a synthesis of detailed fact must not be interrupted by the complicated discussion of a single detail. This question must be set aside for an appendix or, better still, be published separately in a specialized periodical as a scholarly article, where its treatment will clearly and conclusively demonstrate its importance.

But once again, it is not a question here of supplying a rough draft of a treatise on the art of writing: writing a book is a profession that must be learned. Only the principle matters for the moment, and it is clear: in order to do his task well, in order truly to fulfill his function, the historian must also be a great writer. This truth has been overshadowed by the discussions which our predecessors have had on the theme, "History should be a science and not an art."[5] On that point they fought a battle that was necessary in order to separate history from eloquence—from "literature" (the term being used in its most disparaging sense—and in order to obtain recognition of history's law of research and truth. But as always, polemic passion has wrought havoc, and we have been brought to an extreme position close to absurdity.

Many British historians, we are told,[6] try to write "badly" (sacrificing elegance and even correctness) for the sake of being taken seriously. Or again, "if a book which has helped establish truth is excellent into the bargain, that is good luck, and a kind of luxury. A historian is not obliged to write like

5. Cf. the bibliography on this question by H. Berr, *La synthèse en histoire*[3], p. 226, n. 1.

6. This opinion is expressed somewhat paradoxically by G. J. Renier, *History: Its Purpose and Method*, p. 244.

Fustel de Coulanges any more than a biologist is obliged to write like Claude Bernard . . ."[7]

What a strange ideal of literary "beauty"! The "search for artistic effects" would seem to consist of scattering over Truth those *colores atque sententiae* of the rhetoricians of by-gone days—those reflections with a so-called philosophical depth which Chateaubriand thought so necessary for adorning the text of his *Memoires* (otherwise excellent). It is a little like those people who think that poetry is prose with the addition of rime.

No, indeed! History, taken by itself, is the infinitely subtle knowledge that comes slowly to maturity in the historian's mind in the course of a purely technical experience carried out in contact with documents. Its truth, all in fine shadings, is made of the minute and complex coordination of a thousand different elements. Ultimately, truth tends to become almost intransmissible to anyone who has not gone through the same experience. And if this is history, what mastery in the art of writing, what skill with the pen, what felicity of expression will be required—will be indispensable—for presenting it in an authentically valid formulation which will communicate (without deforming it too much) that knowledge which is so precious and yet so easily betrayed.

Here again I speak from experience. The non-professional can imagine only with difficulty the daily struggle that the historian must carry on to find the right expression, the sentence which will say all that he knows, without letting anything escape—but also without hardening the thought, or appearing to know more than he really does, or turning the reader's imagination off onto a wrong track. Being a French historian and obliged to measure myself every day against that exacting language of ours, it sometimes happens (when

7. H. Berr, *op. cit.*, p. 226 (who furthermore immediately corrects this exaggeration somewhat).

I am lazy) that I could feel more happy writing in German, that fluid and docile language, so convenient for camouflaging vagueness in apparent profundity—but that is ungrateful of me, for I well know what progress in precision and accuracy I owe to the very inertness of the robust instrument that I use.

The historian must take great pains with the precise expression of his subtle truth. Who would hesitate to agree that for this he must also be an artist? All the great men are at one with me on this point, from Ranke to G. J. Renier—just think of Dilthey, Simmel or Croce.

If Ranke (more so than Niebuhr) is honored by us as the first modern historian, in the sense in which we are using the word, it is because he was able to combine the penetration and subtlety of an inquiring mind and the breadth of vision of a philosophic mind with the great skill of a master of his language.[8]

However, it is easy to prove that all the great historians are also great artists with words. It is generally agreed that the very greatest philosopher will not always be the man who penetrates most closely to the truth; the greatest theologian will not always be the mystic who is furthest advanced on the way to the unitive experience. But in both instances it is the man with a poetic gift of expression (in the fullest sense of the Greek word—ποιητιχός) whose writing will be the most simple, most appropriate and the most understandable. The same is true of the historian.

I also find something a little too polemic in the attitude (still frequent today) which sees in the historical work only a reflection of the transitory state of research. The most beautiful eulogy conceivable, it is widely felt, will be totally useless and out of date after about thirty years. All its con-

8. Th. von Laue, *Leopold Ranke: The Formative Years* (Princeton, 1950), p. 21.

clusions will be revised by the very progress that it would
itself give birth to.[9] It is just here that we should not forget
that the truth of history is a two-fold truth. It comprises
knowledge of the object itself, and also truth about the historian's effort, and what he introduces of himself. Undoubtedly after thirty years a reader will be highly sensitive to
everything in a work that is out of date. This would seem to
parallel the period of disaffection for the work of a man in
literature, sculpture or painting, that usually occurs in the next
generation. But when sufficient time has passed to allow a
more disinterested judgment of these works, it will be discovered that the historical work (which certainly is more and
more out of date in one sense) has survived because of all
that the author has incarnated of his own humanity. The work
will mellow and rise slowly to the dignity of a historical witness, becoming (as we have shown) a document about the
historian himself, his surroundings and his time.

Who can reread the wonderful preface in Michelet's *History
of the French Revolution* without evaluating all it reveals
of the ideas current in France about 1847, and in a more
precise way about the Jansenist origins of our "laic" tradition?

But that is not the principal thing. The work will survive
not to the extent that it is expressive of a truth about the past,
but because it has an authentic grasp of its object (though
only partial, incarnated in a particular thought). Thucydides
was very much aware of this,[10] and how can we hesitate to
agree with him—we who after so many centuries reread his
history with renewed interest each time? His *History* survives
because we find these truths—the truth about man, his life
and his actions—the things he was able to scrutinize and
reveal. His genius has made the Peloponnesian War the best

9. L. Febvre, *Combats* . . . , pp. 397–398.
10. Thucydides, I, 22, 4.

understood war in history. Every war can be found there and illuminated in some way by parallel or by contrast.

I remember the spring of 1939 at Nancy, when the storm clouds that would sweep over Europe were gathering over Prague and Danzig. I had just taken up once more Thucydides' first book with my students. This analysis of the situation in Greece on the eve of the great conflict, because of its limpid serenity, is most moving. Was not Europe—just as Greece had been—on the verge of war? The counter-arguments went back and forth: sometimes I was on the side of Athens, sometimes on Sparta's side—a democrat with the one and an anti-imperialist with the other . . .

Men of the First World War have had the same experience. Toynbee[11] recalls, in words charged with emotion, how Thucydides suddenly took on a new meaning for him in August of 1914. And in the somber days of March 1918, he read it once again to keep up courage. About this same time Thibaudet, a corporal assigned to guard part of an unused barracks, began to write *La campagne avec Thucydide* . . .

These examples suffice to show in what analogical and profound sense one must understand the famous declaration of Thucydides on the usefulness of his history: "for those who will want to see clearly into past events and into those that are to come, by virtue of the human character which is theirs it will happen again in an analogical manner." Nothing would be farther from the truth than an interpretation in a style à la Maurras, as if history permitted one to isolate in some way the laws of "social physics." No, the analogy is always partial and the likeness shared.

Now, if we admire the genius of Thucydides, it is of course in a very clear-sighted way. We know how to ascertain and define his form and his limits. This "history" is that of

11. *Civilization on Trial*, pp. 15–16. Cf. T. Lean, in *Horizon*, vol. XV (1947), p. 27.

"Thucydides the Athenian," Thucydides son of Oloros, descendant of Miltiades, a man whom we place at such and such a moment in the development of the Hellenic culture. That intelligibility which he knew how to disengage from its object he has elaborated with the means in his power—the instruments of thought that he had received from the teaching of the Sophists and the great human schemas which the Aeschylean tragedy[12] suggested to him. We can easily see how this construction is accomplished, but at the same time these characteristics do not prevent it from being true.

Perhaps one may find the example chosen a little artificial; for lack of direct documentation on the Peloponnesian War Thucydides' *History* itself must function for us as a primary source. Let us then take Tacitus: thanks to the progress in documentation accumulated and exploited by our auxiliary sciences—thanks to the coins, the inscriptions, the papyri—we are able today to know Tiberius, Claudius or Nero in many ways other than through the *History* or the *Annals.* However, we still keep reading Tacitus—I mean as historians. Indeed, here also we clearly see his limits; we know how to criticize his testimony, we know the deformations or the selections that he implies.

It is a representative of the senatorial aristocracy who is speaking and—what is more—an upstart (to a certain extent). Like Saint-Simon, he "puts more into it than there is." Thanks to the Claudian tables of Lyons, which have preserved for us the authentic text of a speech of the Emperor Claudius, we are even able to surprise him in the act of manipulating his sources. J. Carcopino[13] has shown that he had the original text at hand, but he has re-made it entirely, "re-written it"!

But we are not able to elaborate our own vision of Tiberius,

12. Bear in mind the informative book by F. M. Cornford, *Thucydides Mythistoricus* (1907).

13. *Points de vue sur l'impérialisme romain* (1934), pp. 164–189.

of Claudius or of Nero by depriving ourselves of the contribution which Tacitus represents. It is not a matter of the supplementary documentation that he can give us, but once more of the intelligibility, and the human truth he introduces into his story by his effort of thought. The dialogue, in a sense, no longer exists as a private conversation between, let us say, Tiberius and the historian that I am. Tacitus stands there as a third person between us—a noble figure, serious and sometimes a little stilted. And I hear him repeating his famous formulas (. . . *ruere in servitium* . . . *ibatur in caedes*), which I admire not only for their unique verbal magic, but also to the extent that their splendor is pregnant with truth. It is in this sense that the historical work participates in the eternity of the work of art, χτῆμά ἐς αἰεί.

Historical Faith[*]

In a report drawn up on the occasion of the last International Congress of philosophy,[1] the writer discussed the state of convergence which seemed to him manifested "by the recent works devoted to rendering justice to historical knowledge," and risked expressing this imprudent conclusion: Today, it seems, "There is no other critical philosophy of history but one summed up in the formula: history (that is, historical science) is inseparable from the historian." That is indeed going much too far. All minds are not yet equally disposed to greet with sympathy such an effort to bypass the strict objectivism of the positivist theoreticians. Recent bibliography is sufficient witness to this. We find in it very many refusals, expressed turn and turn about with scandalized astonishment,[2] ironic humor,[3] or passion going as far as sarcasm[4]—when it is not invective.[5]

[*]This article was first published in Les Études Philosophiques, April-June 1959, pp. 151–161.

1. International Institute of Philosophy, Philosophy in the Mid-century, a Survey, Florence, 1958, vol. III, p. 178.

2. A. Piganiol, "Qu'est-ce que l'histoire?" in Revue de métaphysique et de morale (July-September 1955), pp. 225–247.

3. M.-L. Guérard des Lauriers, "A propos de la Connaissance historique," in Revue des sciences philosophiques et théologiques (October 1955), pp. 569–602.

4. G. Gurvitch, "Continuité et discontinuité en histoire et en sociologie," in Annales, Économies, Sociétés, Civilisations (January-March 1957), pp. 73–84.

5. F. Chatelet, "Non, l'histoire n'est pas insaisissable!" in La Nouvelle Critique (May 1955), pp. 56–72. See also by the same author, and in a calmer tone, "Le temps de l'histoire et l'évolution de la fonction historienne," in Journal de psychologie normale et pathologique (July-September 1956), pp. 355–378.

Much remains to be done before we can reach the anticipated *consensus,* and many misunderstandings must be dissipated. It is surprising to read, for example (touching a debate on the relations between history and sociology): "One can see that even the most severe critics of objectivity in history, such as R. Aron, admit that certain structures can be disengaged as though read in the reality itself, even before there is any question of a theory . . ."[6] Yes, to be sure, but the historian does not disengage these structures unless he sees them printed as it were in the documentary material which the Past has bequeathed him. But in order to read them there he must first have proposed them as hypotheses submitted for verification, and therefore he must have first formulated them by means of the mental equipment which is his own. In this sense, we cannot reject R. Aron's formula, even though it is a bit abrupt: "Theory precedes history."

Partisans and adversaries both, we have all exaggerated the polemic—so much so that we can no longer see clearly the hidden agreement or disagreement behind the sharp affirmations and the paradoxical provocations which oppose each other in turn. We are surprised when, after denouncing our critical philosophy as a string of naïve misunderstandings and errors, to our surprise the same author will at last propose as his own conclusions that—if they have any meaning—express an exaggeration of the very doctrine which he formerly contested: "Historical truth is the most ideological of all scientific truths. . . . The terms 'subjective' and 'objective'

6. P. de Gaudemar, "Evénement, structure, histoire: limites du rôle de la pensée formelle dans les sciences de l'homme" in *Cahiers de l'Institut de science économique appliquée,* serie M, no. 2, *Recherches et dialogues philosophiques et économiques* (December 1958). p. 35, n. 1. Note that my criticism deals only with the quoted formula; furthermore, I am in agreement with the whole of the development in which P. de Gaudemar justly claims history's right to take a place among the humane sciences and to rise above the level of contemporary experience.

no longer signify anything precise, since the triumph of the
open conscience. . . . Historical truth is not a subjective truth,
but an ideological truth, resulting from a partisan knowledge."[7]

To the misdeeds of polemics we must add those of propaganda (often perfidious), and of popularizing that is deliberately clumsy. Expressed by a journalist, the theory is
summed up in a sentence of the type: "History is only the
projection into the past of the options, chiefly political, of the
present." We would no doubt be more astonished by one of
those who make use of these options in revealing that history
does not belong to any of these "nominalists, idealists and
spiritualists" responsible for our critical philosophy, but rather
to a debased Marxism—that of the Soviet historian N. Prokov-
skij (d. 1932), who knew his hour of glory before being
anathematized posthumously, as he is today.

We must protest against the sophistic interpretation which
attempts to draw critical philosophy within the orbit of scepticism. When it poses "the limits of historical objectivity,"[8]
this philosophy does not go so far as to pretend, as we might
put it, that "what the man of today can know of the man of
yesterday is not *true*."[9] The interpenetration of the reality of
the Past and the contribution of the knowing subject (which
is at the heart of historical knowledge) does not imply the
identification of that reality and that knowledge.[10]

In order to triumph over so many calumnies or misunderstandings, it is undoubtedly necessary for the theory of
history to spend some time in elaborating a more profound
and more complete logic, based on a constantly more precise
analysis of the historian's comportment toward his work. This
is the method obligatory in the philosophy of science. History

7. Gurvitch, article quoted, p. 83.
8. This is the sub-title of R. Aron's thesis, *Introduction à la philosophie
de l'histoire*, Paris, 1938.
9. Chatelet, article quoted (*La Nouvelle Critique*), p. 59.
10. Gurvitch, article quoted, p. 76.

exists—let us say since Herodotus, Hellanicus of Mitylene and Thucydides—insofar as it is a discipline that possesses a method progressively refined through long use and elaborates a knowledge recognized as valid by qualified technicians. The problem is to analyze its structure. A logic will never be sufficiently rigorous, but let us be on our guard here against a false rigidity. We would do well to remember the Pascalian distinction between the spirit of geometry and the spirit of finesse: even though scientifically elaborated, history is not a science of the geometric type.[11] "The geometricians who are only geometricians" become "false and unbearable" when they transplant their reasoning habits into a domain in which these habits are not applicable. The minds of the geometric type are not the best armed to advance the analysis of historical knowledge, because "they are accustomed to the clear cut and 'simple' principles of geometry. They do not reason until they have thoroughly examined their principles and manipulated them; they are lost in things of finesse. . . ."

At the end of a long analysis which sought to show the interpenetration of the known object and the knowing subject in the heart of historical knowledge, I had given as an illustration the comparison between the science of the historian and the art of the portraitist[12] (which an English philosopher had already used before me). A geometrician came along and undertook to give a form to this "analogy of proportionality": "The ensemble of the portraits of an individual is to that individual what the ensemble of the views of the same 'human past' by different historians is to that human past." And he protested to me: "Is it therefore legitimate to create a 'rapprochement' between a human being in his outer ap-

11. The neo-scholastic philosophers are the first to admit this: see for example J. de Vries, *Critica* (Institutiones philosophiae scholasticae des Jésuites de Pullach, II), Freiburg, 1954, §238.

12. See above, p. 240.

pearance, the object of a portrait, and the 'human past,' the object of history?"[13] From this we can see that the mathematicians are scarcely interested in the plastic arts: "What vanity painting is . . . ," Pascal had already written, having profited little on this point from the lessons of the Chevalier de Méré. The truly honest man does not ignore the fact that the painter, whether he be named Holbein, Raphael, Rigaud or Mignard has the pretension, in his portraits, of representing something quite other than "the human individual in his outer appearance." Instead, through that and by means of that, he tries to capture all that he has understood of the human reality of his model. In each case he envisages this his subject, in his most personal psychology or in his social personality (the groups of *Regents* or *Regentes* of Franz Hals are amazing testimonies concerning the Dutch bourgeoisie of the seventeenth century). There is indeed a real analogy between the portraitist and the historian (or at least the biographer); the parallel could be pushed a long way. Just as in the long run all the historians treat "facts," so do the somatic elements of the diverse portraits most often become superimposable. We recognize with perfect objectivity the facial angle, the complexion and the size of Louis XIV—what can I say—even the (excessive) length of Cleopatra's nose. It is when it becomes a question of expressing something else, for instance that she was a "woman of noble mind," full of "sweetness and good grace" (to talk like Amyot's *Plutarch*) that the difficulties begin and different versions of the portrait, as of history, run the risk of diverging. Why? Because in both cases, no matter what the specific differences in the nature of the object (present or past) and of the means of expression (plastic or conceptual) the same type of knowledge is utilized—the knowledge of man by man—and the same inextricable mixture of

13. Guérard des Lauriers, article quoted, p. 584.

subject and object that it implies. This does not mean that within that mixture this knowledge is not capable of truth.

Perhaps we were wrong in insisting too strongly on Dilthey's role—and the tradition which issued from it, "all the uncertain family of its spiritual sons,"[14]—in the development of the critical theory of history. In fact, this tradition is the result of an entire series of convergent efforts. We must take into account the series that starts with Hume,[15] as we must also take into account the diffusion of Bergson's reasoning[16] (I say again with pleasure). Nothing could be more deceptive than to associate our critical philosophy too closely with a particular stage of new-Kantianism.[17] That excellent humanist and historian of history, Arnaldo Momigliano, has most usefully reminded us[18] (surpassing even E. Cassirer's erudition) that that logic of history had already been formulated in its essential points by the classicism of the seventeenth century.

14. Adopting F. Braudel's picturesque expression, "Lucien Febvre et l'histoire," in *Annales* (April-June 1957), p. 181.

15. As in the case of Dilthey or of Max Weber, we must not separate Hume's work as a historian from that of his philosophic thoughts on history. I am surprised that I. Meyerson, in "Le temps, la mémoire et l'histoire," *Journal de psychologie* . . . , (July-September 1956), pp. 344–346, refers to the *History of England* without mentioning the *Essay on Miracles*.

16. See my earlier note, "Bergson et l'histoire," in the first *Mélanges Bergson* (La Baconnière, Neuchâtel, 1941), pp. 213–221.

17. "There is perhaps a little too much of Kantianism in Marrou's approach," writes J. Maritain (*On the Philosophy of History*, New York, 1957, p. 7), and that is a friendly reproach from his pen. But I had referred only to a very exoteric Kantianism which one may consider, with K. Jaspers (*La Foi philosophique*, French translation, Paris, 1953, p. 12), integrated with the *philosophia perennis*. See R. Marlé's remarks (*Recherches de science réligieuse*, 1958, p. 428 and note 15) concerning Bultman's criticisms of my reference to the noumenal object in the additions (pp. 134, n. 2; 135, n. 1; 159, n. 1) to the German edition of the *Gifford Lectures* of 1955 (*Geschichte und Eschatologie*, Tübingen, 1958).

18. *Contributo alla Storia degli Studi Classici*, Rome, 1955, p. 113 (republished from the *Rivista Storica Italiana*, I, 1936).

It has therefore something more than the simple expedients of a capitalism at bay to which the Marxists would like to reduce it. It was also defined precisely by the Jansenists, who were replying both to historical pyrrhonism and to the exaggerated exigencies of Cartesian rationalism. The final chapters of the *Logique de Port-Royal*, which distinguished two general paths leading to *true* knowledge, have been too often forgotten. According to a famous formula of St. Augustine, there was on one hand reasoning and experience, and on the other faith, itself of two kinds: divine and human. And it is from this latter that history arises.

"Human faith is in itself subject to error," Arnauld[19] wrote on this matter, "because every man is a liar, according to Scripture, and it could be that a man who assures us that a thing is true will himself be deceived.[20] Nevertheless, as we have already noted above, there are things which we know only through human faith that we should consider to be as certain and as undeniable as if we had had mathematical demonstrations of them."

We would like to refer certain of our opponents to the *Petites Écoles*. The polemic passion causes them to forget the fundamental distinction between divine faith and human faith. It is as if, when we speak of a knowledge by faith à propos of history, it were religious faith, supernatural faith, that we should understand by it. No doubt it is neither ridiculous nor useless to relate one to the other. Christianity in particular, a historic religion, has been called upon to reflect upon the notion of faith, its nuances (Christian language has distinguished *credere Deum, credere Deo, credere in*

19. *Logique de Port-Royal*, Part IV, Chap. 12 (Ch. Jourdain, 1854, p. 308). Apparently these pages should be attributed to Arnauld rather than to Nicole.

20. And that is why the historian should always "be on his guard" in a way (cf. Piganiol, article quoted, p. 227): a theory of historical knowledge based on the notion of faith does not imply credulity.

Deum),[21] its stages (credibility, credence, belief) and the logic
of history can profit by these analyses. The reciprocal is also
true, as a matter of fact: we must not be too quickly satisfied
by peremptory formulae when considering Christian faith.
Knowledge "absolute, perfect, irrefutable,"[22] economy "perfectly satisfying because of the quality of the Witness,"[23]
because "God can neither mislead us nor be misled."[24] Only a
god (if such a word can have a meaning other than blasphe-
mous here) could be sure of having understood the meaning
of the Word of God, for if God has spoken to us he did so in
a human language, by the intermediary of human instruments
concerning which we could be mistaken. The treatise of the
faith presupposes the elaboration of one on the Church, on
the pedagogue, on the theological sites, and so forth. However it may be, the distinction remains and the notion of
human faith has its place within the theory of knowledge that
is notably historical, and this independently of all reference
to religious faith.

It is the virtue of the logicians of Port-Royal to have known
how to recover that notion in St. Augustine's teaching. (It
was Momigliano's merit to have recalled it to us: it is always
useful to wrest the moderns that we are from barbarity and
the pleasant illusion of rediscovering America.) They have
fully shown, first of all, that the knowledge of faith is not an
irrational act: *credere non possemus, nisi rationales animas
haberemus.*[25] Faith—confidence and belief—issues from a

21. C. Mohrmann: "Credere in Deum," in *Études sur le Latin des
Chrétiens*, Rome, 1958, pp. 195–203 (republished from *Mélanges J. de
Ghellinck*, I, 1951).

22. Piganiol, p. 229.

23. Guérard des Lauriers, p. 595.

24. *Logique de Port-Royal*, IV, 12, p. 308, Jourdain (echoing the
Catechism).

25. Saint Augustine, *Ep.* 122, I (3), to which the *Logique de Port-Royal*
refers explicitly (cited above).

rational conduct that precedes it and legitimizes it (not without degrees, naunces, hesitations, uncertainties):

"To judge the truth of an event, and to decide to believe it or not to believe it myself, I must not consider it in isolation, and in itself, as I would a geometrical problem; but it is necessary to consider all the surrounding circumstances, both internal and external. I call internal circumstances those that belong to the fact itself; external, those that have to do with the persons whose testimony we are inclined to believe. . . ."[26] Logically, if historical knowledge rests in the final analysis on an act of faith, it is true knowledge to the degree that the historian has succeeded in giving this a rational basis. History is true to the extent that the historian possesses valid reasons for giving his confidence to (what he has understood of) what the documents reveal to him of the Past.[27]

The rational character of the historian's work must be insisted upon. I have been happy to note that the philosophers who have listened to me, when I analyzed the mechanics of the elaboration of history, have stressed the fact that the rational scheme of this conduct is to be found (in strictly identical fashion) in any type of human knowledge[28]: history is certainly a scientific knowledge, specified by its own object —the human past—and its methodological technique (heuristic, critical, interpretive) is in itself a function of that object. Human reason adapts itself to the varied missions confided to it, but it is always the same reasoning which is exercised and whose working we observe.

I realize fully that the philosopher is not so easily satisfied.

26. In the same *Logique,* IV, 13, pp. 311–312. As did A. Piganiol, at an interval of three centuries (article quoted, p. 227); it is from the archives of the Constantinian legend that Arnauld borrows an example of the critical problem: IV, 13, p. 312.

27. *Supra,* pp. 143 and 241.

28. B. Brunello, "Sulla conoscenza storica," in *Convivium* (Bologne, 1958), p. 84; Guérard des Lauriers, pp. 576, 577.

If it is difficult for him to contest the fact that history belongs
to one "of the types of knowledge whose modality is the probable," that it is a "knowledge of the faith-type,"[29] he will ask
me: "But what exactly is the formal object of that historical
faith? To what do the *praeambula* which precede that faith
refer?"[30] I will reply, "to the ensemble of the operative procedures by which we force ourselves to reach the Past, to discover
and understand its traces." I do not believe, as a matter of
fact, that the right method consists in distinguishing (to the
point of opposing them) between belief in the document—and
thus rational judgment concerning its credibility—and belief
and credibility relative to the historian himself. Philosophers
(and theologians)[31] seem to me too apt to confer the title of
"science" on the techniques of criticism and the identification
of documents. That is a matter of an organization of operative
procedures regulated by workshop traditions. But the validity
of application is not to be separated from an intervention
of the historian's mind, of a more general character.

I have taken pains to give an example of this critical procedure with respect to a Latin inscription, showing how the
paleographic, diplomatic and archeological analysis of the
document allowed the epigraphist to conclude with certainty
that he had in hand a text concerning the history of the Gallo-
Roman religion and not (as had been believed in the sixteenth
century) the cult of the Saintes-Maries-de-la-Mer.[32] The
essential point of the analysis (which some seem to have
missed) is that this conclusion is true. It possesses a moral
certitude whose probability is practically infinite, because of
an initial act of faith (which alone *thereafter* allowed recourse

29. Guérard des Lauriers, pp. 598, 594.

30. *Ibid.,* p. 595.

31. See for instance S. Harent, in the *Dictionnaire de théologie
catholique,* article on "Foi," col. 446: "We recognize historical *criticism*
as a science . . ."

32. See above, pp. 121-126.

to the proven methods of classic epigraphy). By this faith I decided to accept this text at its face value, confront the problem (a dedication to the *Iunones Augustae*) and—unlike our witness of the sixteenth century—not see in it a cryptogram drawn up by Christians of the first century "as obscurely as they could." It was an act of faith founded on a rational *preambulum*. For a cryptogram to be decipherable one day, it must at least be possible to see that it is a cryptogram.

The mistake of many critics, a mistake often denounced by L. Febvre, is to imagine that historical work is summed up in two acts: 1) Establish the facts. 2) Put them to work.[33] The first operation, they think, has greater security, objectivity and truth than the second. But it is not sufficient to insist on the historian's "starting from facts," as though in our archives, our libraries and our museums a mass of documents awaited us, all ready. It is wrong to think that after an appropriately "scientific" treatment (external and internal criticism, interpretation, and so forth) they can be "exorcised of the historian's present"[34] and made to present us with the "facts" of the past (in a limited way) in the pure state, between which relations must thereafter be established.

No indeed, the document itself does not exist, prior to the intervention of the historian's curiosity. That is what R. C. Collingwood explained, in his paradoxical fashion, by the formula: "Everything in the world is potential evidence for any subject whatever."[35] And this has been well understood by the curators of our museums, libraries and archives, who try to save all that has survived from the past without daring

33. L. Febvre, *Combats pour l'histoire*, Paris, 1953, pp. 6–7 (Opening lesson, Collège de France, 1933); 430–431 (republished from *Revue de métaphysique et de morale*, 1949).

34. Again I quote here Guérard des Lauriers' formulas, cf. article quoted, pp. 590, 595.

35. *The Idea of History*, Oxford, 1946, p. 280 (but see the nuanced commentary of it that I proposed above, pp. 84–85).

to impose limitations on the use that history may make of them in the future. We are very fortunate that they have preserved, for instance, those notarial archives, those parish registers long abandoned and covered with dust, unused and unusable —until the moment when historians preoccupied with economic and social problems thought of the possibility and the means of exploiting them profitably.

For historical science does not progress solely (nor principally) by accumulation—a constantly greater number of notes of the same type abstracted as a result of the same questionnaire. It also experiences revolutions and takes a great step forward when another historical school arises that is animated by a different spirit and consequently led to put new questions to the Past. This leads to an entirely different way of using the documents in our possession, or it may seek out and promote to the dignity of historical documents a category of relics neglected until then. Prior to recent developments in the history of agrarian regimes, who thought of questioning the land registry plans, and the shape of the fields themselves as they appear to us in the rural landscape, in order to discover the system of property and of the exploitation which molded them?

One could symbolize the progressive development of historical work by a parabolic curve. Its support is the "facts" that are turned up in the course of the investigation (corresponding to the summit of the curve, which includes two branches—and not, as is too often unconsciously assumed, a single one). The first takes its point of departure from the depths of the historian's mind (his mentality, his culture, his social roots). He comes upon the "real" little by little, as he formulates problems about it which lead to the elaboration of a heuristic. At this point we are in contact with the documents: criticism, interpretation—here there is a whole operative procedure which logically is very analogous to that used by the experimental sciences. The historian is led to put a precise question to a selected document (this is the equivalent of the scientific experiment). The hypothesis once verified (not without having been revised several times), one ends by establishing a "fact." This latter is not an initial premise, but is the result of all that work of elaboration which constitutes the first part of the undertaking. There is no need to describe the second: the "fact" is no more our destination than it is our point of departure. Once it is established it must be interpreted, explained by inserting it in causal chains, collections of facts, structures, and an ever more vast synthesis that is bringing us by degrees to the same profound regions of the mind from which we started.

I have used the accepted term "historical fact" despite its ambiguity. It is important not to make a sort of atomistic image of this, as if history were composed of a multiplicity of little hard kernels of factual reality. This is true only of ancient history (especially political), which is still close to the chronicle. This is the history that the school of the *Annales* labels somewhat contemptuously with the term "historicizing history." Others call it "anecdotal." It is interested in questions of the type: "When, where and how did Hugh Capet die?" Undoubtedly, history is a knowledge of the concrete—even of the singular. But this is on the condition we understand that the individual instance being studied may be in itself a global fact, embracing a vast sector of humanity, of men who have each lived his own personal life—or of ideas, of values, of cultural creations. The notion of the historical event can apply to a phenomenon of long duration[36]: the historical object can be not only a battle, a war, a dynasty,

36. A type of phenomenon that F. Braudel, in the name of history, rightly refuses to abandon: "Histoire et sciences sociales, La longue durée," in *Annales* (October-December 1958), pp. 725–753.

but also those events constituting an economic crisis, a demographic movement, a social class, a regime—or in the artistic field, a style—a religion, a general system of the organization of society, a civilization (for example, the Ancient City, Feudalism, the Baroque, Islam, Capitalism).

In his thesis,[37] J. Schneider studied the development of an original social class, the patriarchal society of Metz. He based his findings partly on a very carefully constructed, criticized, interpreted and exploited file of some two hundred legal documents concerning financial operations, principally real estate, carried out by the bourgeois of Metz between 1219 and 1324. It would be wrong to imagine that these elementary "facts" are more concrete, more real, more historical than the phenomenon of the collective fact—the transforming of an urban oligarchy into a landholding aristocracy. But in a still more obvious way than in the case of small individual facts, the role of the operative procedures selected by the historian appear to have a decisive role in determining these "facts" of a global type. Nothing is more instructive, for instance, than to attend the impassioned debates between demographers and historians concerning the conditions necessary for applying to the past statistical methods used for the study of contemporary societies.[38] Let us take as an example the problem of variations in mortality for a given rural region of France in the seventeenth and eighteenth centuries. For such an investigation we have at our disposal precious documents: the parish registers. But taking them just as they are, they reflect only an accumulation of elementary "facts" (the baptism or

37. Cited above, p. 67.

38. See for example R. Baehrel, "Statistique et démographie historique: La mortalité sous l'Ancien Régime," in *Annales* (January-March 1957), pp. 85–98), and the polemic between the author and L. Henry (*ibid.*, October-December 1957, pp. 628–638).

burial of one or another parishioner). The discussion of problems of criticism or of interpretation can not practically be located on this level of reality, for the specifically historical problem of mortality and its variations (following, for instance, a war, an epidemic, a famine) makes its appearance only at the moment when the use of a statistical procedure allows us to define with precision (and consequently to grasp) this global fact. But what is the proper method to use? Should we calculate the average age at death, the rate of general mortality, or perhaps something else? We should use none of these, but rather the relationship of the number of tombs to the number of baptisms, or better yet, the number of conceptions (as J. Meuvret proposes, based on his experience of more than thirty years. Here is the problem, and on its solution will depend the truth of the demographic history that is later elaborated.

The foregoing analysis, I hope, will allow the reader to grasp the sense in which the "personalist" historian feels able to answer the question put to him by the philosopher: "What criterion do you give us, and what criterion do you yourself have for your own act of faith?"[39] There is no unique criterion, for the elaboration of historical truth is the fruit of a complex procedure (that I sought to symbolize by the image of a parabola). It plunges its roots—at the very first moment just as at the point of departure—in what is most profound in the heart of the historian's thought, his *Lebens- und Weltanschauung*, his general philosophy.

Its validity depends on the validity of each operation carried out in the course of that procedure, and not only on the intermediate experimental stage of contact with the documents. It remains for us (but that would take us well beyond the limits of a simple note) to define how the verification of

39. Guérard des Lauriers, p. 597.

that validity can be carried out practically—in the eyes of the historian himself first of all, then of his colleagues and peers, and finally of his public. That leads us back to the analysis of what I proposed to call the "existential psychoanalysis" of the historian.[40] (The label—chosen for its picturesque quality—is meant to be taken, of course, *cum grano salis*.)

40. *Supra*, p. 258.

Index

Different type has been used to make the following distinctions: the historical object (Abelard, *Love*), the historian (ACTON), the philosopher or theorist (ALAIN).